The Alchemy of Human Happiness

Also available from Anqa Publishing

Ibn ʿArabī: *The Seven Days of the Heart: Awrād al-Usbūʿ (Wird)*
Translated by Pablo Beneito & Stephen Hirtenstein

Ibn ʿArabī: *Contemplation of the Holy Mysteries: Mashāhid al-Asrār*
Translated by Cecilia Twinch & Pablo Beneito

Ibn ʿArabī: *Divine Sayings: 101 Ḥadīth Qudsī* (*Mishkāt al-Anwār*)
Translated by Stephen Hirtenstein & Martin Notcutt

Ibn ʿArabī: *The Universal Tree and the Four Birds: al-Ittiḥād al-Kawnī*
Translated by Angela Jaffray

Ibn ʿArabī: *A Prayer for Spiritual Elevation and Protection: al-Dawr al-aʿlā*
Study, translation, transliteration & Arabic text by Suha Taji-Farouki

Ibn ʿArabī: *The Four Pillars of Spiritual Transformation: Ḥilyat al-Abdāl*
Translated by Stephen Hirtenstein

Ibn ʿArabī: *The Secrets of Voyaging: Kitāb al-Isfār ʿan natāʾij al-asfār*
Translated by Angela Jaffray

The Lamp of Mysteries: A Commentary on the Light Verse of the Quran,
by Ismāʿīl Anqawarī. Translated & edited by Bilal Kuşpınar

The Nightingale in the Garden of Love: the Poems of Üftade, by Paul Ballanfat
Translated from French by Angela Culme-Seymour

The Unlimited Mercifier: The Spiritual Life and Thought of Ibn ʿArabī
Stephen Hirtenstein

Ibn ʿArabi and Modern Thought: The History of Taking Metaphysics Seriously
Peter Coates

Beshara and Ibn ʿArabi: A Movement of Sufi Spirituality in the Modern World
Suha Taji-Farouki

The Teachings of a Perfect Master: An Islamic Saint for the Third Millennium
Henry Bayman

Muḥyiddīn Ibn ʿArabī

The Alchemy of Human Happiness

(fī maʿrifat kīmiyāʾ al-saʿāda)

Introduction and Translation

STEPHEN HIRTENSTEIN

ANQA PUBLISHING • OXFORD

Published by Anqa Publishing
PO Box 1178
Oxford OX2 8YS, UK
www.anqa.co.uk

First published 2017

British Library Cataloguing in Publication Data.
A catalogue record for this book is available from the British Library.

ISBN: 978 1 905937 59 2

Cover design: meadencreative.com

Back cover MS: Opening page of the chapter in Evkaf Müzesi MS 1859, fol. 16b, in the author's own hand.Courtesy of the Turkish and Islamic Arts Museum, Istanbul, Turkey.

Printed by Independent Publishers Group, Chicago

CONTENTS

ABBREVIATIONS

Divine Sayings = Ibn ʿArabī, *Divine Sayings (Mishkāt al-anwār)* (Oxford, 2004)

EI2 = *Encyclopaedia of Islam*, 2nd edition, P. Bearman et al. (Leiden, 1991–2004)

Fuṣūṣ = *Fuṣūṣ al-ḥikam*, ed. Kiliç and Alkiş (Istanbul, 2016)

Fut. = *al-Futūḥāt al-Makkiyya*, 4 vols. (Beirut, n.d.)

JMIAS = *Journal of the Muhyiddin Ibn ʿArabi Society* (Oxford, 1982–)

SPK = Chittick, William, *The Sufi Path of Knowledge* (Albany, NY, 1989)

SDG = Chittick, William, *The Self-Disclosure of God* (Albany, NY, 1998)

Seal of Saints = Chodkiewicz, Michel, *Seal of the Saints* (Cambridge, 1993)

Secrets of Voyaging = Ibn ʿArabī, *The Secrets of Voyaging (K. al-Isfār)* (Oxford, 2015)

Seven Days = Ibn ʿArabī, *The Seven Days of the Heart (Awrād al-usbūʿ)* (Oxford, 2008)

Unlimited Mercifier = Hirtenstein, Stephen, *The Unlimited Mercifier* (Oxford, 1999)

ACKNOWLEDGEMENTS

I have benefited enormously from the suggestions of many, many others, especially those with whom I first embarked on the task of translating this chapter (Layla Shamash, Cecilia Twinch, Jane Clark and Rosemary Brass), the readers who have been kind enough to comment and give feedback, and the students with whom I have studied the text. Without their help and encouragement, I would not have dared to publish. My heart-felt thanks also go to Yusuf Mullick, Abdul-Rahim Hassan, Andrew Meaden and the ever-calm hand of Michael Tiernan. And my eternal gratitude to my wife and companion Carla, without whose love, support and encouragement this project would never have been completed. Any errors that remain are entirely my own, and will, I trust, be covered by the One whose forgiveness is without end or limit.

THE TRANSLATION

Translation from Arabic to English is never easy, because of the way that the two languages are constructed, and this is especially the case with a medieval writer of the stature of Ibn ʿArabī, who is highly attuned to and utilises the full range of meanings inherent in Arabic words. A Western language, especially those based on Latin roots, develops on the basis of the etymological connections that a single meaning gives rise to: for example, the Latin *verbum*, 'word', gives rise to verb, verbal, adverb, verbalise, verbosity and so on. Arabic, like other Semitic languages, is founded on a tri-literal (or sometimes quadri-literal) root, which has a constellation of meanings inherent in it: for example, *k-l-m* means 'to speak, express, talk', and gives rise to *kalima* ('speech, remark, saying, expression of opinion'), *kalām* ('sayings, speech, theology') and *kalm* ('wound, cut'); *r-w-ḥ* means 'to journey or work in the early evening, to be breezy, brisk, cheerful, to experience relief, to perceive by smelling' and is related to *rīḥ* ('breeze, wind'), *rawḥ* ('ease, relief'), *rūḥ* ('spirit') and *rayḥān* ('sweet basil').

Since Arabic and English are linguistically and culturally quite different, I have opted for certain simplifications to make reading easier. Medieval Arabic has no capital letters or punctuation as Europeans know it, and so any translation into a Western language has to make decisions about where a sentence begins and ends, what a pronoun refers to, what constitutes a paragraph and so on. Even apparent similarities such as the definite article or singular and plural nouns are not really equivalent concepts in the two languages, and often a plural in Arabic is better expressed as a singular in English. Square brackets are used to indicate words that I have added, which are implied but not explicit in the original text, in order to help the flow of the meaning. Italics are used in the text to indicate passages from the Quran or Hadith, with full references given in the footnotes. For the translations from the Quran I have relied on the excellent version by Alan Jones, with minor modifications to suit the context. The standard pious formulae after the mention of God (*taʿālā*, the Exalted), a prophet (*ʿalayhi al-salām*, upon him be peace) or the Prophet Muhammad (*ṣallā Allāhu ʿalayhi wa sallam*, may God bless him and give him peace) have generally been omitted – sometimes in Arabic these are simply used to clarify what a capital letter does in English, although in reality they serve as a reminder of the deep respect for God and His prophets that is inherent in Islamic culture, but rather alien to a modern Western reader. The paragraphs and headings are entirely my own, and have been introduced to allow the reader to follow Ibn ʿArabī's explanation more easily.

Gender issues are also a conundrum when translating from Arabic, which has only two noun classes, masculine and feminine, whereas English has three. In general the word *huwa* ('He' or 'It') is used to denote the Ipseity, the Itselfness of God, but the English neuter 'It' cannot convey the personal quality inherent in the Arabic, so like others I have opted for 'He'. Ibn ʿArabī is very sensitive to the gender implications of words, and sometimes he deliberately emphasises the feminine quality of the receptive soul (*nafs*) or the Reality that is given form (in the final poem) – in those cases I have opted to use 'she' as the referent. We may also note that Ibn ʿArabī makes it very clear in the text that the two travellers who aspire to perfection may be male or female, but in translation I have kept to the masculine 'he' (as he does in the original text) to denote them.

In addition, translating a medieval text on alchemy is fraught with problems of understanding. The technical terminology is occasionally unclear, and the conceptual universe obscure. The footnotes give Quranic references and background on some of the major terms, including (where applicable) the ways in which Ibn ʿArabī uses them in other texts. There are also some indications of where the text is ambiguous or can be read in different ways.

INTRODUCTION

THE AUTHOR of this work and the book from which it is drawn need little introduction. Ibn ʿArabī (1165–1240), known as Muḥyī al-Dīn ('The reviver of religion') and al-Shaykh al-akbar ('the greatest spiritual master'), is one of the most profound mystics and authors in any tradition. His many writings have long been regarded in the Islamic world as essential to the deepest understanding of the nature of Reality and the possibility of human realisation.

Born in Murcia in south-eastern Spain in 560/1165, Ibn ʿArabī spent the first thirty-five years of his life with various spiritual masters in Seville, Cordoba, Fez and other towns in the Maghrib, before leaving his homeland to go on pilgrimage. He arrived in Mecca in 598/1202 at the age of thirty-seven, and almost immediately began work on what would become his magnum opus, *al-Futūḥāt al-Makkiyya* (*The Meccan Illuminations*), which took several decades to complete. Although we do not know the exact date when chapter 167, the particular part of the work translated in this book, was composed, it would seem plausible that it was done sometime within the following ten years, when he was travelling and living in the Mashriq.[1]

The full title of chapter 167 is 'On the inner knowing of the alchemy of human happiness' (*fī maʿrifat kīmiyāʾ al-saʿāda*). This is a clear reference to a well-known work written some 100 years earlier by the great theologian Abū Ḥāmid Muḥammad al-Ghazālī (d. 505/1111), entitled *Kīmiyāʾ*

1. It is possible that Ibn ʿArabī came into contact with practitioners of alchemy in Egypt, when he was visiting friends in 598/1202 on his first visit en route to Mecca, or when he stayed in Cairo in 603/1207 (where his *Rūḥ al-quds* was read).

al-saʿāda (*The Alchemy of Happiness*).[2] Al-Ghazālī's work was written in Persian as a popular abridgement of his much longer Arabic *Iḥyāʾ ʿulūm al-dīn* (*The Revival of the Religious Sciences*). It primarily discusses spiritual alchemy in a fairly standard philosophical manner: beginning with the implications of the famous prophetic hadith 'whoever knows their self knows their Lord', he examines in turn the knowledge of the self, the knowledge of God, the knowledge of this world and the knowledge of the next world. Al-Ghazālī then considers highly practical issues such as whether the religious life is enhanced or hindered by practices such as music and dancing, meditation and abstinence, and whether it is better to be married or not.

Whether he had read al-Ghazālī's work or not, Ibn ʿArabī takes the idea of alchemy in an altogether different direction, and apart from the overall subject matter of spiritual transformation, the two works could hardly be more different in tone and content. Ibn ʿArabī is much less concerned with generalities or practical details, and he links the way alchemists view their art to mystical ascension and spiritual journeying. His concentration is primarily on experiential knowledge (*maʿrifa*) of the heart – a direct immediate knowing – and how this contrasts with intellectual understanding. This difference between two great authors is in itself unsurprising, since Ibn ʿArabī's use of his illustrious predecessor's work was both a mark of respect, a nod to the huge contribution to philosophy, theology and Sufi thinking which al-Ghazālī had made a century earlier, and a way of

2. It has been translated into English several times as *The Alchemy of Happiness*: for example, by Henry Homes (Albany, NY, 1873), Claud Field (London, 1980) and Jay Crook and Laleh Bakhtiar (Chicago, 2008).

demonstrating to his readers that he was writing in a very different way.[3]

Earlier mystical writers viewed alchemy as a means of spiritual transformation: for example, the famous Egyptian Sufi Dhū'l-Nūn al-Miṣrī (d. ca. 245/859), who came from the town of Ikhmīm (Gk. Panopolis), a major centre of Hermetic teaching, is credited with several alchemical treatises drawn from the Graeco-Egyptian Hermes tradition.[4]

Some Muslim philosophers, such as the great master of the eastern Peripatetics who was closest to the Greek philosophical tradition, Ibn Sīnā (d. 428/1037), cast doubt on the power of alchemists to effect real substantial transmutation, viewing it solely as an art of imitation:

> As to the claims of the alchemists, it must be clearly understood that it is not in their power to bring about any true change of species. They can, however, produce excellent imitations, dyeing the red [metal] white so that it closely resembles silver, or dyeing it yellow so that it resembles gold... In these [dyed metals] the essential substance remains unchanged.[5]

This kind of scepticism may partially explain why in this chapter of the *Futūḥāt* Ibn 'Arabī is keen to portray the difference between the mystical and philosophical

3. Several of Ibn 'Arabī's works utilise Ghazalian titles, most notably, *Mishkāt al-anwār* (Niche of Lights) – see *Divine Sayings* (Oxford, 2008), the Arabic text with English translation, by Stephen Hirtenstein and Martin Notcutt.

4. See Peter Kingsley, *Ancient Philosophy, Mystery and Magic* (Oxford, 1995), 388–90, who views early Sufism as incorporating a transmission of Hermetic doctrine from teachers such as Empedocles (5th century BCE) and Zosimos (4th century CE), Fuat Sezgin, *Geschichte des arabischen Schrifttums* (Leiden, 1967), 1/643–4.

5. From Ibn Sīnā's *K. al-Shifā'*, a text originally believed by Western writers to have been written by Aristotle, translated by Eric Holmyard and Desmond Mandeville in *Âvicennae de Congelatione et Conglutinatione Lapidum* (Paris, 1927).

approaches in stark and dramatic terms: his concern is not with whether this transmutation is possible in physical terms but with the inner transformation that is opened up by the spiritual path. He seems to have found it particularly important to emphasise that spiritual transformation is real and attainable, but only as a stage beyond what can be reached through the intellect.

Mystical writers generally make a very clear distinction between 'divine alchemy for the soul', practised within, and human alchemy whose obsession with physical gold was viewed as a major distraction from the spiritual path. In a story about a king (who symbolises the Universal Spirit) and his six sons, related by 'Aṭṭār (d. 618/1221) in his 'Book of the Divine' (*Ilāhī-nāma*), the sons reveal to their father their dearest desires: the sixth child is keen to know the science of alchemy, in order to transform the world into a place of faith and to allow everyone to enjoy wealth (and make poverty history). He is warned by his father against being overpowered by greed, pride and ambition. While the son believes that the alchemical art can benefit both the worldly and religious life, the father emphasises that it is impossible to have gold and religion, and true happiness can only be achieved through the elixir of suffering. Commenting on a story about Plato, 'Aṭṭār reminds the reader to 'turn your body into a heart and turn your heart towards pain – this is the way that true men practise alchemy'.[6] His final story tells of a deer which eats nothing but one or two sweet flowers for 40 days (the traditional period of retreat), and then breathes in the new dawn's air: 'when that breath passes into its life's blood,

6. *Ilāhī-nāma*, ed. Shafi'i Kadkani (Tehran, 2014), v. 6179 – discourses 19–22 are dedicated to the sixth son's desire for the elixir and various stories of spiritual transformation; see also Hellmut Ritter, *The Ocean of the Soul* (Leiden, 2003), 7–8.

musk flows from its navel... who knows this kind of breath in the world, by which blood is turned into musk in a single instant?... Practise this alchemy if you are a man of the Way, for this is a divine alchemy for the soul."[7]

Like 'Aṭṭār, Ibn 'Arabī views alchemy according to its underlying meaning but is not so disparaging about it as a human endeavour. He uses the principle of transformation or transmutation as the basis for explaining alchemy as a science that is at once physical, spiritual and divine. He equates the knowledge of alchemy with the return to the original state of what the Quran calls 'the finest stature' (*aḥsan taqwīm*), according to which God created the human being.[8] The juxtaposition of alchemy, ascension and happiness, as well as an almost scientific classification of mystical knowledge, makes this one of the core chapters of the *Futūḥāt*. It is a tour de force, almost novel-like in its use of characterisation and story-telling.

Chapter 167 within the Futūḥāt

The 167th chapter from the *Futūḥāt* can be found approximately one-third of the way through this work, within the second section on spiritual behaviour (*faṣl al-mu'āmalāt*). For the purposes of this translation we have treated it as self-standing, partly because it is unusually designated by the author as a complete 'part' (*juz'*) in itself.[9] It is possible

7. Ibid. vv.6325–7.

8. 'Indeed We have created the human being according to the finest stature (*aḥsan taqwīm*), and then We brought him down to the lowest of the low' (Q.95.4–5). See *Fut*.I.152.

9. Evkaf Müzesi MS 1859, vol. 15, fols. 16b–43b, *juz'* 108. *Fut*.II.270–84 (Mansoub edn., 5/481–508). Given Ibn 'Arabī's close interest in and sensitivity to numbers, the

that this chapter was originally written at an earlier date as a treatise in its own right, perhaps even under a different title, before being incorporated into the *Futūḥāt* – one feels that there is a certain completeness about the way it is constructed and the way it manages to touch upon all of Ibn 'Arabī's teaching in a succinct and comprehensive manner. At the same time, it is very much part of a whole book, one chapter amongst many, having a particular place within a vast network.

The division of the original *Futūḥāt* (autograph Evkaf Muzesi, 1845–81) is complex: its 560 chapters (*bāb*) are spread across thirty-seven physical volumes (*sifr*), each of which consists of twenty quires of paper (a quire being eight leaves or sixteen sides of paper, or parchment in medieval times), i.e. totalling over 11,000 pages of handwriting. Each volume is divided into seven parts, making a total of 259 'parts' (*juz'*). The whole book is also divided into six 'sections' (*faṣl*) that are designated in the table of contents (*fihris*), and these have attracted some detailed study, most notably by Michel Chodkiewicz.[10] As a result, the 'parts' have tended to be relegated to secondary importance, yet they reveal a most interesting structure in their own right. The long chapters of the *Futūḥāt* comprise several parts: for example, the 73rd chapter (which opens the second volume in the printed Beirut edition) contains five parts (*juz'* 75–9) on the various types of spiritual men (*quṭb*, *abdāl*, etc.), followed by twelve parts (*juz'* 80–91) on the answers to al-Tirmidhī's questionnaire. After a further twelve parts (*juz'* 92–103) in which he discusses the many stations (*maqāmāt*) of spiritual endeavour and how

fact that 167 is a prime number may have played some part in this.

10. For an overview, see Ibn al-'Arabi, *The Meccan Illuminations*, introduction by Michel Chodkiewicz (New York, 2004), 7–12.

to go beyond them by 'abandoning' (*tark*) them, Ibn 'Arabī turns his attention to divine friendship or sainthood (*walāya*) at the end of Part 104 (chapter 152) and follows it with:

Part 105 (chapters 153–6): on the forms of sainthood and the station of prophethood;

Part 106 (chapters 157–61): on prophethood and messengerhood in its various forms and the station of closeness;

Part 107 (chapters 162–6): on the poverty of total dependence upon God (and its complement, independence), *taṣawwuf* (Sufism), realisation and wisdom (especially in relation to the people of blame, the *malāmiyya*), i.e. the various ways that closeness can be viewed;

Part 108 (chapter 167): on the alchemy of happiness.

In other words, this chapter builds on an analysis of the various typologies of spiritual human beings and degrees of attainment, the differences among those charged with announcing truths (saints, prophets and messengers), and the principles of spiritual realisation.

In addition, a close reading of the text shows more or less explicit links from one chapter to the next provided by the author, often in the final sentence. For example, chapter 164 ends with the line 'May God make us one of the Sufis who uphold the rights (*ḥuqūq*) of God and prefer the side of God', *ḥuqūq* (the plural of *ḥaqq*) being related to the actualisation or realisation of these rights (*taḥqīq*), which is the subject of chapter 165. Chapter 166 concludes with 'The sages have rulership in the world by virtue of the path established by revelation, which God has prescribed for His servants that they might follow it and thus be led to their true happiness', happiness (*sa'āda*) forming the central theme of chapter 167.

Chapter 167 itself is set out as two distinct divisions: the first deals with alchemy (*al-kīmiyā'*), making this text one of the major surviving examples of Islamic alchemy; and the second with spiritual ascension (*mi'rāj*), a subject that Ibn 'Arabī discusses in many different ways. It is clear from Ibn 'Arabī's exposition here that the reader is meant to contemplate alchemy within its deeper context of spiritual transformation: how the base lead of ordinary humanity may be transmuted and perfected into the gold of true human nature.

Alchemy and the Hermetic Tradition

Although often portrayed simply as the forerunner of modern chemistry, alchemy in itself was a coherent and integrated view of the world. It tends to be understood by scholars today as a science of quite diverse conceptions and definitions, spanning the Chinese world (with their emphasis on attaining spiritual perfection, making imitation gold, and finding mineral elixirs), India (*rasāyana*, the science of rejuvenation, and tantric alchemy) and the West, specifically Greece and Egypt. Usually it was seen as part of a whole psycho-medical tradition.

The English word 'alchemy' derives from the Arabic *al-kīmiyā'*, itself a loan-word from Syriac *kīmīyā* which in turn was taken from the Greek *χημεια*, meaning 'the art of casting metals'. The earliest surviving alchemical texts in the West, which are written in Greek, hardly ever use the word *χημεια* and refer to their practice as 'The Work', 'the divine and sacred Art' or 'The making of gold'. A large quantity of these Greek writings were translated into Arabic in the 2nd/8th and 3rd/9th centuries. The fundamentals of Arab alchemy remain somewhat obscure, as relatively few manuscripts have survived. While the Greek *χημεια* has given rise to our word 'chemistry', its Arabic derivative is responsible for the term 'alchemy'. This etymological history shows the way that scientific knowledge spread in medieval times from the highly developed and sophisticated Arab world to Europe, via writers and translators such as Abelard of Bath.

Some have also derived 'alchemy' from the Egyptian *kême*, the oldest official name for Egypt, meaning 'black', a reference to the 'black earth' of all Egypt.[11] The rich arable land on either side of the Nile, which gave rise to the ancient Egyptian culture, became the basis for identifying Egypt as the land of special esoteric knowledge. This knowledge was held by the priests, and was not available to the ordinary public. It was understood that speaking the right words and applying the right mixture of potions could effect physical, psychological and spiritual change, and such secrets needed to be guarded.

Historically alchemy was absorbed into the Western religious traditions with relative ease. In Hellenistic Egypt, where practitioners of alchemy were versed in the Greek version of the Bible, the science of alchemy was traced back to biblical prophets, beginning with Adam and passing through Seth, Noah, Abraham and so on.[12] According to Maria the Jewess (flor. Egypt 2nd or 3rd century CE), only 'the seed of Abraham' were entitled to delve into the mysteries of alchemy. From the Christian point of view, the philosophers'

11. keme.t = the black woman, the black cow, the black nation, as opposed to deshr.t = red, as in 'red devils', light-skinned people.

12. See Raphael Patai, *The Jewish Alchemists* (Princeton, 1994), 18ff. and chapter five for Maria the Jewess.

stone that turns base metals into silver and gold symbolises Christ. Since any pre-Islamic art or science was understood to be a wisdom inherited from earlier prophets, the Arabs regarded the science of alchemy as deriving from the ancients and wise men of legend, such as Hermes, but were keen to interpret it as springing from the sacred tradition of revelation. This was part of a general concern, common among writers from all three Abrahamic traditions, to show how the Semitic prophetic tradition had given rise to all forms of known wisdom and science, including Egyptian, Persian and Chinese traditions and Greek philosophy.[13]

It was generally believed that the science of alchemy had been founded by Hermes Trismegistos, the 'thrice-greatest Hermes'.[14] This epithet seems to have been devised by unnamed sages, living in Roman Egypt and writing in Greek in the first centuries of the Common Era. It originated from an old Egyptian title of Thoth, found in Greek as 'the greatest and greatest great god' (*megistos kai megistos theos megas*), and thereby distinguished him from being confused with the Greek Hermes, messenger of the gods. In the Hellenistic tradition Hermes Trismegistos was identified with the Egyptian god Thoth ('He who is like the ibis'), the God of knowledge and wisdom, scribe of the gods/underworld, inventor of writing, the author of all works of science, religion, philosophy and magic – i.e. the priestly arts and sciences.

13. Likewise, scholars in Sasanid Persia tended to promote the idea that all 'foreign' science had its origins as part of an ancient Persian heritage, which the early Sasanid emperors had resuscitated. For example, Hermes was said to be from Babylon and had taught the sciences of ancient Persia to the Egyptians.

14. For a detailed discussion of the whole Hermes tradition, see Kevin van Bladel, *The Arabic Hermes* (Oxford, 2009). For an overview and translation of Hermetic or Trismegistic literature, see G.R.S. Mead, *Thrice-Greatest Hermes* (London, 1906), vols. 1–3.

The Arabs, on the other hand, portrayed Hermes as a primordial Egyptian sage, who founded human religion before the Flood, ascended to the heavenly spheres of the planets and then returned to instruct his people in the sacred arts and sciences, especially astrology, alchemy and medicine. He was identified with the Quranic figure of Idrīs (considered identical to the biblical figure of Enoch, the great teacher of humankind),[15] a major prophet in the Islamic tradition like Moses, Jesus and Muhammad, and he was said to have been the first to teach writing and the study of books (*dars al-kutub*). Hermes' teachings had been handed down by successive philosophers of the past, including Pythagoras, Socrates and Plato, or had been rediscovered on tablets hidden in Egyptian temples or in underground tunnels. Hermes was not regarded as a proper name but as a title like the Roman Caesar or Persian Khusraw. His epithet of Trismegistos (Latin: Trismegistus) was explained as three separate persons connected to Egypt: a pre-Flood Hermes who was the prophet Idrīs, lived in Egypt and built the Pyramids; a post-Flood Hermes, who lived in Babylon, revived the original sciences and taught Pythagoras; and a later Hermes, who lived in Egypt, wrote about various sciences and crafts including alchemy and taught Asclepius, the Greek god of medicine.[16] For example, the 4th/10th century writer Ibn al-Nadīm (d. 380/990) wrote:

15. His name Idrīs is an intensive form from a root *d-r-s* meaning 'to learn, study' as well as 'to erase, eliminate'. See Q.19.56–7: 'Mention Idrīs in the Book: he was truthful, a prophet. We raised him up to a high place', and *Secrets of Voyaging*, 214–17.

16. Quoted by Ibn Juljul (d. post 384/994) from the writings of the astrologer Abū Ma'shar al-Balkhī (d.272/886), whose *Book of Thousands* is now lost but much quoted by later authors. For a translation and analysis of Ibn Juljul, see van Bladel, *The Arabic Hermes*, 122–7.

> The practitioners of the art of alchemy, which is the art of producing gold and silver from other minerals, maintain that the first person to speak of the science of the alchemical art was the sage Hermes the Babylonian, who emigrated to Egypt when the people were dispersed from Babylonia, and ruled over Egypt. He was both a wise sage and a philosopher. He initiated the art (of alchemy) and wrote numerous books on the subject.[17]

Ibn al-Nadīm goes on to give other versions of who Hermes might be, relating him to the Pyramids, and then gives a list of practitioners who wrote on the subject (including Zoroaster and Pythagoras) and those who he says discovered the mysterious elixir. The Ikhwān al-Ṣafā' (Brethren of Purity) taught that Hermes Trismegistos, 'who is the prophet Idrīs, ascended to the sphere of Saturn and resided there for thirty years, until he had witnessed all the states of the sphere; then he descended to the earth and instructed people in astrology.'[18] Later writers such as Jalāl al-Dīn al-Suyūṭī (d. 911/1505) also followed this ancient tradition of identifying Idrīs with Hermes, adding that the epithet 'thrice-greatest' (Trismegistos, rendered into Arabic as *al-muthallath bi-l-ḥikma*, 'triplicate in wisdom' or 'thrice-wise') referred to his being a prophet, king and sage, and that 'he could make lead into shining gold'.[19]

17. Ibn al-Nadīm, *The Fihrist*, ed. Ibrahim Ramadan (London, 1994), 431.
18. *Rasā'il*, 1/138.
19. Al-Suyūṭī, *Ḥusn al-muḥāḍara fī ta'rīkh Miṣr wa al-Qāhira*, ed. Abū al-Faḍl Ibrāhīm (Cairo, 1968), 60, citing as his sources al-Kindī and the Egyptian historian Ibn Zūlāq (d.ca.387/997). This doctrine found its way into Italian Renaissance thinkers such as Marsilio Ficino.

In these accounts we can see many of the themes that are addressed by Ibn ʿArabī in chapter 167: alchemy, the transformation of lead into gold, the ascension of the spirit into the heavens in order to be taught wisdom, and so on. These topics had been much discussed by Neoplatonist Gnostics and the various followers of Hermes, including the Sabians of Harran. However, unlike Ibn ʿArabī's depiction, the context for discussing them was an intelligible hierarchy as expounded by Plotinus, from the 'visible gods' (the planets) rising up to the Universal Soul and then the Intellect and finally the One Itself.[20] According to al-Kindī (d. ca. 260/873), the first significant Islamic philosopher to appropriate the Greek tradition,

> Plato... states... that the abode of intellectual souls, when they are detached [from the material world] is... beyond the sphere, in the world of Lordship, where the light of the Creator is. But not every soul upon parting from the body comes to be in that place immediately. Some souls part from the body having in them filth and impure things, so that some of them come to be in the sphere of the moon, and remain there for a period of time; until having been refined and purified, they ascend to the sphere of Mercury, and remain there for a period of time... When they come to be in the highest sphere, and have been utterly purified, ... they ascend to the world of the Intellect, passing beyond the spheres, and come to be in the loftiest and noblest of places, where nothing is hidden from them.[21]

20. See *Ennead* V.8.3ff., *On the Intellectual Beauty*. For Plotinus' famous description of his own ascension, see *Ennead* IV.8.

21. *Al-Qawl fī al-nafs*, 277ff., trans. in E.K. Rowson, *A Muslim Philosopher on the Soul and its Fate* (New Haven, CN, 1988), 244.

This Arabised Neoplatonist view, which had appropriated the teachings of Plato into a Hellenistic mindset concerned with the single source of all things, dominated most philosophical discussions in the Islamic world, until Ibn 'Arabī reviewed it in the light of the Prophet Muhammad's ascension (*mi'rāj*): in contrast to those in the philosophical tradition, he followed the Prophet's example by situating the human prophetic realities rather than the planets at the very centre of the spheres.

Ibn 'Arabī inherited a long tradition of hierarchical correspondence between the macrocosmic universe and the microcosm of the human being, and gave it his own unique twist. In his early years in al-Andalus, he came into contact with the teachings of Ibn Masarra of Cordoba (d. 319/931) and the Ikhwān al-Ṣafā' (the Brethren of Purity), and many Neoplatonic doctrines of alchemy, cosmology, astrology and magic. His treatment of the macrocosm–microcosm can be found in various works, particularly those written in his early years in al-Andalus such as *al-Tadbīrāt al-ilāhiyya*.[22]

Transmutation into Gold

Alchemy came to mean primarily the art of transmuting metals, in contrast to metallurgy or the fabrication of glass or imitation precious stones. This transmutation or 'divine Art' was understood as making gold or silver without returning to the baser metals, or altering the specific qualities of mineral

22. See Appendix B for a summary of the conceptual framework that was incorporated from the *Tadbīrāt* into the *Futūḥāt*. For the relationship between Ibn 'Arabī's thought and the doctrines of Ibn Masarra and the Ikhwān al-Ṣafā', see Michael Ebstein, *Mysticism and Philosophy in al-Andalus* (Leiden, 2014).

substances so that gold or silver could be obtained. The fact that chemistry shares a common linguistic root with alchemy should not obscure the fact that they belong to quite different conceptual universes: alchemists were not concerned with the specific chemical composition of a substance or in natural phenomena as such, except insofar as that might lead to their primary aim, the transmutation and elevation of base metal into gold, a process at once physical and spiritual.

Gold has long been perhaps the most powerful earthly symbol of perfection, something of priceless value, amongst various cultures.[23] For the ancient Egyptians, who had abundant mineral resources and whose empire was built on gold production,[24] gold was a sacred substance, associated with the immortal light of the sun. The pharaohs, who were deemed the offspring and manifestation of the sun god Ra, bedecked themselves in golden finery to emphasise their divine origin and to show that they were, literally, the light of their people. The immutability of gold was associated with immortality, its rarity with the uncommon appearance of spiritual perfection and kingliness.

Such a viewpoint is a long way from that of modern people, who are used to a world where any object can be made to appear as gold and silver by the process of electroplating: when this surface technique was patented by George Elkington in Birmingham in 1840, it confirmed the now ubiquitous mindset that alchemy was a thing of the past, a mixture of superstition and mystical mumbo-jumbo, and that chemistry and its scientific counterparts were the true

23. Among Amerindian cultures such as the Tairona in modern Colombia, gold is evidence of the earth's fecundity: it was formed when the earth first became fertile.

24. The Turin Papyrus map, which is housed in the Turin Museum in Italy, dated to 1100 BCE, shows the many gold-bearing regions in the eastern desert.

understanding of the natural world. In the process of putting gold, whether authentic or not, in the hands of everyone, its symbolic function was forgotten or ignored. Gold became quantified as a simple metal and took its place in the periodic table: Au, with an atomic number of 79 (i.e. 79 protons/electrons), a cubic crystal structure and 118 neutrons. These numbers are not regarded as significant, except as a way of delineating gold from other metallic structures. Gold still retains its financial value in the world's banking institutions, although it has taken second place to the US dollar as the reserve currency on the global monetary system. In other words, gold has become a commodity to be traded like any other, and is no longer viewed as the basis of a universal currency. Whatever we take as 'the gold standard' nowadays, in whatever domain of life, is far more subject to change than gold in pre-modern thinking.

Cosmic Order

Alchemy relies, above all, on the idea that the universe is a beautifully ordered place, where the original infinite and indeterminate state of Being (Gk. 'chaos') has been differentiated into an order of knowable patterns (Gk. 'cosmos'), revealing truths about the world and about human beings. The essential Unity of all things is one substance, and all the varied physical bodies and forms are manifestations of that substance.

This cosmic order is observable in the interactions of the four elements (earth, water, air and ether/fire), a theory expounded by Empedocles, Plato, Aristotle and others:[25]

25. For an analysis of early Greek texts on the four elements, see G.S. Kirk et al., *The Presocratic Philosophers* (Cambridge, 1983). The interplay of elements has long

these arise out of the same substance (*materia prima*) and can be converted into each other. Each element is regarded as having two qualities or humours: earth is cold and dry; water is cold and wet; air is hot and wet; ether/fire is hot and dry. The four elements are considered to be different forms or appearances of prime matter, so that all visible, material things are a specific combination of hotness, dryness, coldness and wetness. A thing's appearance in one form does not preclude its transmutation into another.

Secondly, there is a close and important correspondence between macrocosm and microcosm. Both the universe ('the great world', *al-ʿālam al-kabīr*) and the human being ('the small world', *al-ʿālam al-ṣaghīr*) are expressions of the same reality. Indeed these correspondences link what might otherwise appear as disparate worlds (the world of heaven/planets and the world of earth/elements, the universe 'out there' and the human individual consciousness), and thus the science of astrology developed as the key to understanding the formation and transmutation of elements and metals.[26] It is worth noting that according to Plato and Aristotle, all earthly objects are under the power of the moon, and are in a state of constant flux[27] and transformation: in this natural state of change, which the alchemical art seeks to imitate and utilise, earth can be changed to water if its 'dryness' is converted into 'wetness' and it remains 'cold', or air can

---

fascinated writers of different persuasions, from Dante to T.S. Eliot (whose *Four Quartets* is structured according to the elements).

26. See Arthur Hopkins, *Alchemy* (Morningside Heights, 1934), 28. For the correspondence of human being and universe in the Ismāʿīlī tradition and the *Rasāʾil Ikhwān al-Ṣafāʾ* as well as in Ibn ʿArabī's work, see Ebstein, *Mysticism and Philosophy in al-Andalus*, 189–200, 205–12.

27. For a discussion of the idea of flux in Plato, see Andrew Mason, *Flow and Flux in Plato's Philosophy* (London, 2016).

become fire if its natural moisture is replaced by 'dryness'. This condition of macrocosmic flux was seen to mirror that in the microcosm, i.e. in the incessant play and interplay of thoughts within the human mind.[28]

Thirdly, the processes of growth and development reflect each other. The fundamental doctrine of medieval alchemy, derived from Aristotle's *Meteorology* and current until well into the 17th century CE, was that metals 'grow' within the earth, just as plants and animals grow upon the earth. One basic substance metamorphoses into all the known metallic forms (seven were known in medieval times, which were linked to the seven known planets). The immediate parents of these metals are sulphur (identified with fire, hot and dry) and mercury or quicksilver (identified with water, cold and wet). These two principles, the former 'male', the latter 'female', which together contain all the possible diversity of the elements, interact within the earth in the form of vapours or exhalations, and under particular conditions metals are formed. In Hellenistic alchemy, sulphur is the masculine principle, the dragon and the sun, which fixes the feminine quicksilver, the ourobouros and the moon. Sulphur and quicksilver are like brother and sister. While sulphur has the power to dissolve, kill and bring metals to life, quicksilver is a healing elixir but highly volatile: it is the most difficult to define and highly elusive, often called the *cervus fugitivus* (fugitive stag). Quicksilver was regarded as the primordial water of creation, a solvent in which metals decompose and the water of resurrection from which transmuted metals arise.

28. This 'elemental' structure can be seen in the fourfold division of thoughts into divine, angelic, psychic and satanic. See *Fut.*I.666 and *K. al-Inbāh 'alā ṭarīq Allāh*, trans. Denis Gril, *JMIAS* 15 (1994), 13.

Thus the idea that there is a single substance which splits into two progenitors, and these in turn give rise to their metallic offspring, directly parallels the human creation which is spoken of in the Quran as deriving from Adam: 'O humankind, fear your Lord, who created you [all] from a single soul, and who created from it its fellow, and who spread many men and women from the two of them.'[29] In both the human and the metallic world, as in the universe itself, the crucial factor was to understand how a multitude of different forms could have come about from one Origin. In numerical terms, this is identical to the Pythagorean understanding of the way in which the number 1 is doubled to become 2, and how from that principial division all number proceeds.

Each metal represents a different stage of growth or development within the earth. If left to develop and mature naturally in the earth under the right conditions, it was believed that the metallic substance would eventually turn into gold. This 'ripening' process results in a hierarchy of metals, with gold and silver occupying the two highest positions. Mining was viewed as a kind of natural obstetrics, delivering the 'baby' metal out of the 'womb' of the earth. Since all metals are striving to reach their ultimate stage of development of gold, the alchemist's task is to intervene in order to hasten the transmutation of that metal into gold, achieving in a day what would take Nature hundreds of years. The reason that metals appear different is that the 'quantities' of their progenitors, sulphur and quicksilver, were not in balance at the time of their origination, and that subsequently 'accidents' befall them in the relative world. They were called accidents because they were not considered to

29. Q.4.1.

be fixed: they were thought to have occurred because the metals' development had been interrupted, either as a result of temporal conditions or conditions within the earth, or through being affected by the movements of the heavens. The planets, therefore, were seen as playing a direct part in the formation of particular metals and in the natural evolution towards gold.

The Elixir

The prime agent employed by the alchemist in the transmutation process was known as the elixir (from the Arabic *al-iksīr*).[30] This was referred to by various pseudonyms including the philosophers' stone (*ḥajar al-falāsifa* or *ḥajar al-ḥukamāʾ*). There were two versions: a white elixir (*al-iksīr al-abyaḍ*), equivalent to the moon, which transmuted copper into silver, and a red elixir (*al-iksīr al-aḥmar*), equivalent to the sun, which converted silver into gold. The 2nd/8th-century father of Arab alchemy, Jābir b. Ḥayyān (known to the Latin world as Geber), had set out the theory that as each metal was a particular combination of the four elements, by rearranging the proportions of these basic qualities the metal could be transmuted.[31] The agent for this change was the elixir, which was thought to be capable not only of producing the transmutation into gold or silver but also of healing illnesses and prolonging life. The red elixir was also known as the red sulphur (*al-kibrīt al-aḥmar*), and became a technical term for designating the transformational action of a true spiritual

30. *Al-iksīr* is derived from the Greek τό ξήριον, and originally meant a medical powder.

31. See Ebstein, *Mysticism and Philosophy in al-Andalus*, 97.

master. Ibn 'Arabī uses the term in the *Tadbīrāt* in the context of what he calls 'the revered stone' (*al-ḥajar al-mukarram*), which 'is found in every existent and in every thing' and is identical to the elixir, and he states that the red sulphur is the reality that 'can be cast upon a disobedient person and it will make them become obedient, or upon someone who covers up the truth and it will make them become a person of truth and faith.'[32] He himself was later referred to as 'the red sulphur' in recognition of his mastery of spiritual alchemy.[33]

Originally the elixir was a term used for an externally applied powder for treating various medical ailments, and it retained this therapeutic dimension in mystical writing. Alchemy and medicine functioned not merely as sister sciences, but as identical activities: throughout the centuries, most of the Jewish and Muslim alchemists were physicians as well. Medicine was perceived as the same process working on different levels or in different domains: the healing of a sick person was understood to be the transmutation of a sick body into a healthy one; the transmutation of copper into gold was understood to be the healing of a sick metal and imparting health to it; the healing of a sick mind or spirit was understood to be the completing of human purpose here in this life, so that the human being can really become God's

32. *al-Tadbīrāt*, 138. This phrasing is very similar to that found in the opening poem of chapter 167 – see text p. 49. It is noteworthy that he speaks of another stone, 'the stone of bewilderment' (*ḥajar al-baht*), 'the essential point within the heart' which has a light that confounds the intellect and other faculties (134–5). It is unclear whether this refers to the white elixir that others mention.

33. Most notably by al-Sha'rānī (d. 973/1565), who presented Ibn 'Arabī's teachings in his *al-Kibrīt al-aḥmar fī bayān 'ulūm al-Shaykh al-Akbar* ('The Red Sulphur in explaining the knowledges of the Greatest Master', written on the margin of his famous *K. al-Yawāqīt wa al-jawāhir*). See Richard McGregor, 'Notes on the Transmission of Mystical Philosophy', in *Reason and Inspiration in Islam*, ed. Hermann Landolt and Todd Lawson (London, 2005), 380–92.

vicegerent or representative (*khalīfa*) on earth. This correspondence is the basis of Ibn ʿArabī's exposition in chapter 167, linking the process and goal of alchemy to the aim of the spiritual path, true human happiness and perfection.

Chapter 167: Contents and Themes

The wording of the chapter heading provides two fundamental concepts: alchemy (*kīmiyāʾ*) and happiness (*saʿāda*). The English word 'happiness' does not really convey the depth of the Arabic, which draws both on the Quranic usage (those who are 'happy' as opposed to those who are 'unhappy', terms linked directedly to the afterlife) and a long tradition stretching back to the Greek idea of *eudaimonia* (usually translated as 'happiness' but also as 'human flourishing' or fulfilment). Happiness in this context is something to be striven for in this world, not simply as an ethical excellence that is part of a good life but as the fulfilling of one's potential as a human being capable of knowing God. In stating that 'all happiness lies in knowing God',[34] Ibn ʿArabī emphasises the crucial importance of knowledge and of recognising God in every divine manifestation, in other words in whatever form or Name that He reveals Himself through. As he makes clear in this chapter, it is the attainment of perfection that is the central issue of the alchemy of happiness: 'not everyone who has found happiness is accorded perfection, for while all who are perfect are happy, not every happy one is perfect. Perfection means reaching and joining with the highest degree, and that is assuming the likeness of the Source.'[35]

34. *Fut.*IV.319.
35. See text p.63.

The seven-line poem that opens the chapter starts with the word 'elixirs' (*akāsīr*), suggesting that the primary focus of this chapter is on the many forms that effect spiritual transformation, which can transmute a basic or debased person (*bashar*), whose humanity is only skin-deep, into a fully developed human (*insān*), who is familiar with every aspect of reality and has assumed the divine likeness.[36] Ibn 'Arabī introduces his theme by outlining two distinct kinds of alchemy, which he calls 'origination' and 'elimination of defect and ailment'. The first is a creative process whereby things come into being according to their inherent nature; the second implies that the natural process of development has been hampered in some way by an accidental sickness or ill-health, and requires a therapeutic intervention. To eliminate the defect requires the special art of the alchemist, who understands the cosmic order and works with it to bring things back into balance.

One of the major features of Ibn 'Arabī's approach is that he starts with wholeness and integration. The development or evolution of the human being towards perfection is seen not simply as a process that involves going from ignorance to knowledge, or clearing obstacles on the way to a future happiness, but as beginning and being rooted in an already existing perfection or wholeness. In alchemical terms, the original metallic ore precedes all the possible forms of its existence, and its journey in time and space is a process of realising its full potential, which is gold. He finds corroboration for this standpoint in the Quranic saying 'He gave to everything its nature and then He guided it', where a thing

36. In Arabic, these two terms for 'human being' are etymologically quite different: *bashar* is related to 'skin' or 'surface' (*bashara*), while *insān* is related to 'familiarity' (*uns*).

is created whole and perfect and then begins its development and completion in time, under the aegis of divine guidance. In human terms, this development culminates in the degree of completion (*kamāl*), which is being God's representative (*khalīfa*) on earth, or acting in the full likeness of the divine image, according to which the human is created. This completion is explained by one who has already attained, and who has returned to act as instructor for those in a lower state of development, who are starting to undertake such an inner journey.

The second part of the chapter develops the theme of how the human being should travel to reach completion. It can only be achieved through a process of spiritual ascension (*mi'rāj*), returning from the lowest of the low to the full height 'for which the human being is created'. In Ibn 'Arabī's depiction, the ascent passes through all the degrees of existence in a re-enactment of the Prophet Muhammad's ascension through the seven heavens and beyond. As the Quran puts it, 'Glory be to Him Who made His servant journey by night from the Sacred Mosque to the Furthest Mosque, whose neighbourhood We have blessed, to show him some of Our Signs.'[37] Unlike previous mystics such as Abū Yazīd al-Bisṭāmī, Ibn 'Arabī is particularly faithful to the Prophet's example – for him, this was not simply a metaphorical journey, which each replicates in their own unique fashion, but one that follows the prophetic model most precisely. The heavenly journey experienced by the mystic in the course of following in the Prophet's footsteps is a graphic depiction of a central principle: the process of return to and union with Reality, whilst still living in this world.[38] It is a voyage

37. Q.17.1.

38. From a human perspective, ascension can never be considered without two

of vision, and of realising the truth of one's being in a way utterly different to any other kind of knowledge.

The ascension takes place where the level of earth ends, beyond the four elements of this world.[39] It begins with the first heaven or sphere of the moon, which is under the spiritual rulership of the prophet Adam, and continues through the various heavens up to the seventh, where Abraham resides. These heavenly spheres were regarded as one nested with another, and as spherical in shape.[40] Then the traveller passes beyond into realms that are unlimited in scope and portray successive universal principles.

Elsewhere Ibn ʿArabī reminds his readers that all vision and ascension is actually a two-sided affair: 'vision of the True God only occurs in a mutual encounter comprising an ascent and a descent. The ascending is from our side, the descending is from Him.'[41] Mutual 'confronting' (*munāzala*), the face-to-face encounter between the divine and the human, is a movement that involves both parties. It occurs within the realm of Imagination, where meaning and form interpenetrate each other. All the descriptions of spiritual

---

other journeys: the first, a descending journey which has brought us into the world of multiplicity from our origin when we are born; and the third, a journey of return from union, coming back into this world in full awareness and knowledge.

39. The initial 'earthly' stage of the journey is represented as 'a night-journey' (*isrāʾ*) that is 'horizontal' (from Mecca to Jerusalem), while the ascension (*miʿrāj*) is represented as 'vertical' (through the heavens and beyond). See *Unlimited Mercifier*, 115–22.

40. This was the conventional Ptolemaic view of the universe. See Rowson, *A Muslim Philosopher on the Soul and its Fate*, 241.

41. *Fut*.III.117 (chapter 331). The word *munāzala* is sometimes translated as 'mutual waystation', which might suggest that it is some kind of external 'place' on the road travelled by the mystic. Corbin (*Creative Imagination in the Sufism of Ibn ʿArabī* (Princeton, NJ, 1969), 156) translates it as 'condescendence', in which God and the human alight. Although this is true to the original root meaning of the word, Ibn ʿArabī specifies that it is only the divine that descends.

ascension are best understood as a series of encounters, in which the mystic comes into direct contemplation of the divine Presence through the 'Signs' which He reveals. On the one hand, this entails an endless journey of revelation, in which there is no repetition.[42] On the other, specific degrees or levels of existence need to be delineated, so that the journey can be characterised as having a beginning, middle and end.[43]

The Two Travellers

While the ascension motif appears in various forms in Ibn ʿArabī's different writings,[44] and we find mystical transmutation as a central theme throughout Ibn ʿArabī's life, Ibn ʿArabī depicts the ascent in chapter 167 in a most unusual way. The emphasis is on two specific modes of spiritual travelling and learning, the mode of intellectual endeavour and the mode of spiritual insight.

First of all, he describes how people question their existence and seek the meaning of being in charge of a body. Who or what has created them in this way? What kind of Being

42. A point often emphasised by Ibn ʿArabī – see for example: 'In the Divine Presence, due to its vastness, nothing is ever repeated. This is the truth upon which one can fully depend', *Fuṣūṣ*, chapter on Seth, 42.

43. See Appendix A.

44. For example, *Kitāb al-Isrāʾ* (*The Book of the Night-Journey*, written in allusive rhyming prose shortly after his first major ascension experience in Fez in ca. 594/1197, at the age of thirty-three); *Risālat al-Anwār* (*The Epistle of Lights*, written in 602/1205 in Konya); and chapter 367 of the *Futūḥāt* (corresponding to the 17th Quranic sura, the Sura of the Night-journey), in which he gives an account of the Prophet's ascension and his own spiritual journey). See also *Seal of Saints*, 155–71 (chapter 10: The Double Ladder), where Chodkiewicz analyses the account of the ascension and return in *R. al-Anwār* and chapters 167 and 367.

is He or She? Then he portrays the coming of a prophetic figure whose role is to instruct people in 'sound knowledge', and 'to clarify for them the way of knowledge that leads to Him'. This instructor is met with two reactions: one of acceptance and a desire to learn from the instructor, and one of scepticism and a desire to learn for oneself, without reference to anything but reason. Ibn 'Arabī characterises the first as an 'imitator' (*muqallid*)[45] or 'follower' (*tābiʿ*), and the second as a 'rational thinker' or 'speculative theoretician' (*ṣāḥib al-naẓar*).[46]

Both of them seek the knowledge they have heard about, and undertake a journey of ascent together. The follower, who is shown reality through the 'private face', is given preferential treatment by the prophet who rules over each heaven, whereas the rational thinker is left increasingly out in the cold as he rises through the heavens and finds only the planets and what they can teach him.

This has very strong echoes of the famous story of his own meeting with the great philosopher Ibn Rushd (d. 595/1198) in Cordoba, especially the question that Ibn Rushd posed to the young Ibn 'Arabī: 'What kind of solution have you found through divine unveiling and illumination? Is it identical with what we have reached through speculative

45. In traditional Islamic jurisprudence (*fiqh*), *taqlīd* meant accepting the judgment of another person, specifically the rulings of the scholars (*'ulamā'*) who gave a judgment in particular situations according to the Quran and Sunna. However, Ibn 'Arabī is here referring to the more direct meaning of personally adhering to the Prophet's teaching, without intermediary.

46. *Naẓar* can also be translated as 'observation' or 'mental consideration'. Al-Ḥallāj uses the term in a similarly negative vein in one of his poems: 'My *naẓar* is the beginning of my illness; alas for my heart and what it has done' (*Sharḥ Dīwān al-Ḥallāj*, 165). The term is also found in a poem by Awḥad al-Dīn Kirmānī, whom Ibn 'Arabī met in Konya in 602/1205 (no: 92, *Heart's Witness*), but used in the very different meaning of 'someone possessed of true observation', i.e. a person of inner knowledge.

thought?'[47] His question is entirely reasonable, whether the intellect is equal in scope to mystical illumination and can afford the same results, and within the terms of the human mind, the answer to be expected should be either a simple Yes or a clear No. The reply given by the young Ibn 'Arabī – Yes and No – indicates unequivocally that revelation is simultaneously reasonable and beyond reason. The doubts implicit in the theoretical view, which is of necessity limited, are annihilated in the shift to seeing or being informed with the certainty of direct experience.

As these two figures are central to the story that Ibn 'Arabī tells in chapter 167, it is worth examining more deeply what he might mean by them. At first sight the 'follower' and the 'rational thinker' appear to be personifying a simple conflict between belief and reason. In modern times, especially in Western societies where church and state have long been separated, and where scientific endeavour and reason are normally regarded as paramount in underpinning civilisation and culture, religious belief has less hold on society and tends to be treated more as an individual matter of conscience. When the simplistic polarity of religion versus rationality or fundamentalism versus science appears, most educated people today naturally opt for the latter. It was not always so: in Ibn 'Arabī's day there was no sense of science divorced from religion, and it was unthinkable for any medieval society to have functioned fully without reference to the civilising effects of religion. As William Chittick has remarked,

> To say 'mysticism versus philosophy' in the context of Islamic civilisation means something far different

47. *Fut.*I.153–4. See *Unlimited Mercifier*, 57–8.

> from what it has come to signify in the West, where many philosophers have looked upon mysticism as the abandonment of any attempt to reconcile religious data with intelligent thought. Certainly the Muslim mystics and philosophers sometimes display a certain mutual opposition and antagonism, but never does their relationship even approach incompatibility.[48]

What Ibn ʿArabī is really pointing to with these two figures is less an external dichotomy of religious belief versus rational thought (mental structures which are subject to change over time), and more a fundamental internal framework for understanding the reality of the self and the world, and how learning takes place. In other words, this dichotomy is very much part of everybody's experience. For example, when we are presented with some new understanding, there are two possible approaches: either to accept it as coming from beyond our current perspective and seek to know it on its own terms, or to try to shape it into the knowledge that we already have. The 'imitator' pursues the first course, something that everyone does when learning their first language as a baby, absorbing by copying their mother and father and other adults – this direct imitation is sometimes called 'mimesis' and relies on accepting things as they arise. It is a fundamental ingredient in successful learning. However, mimesis is not the only factor in learning, and the learning process does not stop with simple imitation. As a child develops a sense of self and rationality, then analytical and critical thinking come to the fore, and everything that is presented is subjected to ideas of right and wrong, liking

48. William C. Chittick, 'Mysticism versus Philosophy in Earlier Islamic History', *Religious Studies* 17/1 (1981), 87.

and disliking, accepting and rejecting etc. In short, all experience becomes assimilated through a growing sense of 'I' (I think this, I feel that), in opposition to the 'you/he/she' of others. Spiritual training seeks to develop a further level of integration, where such explicit mental and emotional constructs, which are based on habits of mind and already established connections, do not cloud or interfere with the direct mimetic capacity we have for seeing things as they are, and where the constructed sense of self is no longer centre-stage. In order to see the whole, we have to transcend or leave behind our current vision of the parts. This does not mean abandoning clarity or precise thought, but rather putting it in service of the vision of the whole. The aim is to integrate these two cognitive processes into a new kind of fusion, a new realisation of balance. If the journey of re-integration is successful, it will result in true happiness.

The kind of 'imitation' or 'following' that Ibn 'Arabī intends here is not slavish copying without any understanding, nor simply believing something to be so, but a constant exercise of open receptivity and imaginative identification. As has recently been suggested by a modern neuroscientist in analysing the left and right hemispheres of the brain, 'the enormous strength of the human capacity for mimesis is that our brains let us escape from the confines of our own experience and enter directly into the experience of another human being... it comes about through our ability to transform what we perceive into something we directly experience. It is founded on empathy and grounded in the body.'[49] This kind of imitation, which involves intention, aspiration, attraction and empathy and is what all of us used in our

49. McGilchrist, *The Master and His Emissary* (New Haven, 2009), 248.

development as babies and children, is very different from mere copying. Copying is mechanical and is the rational mind's way of understanding imitation. Mimesis is a mythic identification, an imaginal empathetic embodiment. This is why extreme care is needed with the imaginative faculty: we are not simply projecting neutral images onto a screen, we are participating directly in what we imagine, forming models and patterns. What we imagine becomes part of us. We are 'making ourselves', making our own reality and creating our own happiness. Modern research into mirror neurones seems to demonstrate how 'thinking about something, or even just hearing words connected with it, alters the way we behave.'[50] This insight led many in the past to observe that the path to virtue is by imitation of the virtuous:[51] in some sense we really do create our own destiny. It is this that makes the ascension story such a potent symbol of transformation. It provides a framework for contemplation of the deepest levels of reality, including human models at different degrees of integration (symbolised as spheres of wholeness), whose unceasing prophetic function is precisely to guide those who aspire to their own fulfilment.

The chapter includes detailed conversations with the prophets associated with the seven heavens and on the knowledge which is linked to each degree of existence. In Ibn ʿArabī's account of the two travellers, the left-brain rationalist only succeeds in knowing and understanding the universe of planets or planetary bodies, i.e. how the planets affect the material realm (as in astrology), while the right-brain mimetic follower is educated by the prophets into

50. Ibid. 251.

51. This is the founding principle of all Christian monastic tradition. See, for example, St Augustine in *On the Free Choice of the Will*.

various truths about the nature of Reality, and is allowed to travel into regions closed off to the rational mind, such as being 'plunged into the supreme light, where love-ecstasy overcomes him.'[52] As a result the mystic encounters God in everything, and in a shining rejoicing realises the real meaning of Unity: in Ibn 'Arabī's words, the soul realises that 'she has seen Him only through Himself, not through herself, and that she loves Him only through Him, not through herself, since in reality He is the One who loves Himself.'[53] Elsewhere he describes the realisation in autobiographical terms:

> I gained in this night-journey the true meanings of all the Names, and I saw them all returning to a single Named and a single Source. This Named was my very object of contemplation, and that Source my very being. My journeying took place only within me, and my direction was only towards me. Through this I came to know that I am a pure servant, without any trace of lordship in me.[54]

The follower's journey ends with a return to the world, but along a path that has never been travelled before, while the rational thinker returns in the same way that he ascended. In other words, the follower has been transformed alchemically the first time round, while the rational thinker remains the same and simply gains some additional knowledge – the thinker doesn't move beyond his condition of Sisyphean labour until he takes the path of following and direct self-knowledge. What Ibn 'Arabī also alludes to,

52. See text p.141.
53. *Fut.*III.331.
54. *Fut.*III.350.

by speaking of the two figures undertaking their journey *together* and the rational thinker returning to the beginning and re-ascending in the manner of a follower, is what we in the modern world might refer to as a rebalancing of the right and left hemispheres of the brain in a new vision of reality.[55]

This vision is evoked in startling imagery in a remarkable poem on the unveiling of Reality: all that seems solid (stars in the heavens, mountains of rock) is liquefied, and Paradise is no longer a far-off destination, but 'is brought close'. What God desires for a human being, we are told, is that the 'wild beasts' of potential should be 'driven together', brought into alignment and harnessed into service.

The chapter then ends with a profound re-evaluation of the worth of accumulated knowledge, and an account of a personal encounter with a 'doctor of philosophy' who was given an insight into the nature of faith and knowledge and their fruits in the next world.

The Private Face (al-wajh al-khāṣṣ)

One of the key distinguishing characteristics of the 'follower', which enables him to learn from the prophets directly, is knowledge of what Ibn 'Arabī calls 'the private divine face'.[56] The rational thinker, he says, 'has no knowledge of this face at all'. To know this private face is to possess the elixir of

55. For a description of the functions of the right and left brain hemispheres, in terms of breadth and focus, possibility and predictability, integration and division, insight and rationality, and how they may relate to each other, see McGilchrist, *The Master and His Emissary*, 37–66 et passim.

56. See text p.76.

the mystics, because it transforms what appears as outer 'objective' experience into inner 'subjective' experience.

Everyone has two faces or ways of looking: one towards the single centre of being, which is 'private' or special to the individual concerned and constitutes their direct relationship with reality, and one towards the circumference of manifestations, which is shared with others. It is through the private face that one's utter neediness is recognised. This applies to everything in existence, not only human beings.[57] Everything that exists in the world has a private face to its Creator, and all are given knowledge and educated through this private face, whether they are aware of it or not. The only thing that distinguishes people of God from each other is their knowledge of this face: 'some know that God reveals Himself to every existent from this private face, and some do not.'[58] One aspect of this knowledge is the recognition that all actions are really divine action, and someone who realises this is said to have been 'freed from the bondage of secondary causes'.[59] In this connection it is interesting to note an apparent paradox: in this spiritual ascension the follower receives knowledge through the private face directly from God and yet at the same time he meets the prophets in each heaven, who act as instructors. These apparent prophetic 'intermediaries' are really nothing but ways in which divine knowledge is disseminated, depositories of secrets and mysteries who know that they are inseparable from their origin – like a candle whose light comes from having been lit, and which can transmit its light to any other as yet unlit candle. As is explained elsewhere by Ibn 'Arabī, the recognition of utter need towards

57. *Fut.*II.423.
58. *Fut.*IV.222.
59. *Fut.*IV.199.

God includes all forms of interaction, and being free from secondary causes and knowing the original Causer does not mean eradicating or interfering with the apparent order of cause and effect. 'God affirms that human beings are utterly needy towards Him and not towards anything else, so as to make clear to them that He is the One who is revealed in the forms of secondary causes, and that the secondary causes, which are the forms, are a veil over Him.'[60]

Idrīs, the Prophet of Alchemy and Medicine

Many of the themes in chapter 167 are prefigured in an earlier chapter of the *Futūḥāt*, chapter 15 on the inner knowledge of 'the spiritual breaths' (*anfās*), which he describes as 'the fragrances of divine closeness'. Not only does this chapter include his meeting with Ibn Rushd, which we referred to earlier, but it also mentions a mysterious teacher whom he calls 'the Healer of Wounds', a prophetic instructor whose alchemical message is both transformative and restorative. In the previous chapter,[61] he mentions the same figure as second in a series of prophetic personages whom he saw in a vision in Cordoba: they are referred to by their inner quality rather than by name, since they are not viewed as separate individuals but as instances of the Spirit of Muhammad extending help to humankind. The list begins with 'the Separator, Distinguisher' (*al-mufarriq*), 'the Healer of Wounds' (*mudāwī*

60. *Fut.*II.469.

61. Chapter 14, on 'the inner knowledge of the secrets of the prophets, i.e. the prophet-saints and perfected poles of the communities that existed from the time of Adam to Muhammad, and the fact that the pole is only one [person] since God created him, never dying, and where he resides' – *Fut.*I.149ff.

al-kulūm) and 'the Tearful, Weeper' (*al-bakkā'*). The Healer of Wounds is singled out as 'expert in [all] the woundings caused by subjective love and inclination, opinion and speculation, this low world, Satan and the soul, [speaking] in the language of every prophet, messenger or friend (*walī*)... we ourselves have taken comprehensive knowledge from him in a different manner [to other people].'[62] Ibn 'Arabī goes on to mention six further instances of this wisdom's appearance among human beings at different times. Each figure is mentioned under a particular quality (for example, 'the Submitted to destiny and fate', *al-Mustaslim lil-qaḍā' wa al-qadr*), rather than their actual name, although at one point he suggests that 'the Bringer of Wisdoms' (*wāḍi' al-ḥikam*) might be the prophet Luqmān, but he is not sure. We may note that this psycho-spiritual science of healing is described as being brought originally by a prophetic figure, the Healer of Wounds, and then transmitted from generation to generation by a series of sages.[63]

Although not directly named, 'the Healer of Wounds' clearly refers in the first instance to the prophet Idrīs (with Adam being the 'separator' and Noah the 'tearful'). The healing power or spiritual alchemy of which he speaks in chapter 15 is one of the many sciences Idrīs brought to the world. Idrīs is seen as the great bringer of scripture, teacher of reading and of book-learning, as well as the greatest doctor,

62. *Fut.*I.151. The particular expertise ascribed to the divine Healer covers all the four topics mentioned by the early Sufi Ḥārith b. Asad al-Muḥāsibī (d. 243/857), in his *K. al-Ri'āya fī ḥuqūq Allāh* and *R. al-Mustarshidīn*, as being the enemies of humankind: this world (*dunyā*), the self/soul (*nafs*), passions (*hawā*) and Satan (*shayṭān*).

63. Ibn 'Arabī's view of successive revelations through the prophets, culminating in the appearance of Muhammad, stands in contrast to conceptions such as Marsilio Ficino's *prisca theologia*, which held that the religious message given by God in antiquity runs through all religions but is in increasingly diluted form.

one who eliminates spiritual and physical ailments and defects by returning a person to their reality. As Ibn ʿArabī observes elsewhere,[64] there is a fundamental link, linguistically and semantically, between words (*kalim*, *kalām*) and wounds (*kalm*, *kulūm*): both can injure a person, and both can educate. The linkage, which may appear strange to Western readers, conveys the contemplative notion that just as a cut opens up a physical body and reveals what is hidden beneath the skin, so words open up a world of meaning that lies beneath the forms of speaker and listener. The physical world being the outer visible aspect of the Spirit, words convey meaning by revealing the hidden.

In chapter 15 Ibn ʿArabī describes how those who know through direct inner experience (*ʿārifūn*) are inwardly aroused by inhaling some of the divine fragrance that has wafted towards them from the realm of Reality. Suffering the pangs of yearning for Truth, they look for a person of realisation and wisdom (*muḥaqqiq*, *ḥakīm*) who can impart to them all that they need to know for their own salvation and happiness. Then they are

> made acquainted with a divine individual, one who possesses the secret they are looking for and the knowledge they desire. The Real raises him up amongst them as a pole around whom their spiritual ship sails and a leader through whom their possession is set in order. He is called the Healer of Wounds, and he disseminates among them knowledge, wisdom and mysteries that cannot be contained in a book.[65]

64. *Fut*.I.747.
65. *Fut*.I.152. Note the similarity between this account and the one given in chapter 167 – see text pp.68–9.

It is crucial to notice that for Ibn 'Arabī 'the Healer of Wounds', Idrīs, is not simply the prophet who instructs his people in the study of books (*dars al-kutub*), as is commonly thought, but someone who conveys an essentially esoteric teaching, which 'cannot be contained in a book'.

Ibn 'Arabī then speaks of the two ways of alchemy which he also expounds in chapter 167: the first can transmute iron into silver through the alchemical process and art, a cleansing process which takes place over time like the effect of medicine; and the second can effect the transformation into gold 'through a special way', which he simply describes as 'an astounding mystery' – he is referring to the instantaneous realisation of perfection, which is the effect of red sulphur.

> This course is not pursued in the hope of wealth and riches but out of a desire for the best of outcomes, so that one can thereby reach the level of perfection (*kamāl*)... Everything that is engendered in the mine is seeking its goal, which is perfection – and that is gold. Within the mine, however, defects and ailments befall it due to an excess of dryness or moisture or of heat or cold which remove it from equilibrium. This sickness has an influence upon the [mineral] form, so that it is called iron or copper or lead or some other metal. The wise teacher imparts direct knowledge of the medicines and remedies, whose efficacy removes the ailment that has overtaken the individuality of the one who is seeking the degree of perfection amongst the minerals – gold – and so he removes it. He restores to health and proceeds until it reaches the level of perfection... The only goal is the degree of human perfection in terms of servanthood: God created the

human *in the finest stature*, then He *brought him down to the lowest of the low, except for those who have faith and act righteously*[66] and who remain in original health. In other words, it is in a person's nature to pick up defects that come from the accidents [of life] and the ailments of self-interest. This sage desires to bring the person back to *the finest stature*, according to which they are created by God. This is what an intelligent person aims for, through the direct knowledge of the art which is called alchemy – and that is nothing but the science of weights and measures.[67]

The 'spiritual breaths' that form the subject of chapter 15 are essentially an expression for that which brings someone back to their original nature, 'the finest stature' of human perfection. They are like medicines that cleanse a person of all the ailments of self and self-interest that have occurred through living in the world. The prophetic instructor is thus a doctor of the soul, whose wisdom heals all wounds.

Another aspect of this spiritual healing is brought out in the context of the relation between Idrīs/Hermes and the various philosophical teachings that he is said to have imparted to humankind, which are known as the Hermetic sciences. In the following passage Ibn 'Arabī focuses on the dichotomy between intellectual inquiry and spiritual insight, on his own method of receiving knowledge and the crucial

66. Q.95.5–6.

67. Ar: *ma'rifat al-maqādīr wa al-awzān* (*Fut*.I.152). This phrase, literally 'the inner knowledge of quantities and balances', is precisely how Ibn 'Arabī defines alchemy at the beginning of chapter 167. In Chapter 15 he then goes on to describe the creation of the human body in terms of the four elements and how the four internal humours (black bile, phlegm, blood and yellow bile) correspond to macrocosmic principles. See Appendix B.

importance of understanding the limitations and dangers of intellectual interpretation:

> I proceed in accordance with how the Idrīsian reality is unveiled. This came about when I examined the states of the philosophers and the traditions they pass on about [Idrīs], and the way they have [formed] different opinions about him. I said to myself: I want to take this matter directly from him and understand what has caused them to go wrong. So I went into a retreat for 36 days, and I came to know the matter from [Idrīs] exactly as it is... I saw how error had affected the ancients because of their own souls: this was because they related what he had said, then they interpreted [it] and held different opinions [about it]. This is just like the way the traditions (*ḥadīth*) of the Prophet have come to us, and then one person declares permissible what another says is forbidden, based on their capacity to understand what he said.[68]

Given the ancientness of the Hermes–Idrīs figure as the primordial instructor of humanity, the statement that Ibn ʿArabī received knowledge from him directly through unveiling is quite remarkable. It puts in sharp relief the crucial importance that Ibn ʿArabī gives to direct knowledge, unveiling (*kashf*), and the unlimited capacity of the heart in contrast to the intellect. It is also a comment on the way that human beings are limited by, and to, their own viewpoint unless they engage in specific spiritual work, polishing the heart and being empty of reflective thinking, in order that

68. Reported by Ibn Sawdakīn from Ibn ʿArabī in *Lawāqiḥ al-asrār*, no. 154 (ed. Abdel Baqi Miftah). This passage is paraphrased in ʿAbd al-Wahhāb al-Shaʿrānī, *K. al-Yawāqīt* (Cairo, 1277/1860), 130.

they may be shown the truth of things as they are, without distorting them through the lens of their own viewpoint. However, a deeper aspect can be seen in the fact that in Ibn ʿArabī's teaching, Idrīs is the spiritual Pole or 'axis' (*quṭb*), the stable unmoving point around whom the whole 360° cycle of human existence turns and is in constant motion. This is why he resides in the sphere of the sun, at the centre of the heavens and of all existence (the mid-point of the 28 degrees). Taking knowledge directly from him is equivalent to taking knowledge from the central point of equilibrium, from which all things are seen exactly as they are.[69] His ability to heal is a function of his place at the centre of things: only one who possesses perfect inner balance is capable of healing the sick.

As a prophet before Abraham and Noah, Idrīs' prophethood can be considered to have occurred before what is normally regarded as the Western monotheistic tradition, in a period that is sometimes described as henotheistic or monolatrous (where a single god was worshipped alongside the existence of other deities). As Ibn ʿArabī makes clear elsewhere, the wisdom of Idrīs, which 'cannot be contained in a book', is the knowledge of *tawḥīd* (which may be translated as either Unity or the affirmation of Unity), not as a religious formula or a concept but as a reality to be witnessed and lived. This is the inner reality of the words of Idrīs to Ibn ʿArabī during his own ascension: 'I was a prophet, calling them to the word of *tawḥīd*, not to *tawḥīd* [itself] – for no-one has ever denied *tawḥīd*... we did not say [what we communicated

69. This also explains why Ibn ʿArabī insists that all those who are known as 'poles' (*aqṭāb*) are in reality nothing but deputies and heirs of Idrīs, the perennial solar heart of the universe, who is both the centre of the circle of the universe and its circumference, place of God's peace through perfection (*salām*). See *Fut.*II.6 and 571, and *Seal of Saints*, 91–4.

to people from God] on the basis of reasoning (*naẓar*); we only said it on the basis of a single direct relationship [with Him].'[70] This single direct relationship is equivalent to the private face mentioned in chapter 167.

We may note that the '36 days' he mentions in relation to his retreat is by no means an arbitrary number: in chapter 198 of the *Futūḥāt*, Ibn 'Arabī analyses thirty-six specific forms of *tawḥīd* that are found in the Quran (*lā ilāha illā hū*), which he describes as arising from 'the Breath of the Compassionate' (*nafas al-raḥmān*). Again we notice the mention of 'breath' in the context of a transformative act, here 'remembrance' (*dhikr*) of God. The 36th Sura in the Quran is Yā Sīn, traditionally regarded as the 'heart' of the Quran, and it may be no coincidence that the two letters of this Sura are also the final two letters of Idrīs' name. 36 is equally the numerical *abjad* value of the word *ilāh* (*alif* + *lām* + *hā'* = 1 + 30 + 5), meaning 'god', and may be understood as the number that points to whatever human beings take as a way of worship, whatever is worshipped as 'divine'. In one respect this is the primordial religion, prior to any religions of the Book.[71] Humans are spiritual creatures, inherently orientated towards worship and finding meaning in life. Not all religions have been outwardly theistic, but they have all taught an appreciation of the ineffable reality or unity underlying every moment, every state, every viewpoint.

Chapter 167, therefore, points the reader clearly towards *tawḥīd* as the universal message brought by all the prophets

70. *Fut*.III.348, trans. J.W. Morris in *The Meccan Illuminations* (Paris, 1988), 370–1.

71. I am very grateful to our friend Abdel Baqi Miftah for pointing out in private correspondence these and many other instances of the number 36 and its relation to Idrīs.

and saints, and its special role as medicine for the sicknesses that overcome human beings in the relative world. As a later Ottoman follower of Ibn ʿArabī, Mehmed Üftāde (d. 988/1580), put it, 'union is the only remedy for separation'. As is always stressed in alchemical writings, the knowledge of realities is only imparted to those who are worthy of it, i.e. those who are open to unveiling and allow themselves to be healed by the redemptive power of the revealed word as meaning. It is a chapter on the limitations of intellectual inquiry, the sadness it engenders, and how the illness that afflicts everyone may be treated. It is a chapter of redemption and transformation, as exemplified by the unnamed philosopher at the end, who is brought weeping to a new realisation of his situation and a new life. In short, it is a chapter that speaks to everyone, whatever our stage in life or the times we live in, whatever our degree of understanding.

IBN ʿARABI

The Alchemy of Human Happiness

TRANSLATION

by Stephen Hirtenstein

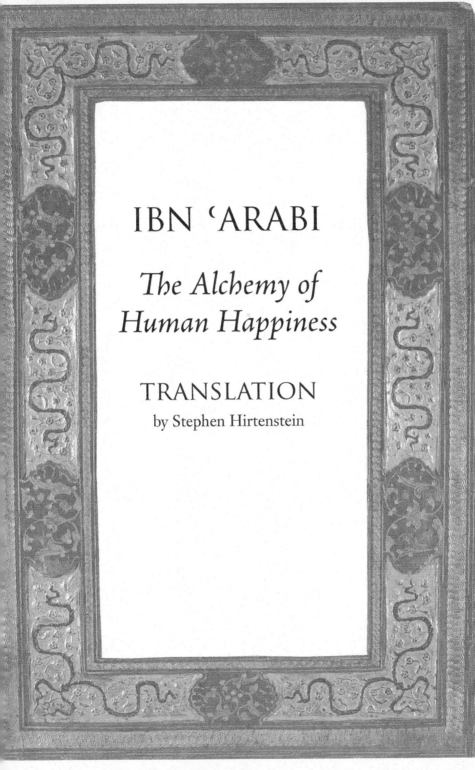

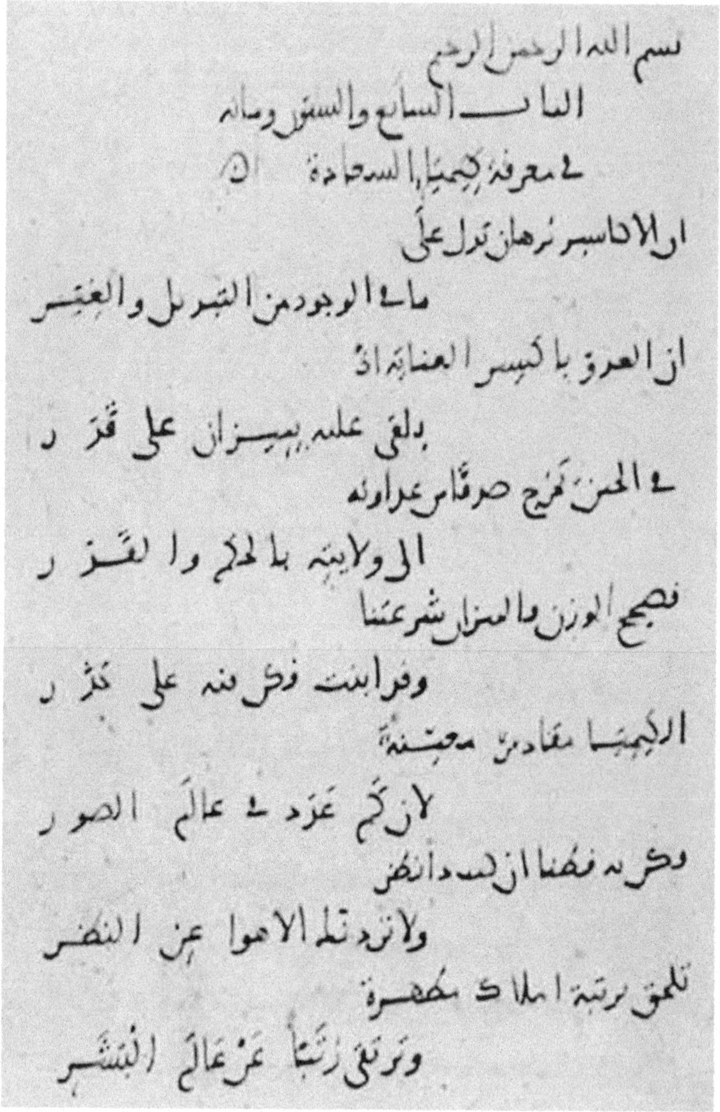

بسم الله الرحمن الرحيم
الباب السابع والستون ومائة
في معرفة كيمياء السعادة
ان الاكسير برهان تدل على
ما في الوجود من التبديل والغير
ان العروق باكسير العناية اذ
يلقى عليه بميزان على قدر
في الحين تخرج صرفا من عوارضه
الى الولاية بالحكم والقدر
فصحح الوزن والميزان شرعتنا
وقد ابنت لكم منه على قدر
الكيميا مقادير معينة
لان كم عدد في عالم الصور
وكم به نقصا ان لم يسد انتقص
ولا ترد تلك الاهوا عن النظر
تلحق برتبة املاك مطهرة
وترتقي رتبا عن عالم البشر

The opening page of the chapter in Evkaf Müzesi MS 1859, fol. 16b, in the author's own hand. Courtesy of the Turkish and Islamic Arts Museum, Istanbul, Turkey.

Part I

ALCHEMICAL ELIXIRS[1] are an evident proof,
showing what can be altered and replaced
in [the realm of] existence.

If an enemy[2] has the elixir of divine Grace[3]
cast upon him in a proper balanced measure,

he can truly pass in time from his [state of]
enmity to [the degree of] His friendship[4]
with the power of judgment and decree.

1. It should be noted that Ibn ʿArabī uses the plural form here to indicate that there are several (more than two) kinds of elixir, both in the visible realm and in the invisible.

2. Ar: *ʿaduww*, which means both a hostile party and someone who is remote. It is the opposite of the term *walī*, which means both a friend and someone who is close. These terms are commonly used to describe the enemies and friends of God.

3. Ar: *ʿināya*, divine providential care or grace. In addition to the well-known attributes of being Knowing, Willing, Powerful etc., God is profoundly Caring towards His creatures, an idea which is founded upon the all-embracing divine Mercy (*raḥma*). The divine solicitude or providential grace which God lavishes on certain beings occupies a central place in Ibn ʿArabī's teaching. It conveys the sense of a special divine favour, given directly to a servant without any intermediary, and ultimately is what determines whether a person becomes a knower of God – see, for example, *Fut.*II.289: 'the light of faith bestows felicity, and in no way can it be gained through proofs. It derives only from *a divine grace* towards the one in whom it is found' (quoted in *SDG*, 169). Later in this chapter, Ibn ʿArabī describes how the giving (or withholding) of this grace is the real cause of superiority appearing among human beings in this world.

4. That is to say, he becomes a friend of God, in other words a saint (*walī*). The personal pronoun here is ambiguous. So this line could also be read as: he can pass from his state of enmity or distance to his state of friendship or closeness (i.e. a movement from a negative quality to a positive one) by the power of God's decree.

Correct the weight, [using] the scales of our
revealed Law – I have explained clearly, so
be on your guard!
Alchemy is [a science of] determined measures –
how much or how many is a figure[5] in the
world of forms.

Be aware of that if you are someone who reflects,
and do not let desires remove you from clear
observation.

Then you will be admitted to the degree of pure
angels,[6] and you will ascend in rank beyond the
world of mere human.[7]

'Alchemy' is an expression for the knowledge that pertains to weights and measures, as regards all the bodies and meanings, in the sensible and intelligible realms, that can be quantified and measured, and their power to change and be transformed – by which I mean the changing of states that come upon the one essence.[8] It is a knowledge that is at once natural, spiritual and divine. We call it divine because there appears [the attribute of] being seated,[9] descending,[10]

5. Ar: *'adad*, literally a number or something that can be counted. In other words, it is a quantity composed of units and therefore different to the simple nature of the One.

6. The model of the human angelic realisation is the prophet Idrīs, of whom it is said 'We raised him up to a high place' (Q.19:57).

7. Ar: *bashar*, meaning the ordinary, unregenerate human being. The *bashar* level is below the angelic purity and represents what the angels saw when they spoke of mankind as 'sowing corruption' (Q.2.30), while the true human being (*insān*) is the Adamic level to which they were commanded to prostrate.

8. Ar: *al-'ayn al-wāḥida*. *'Ayn* means both essence and source.

9. Ar: *istiwā'*, a word associated with the Compassionate Mercy being seated or establishing Himself upon the Throne (Q.20.4–5: 'A revelation (*tanzīl*) from Him who created the earth and the high heavens, the Compassionate (*al-Raḥmān*) who seated Himself upon the Throne').

10. Ar: *nuzūl*, a word indicating the descent of God to creation and the sending-

'withness'[11] and the numerousness of the divine Names in relation to the One Named by virtue of the diversity of their meanings.

The cosmic order is either concealment
or unfoldment,[12]

just as mode and quantity are states of
measurement.

Our constitutions[13] pride themselves over
their constituent elements,

extolling their degree of distinction due
to an inviolate mystery.[14]

---

down of inspiration and guidance to the human being. For example, see the hadith 'Our Lord descends to the heaven of this world every night and asks: "Is there any repenter? Is there any supplicant? Is there anyone asking for forgiveness?"' Cf. *Mishkāt al-anwār, khabar* 16 (*Divine Sayings*, 65).

11. Ar: *ma'iyya*, alluding to Q.57.4: 'He is with (*ma'a*) you wherever you are.'

12. Ar: *bayna al-maṭwī wa al-manshūr*, literally 'between rolling-up and unrolling'. Both terms refer to the way parchments were rolled up (closed) or unrolled (open), and are used in connection with the Day of Resurrection in the Quran: 'and the whole earth shall be His Handful [i.e. in His sole possession] on the Day of Resurrection, and the heavens will be rolled up (*maṭwiyyāt*) in His right Hand' (Q.39.67). Likewise, the 'unrolling' alludes to the revealing of the truth of one's actions in the next world: 'Every human being's fate have We fastened to his own neck; and on the Day of Resurrection We shall bring forth for him a book which he will see spread open (*manshūr*); [it will be said to him] "Read your record! Today your soul is a sufficient reckoner against you"' (Q.17.13–14). These correspond to what the physicist David Bohm called the implicate (enfolded) order and the explicate (unfolded) order of reality (see his *Wholeness and the Implicate Order*). We may note that this poem plays on various opposites (mode vs quantity, constitution vs element, prohibition vs command).

13. Ar: *marākib*, plural of *markab*, a term that also suggests a mount or steed, something which is ridden or which allows one to travel. It is contrasted with the simple elements (*basā'iṭ*, i.e. earth, air, fire and water), which constitute all things.

14. This seems to refer to the idea that our human constitution is composed of, or evolves from, bodily elements, into which the soul or spirit has to descend from the intelligible realm. Thus the individual self-consciousness has a greater rank than what he or she is composed of, because it is the 'place' where the divine mystery is manifest.

Revelation[15] brings down rules, manifested
as law;

judgment contains both prohibition and
command.[16]

The science of alchemy, which is knowledge of the elixir, has two parts, I mean in terms of its action. On the one hand, there is the originating of something,[17] like gold ore; and on the other hand, there is the eliminating of a defect and ailment, like alchemical gold,[18] which is classed as equal to natural gold – this is like the development of the other world and this world in the search for equilibrium.[19]

15. Ar: *waḥy*, a term which covers many kinds of revelation: 'revelation may be given to every kind of creature, including angel, jinn, human, animal, plant and inanimate object. Among animals God mentioned the bee (Q.16.68) and among the inanimates He mentioned the heaven (41.12) and the earth (99.5)' (*Fut.*II.631–2). More specifically, it refers to what the angel brings to a prophet or messenger, which no longer takes place after Muhammad, and to what the friends of God receive directly from the Real without intermediary (see *SPK*, 403–4).

16. This poem is also included in Ibn 'Arabī's poetic collection, *Dīwān al-ma'ārif*, Paris BN 2348, fol. 201b.

17. Ar: *inshā' dhāt*, meaning that something (literally, an 'essence' or 'substance') is brought into being or produced for the first time; it also suggests the idea of development or evolution according to the thing's inherent nature.

18. Literally, produced or worked gold (*ṣinā'ī*). This refers to the production of gold through the alchemical process of removing 'sickness', i.e. the gold that results from transformation, which is not exactly the same as gold ore but equivalent to it according to Ibn 'Arabī.

19. Ar: *i'tidāl*, the principle of right proportion, or the golden mean, the desirable balance between excess and deficiency, an idea emphasised by the Greeks, especially the Pythagoreans, Plato and Aristotle. It is also alluded to in the Quran: 'the One who created you, formed you beautifully and proportioned you well' (Q.82.7) and 'We have created everything in due measure' (54.49). Inherently the spirit is always in harmony and balance, but through its connection with the body, it comes into the relative world, where there is both equilibrium and disequilibrium. It is the job of the divine physician to cure the imbalances of the soul, just as the physical doctor seeks to cure the sickness of the body and restore the natural equilibrium. At the divine level, the divine Names yearn for existence and seek fulfilment through the

Know that all minerals[20] stem from one fundamental source, and that source by its inherent nature always seeks to be united with the rank of perfect completion and fulfilment, which is 'goldenness'.[21] However, since [the source] becomes conditioned by the natural world on account of the effects of the divine Names, with all their various properties, then on its journey [through the degrees] defects and ailments[22] befall it due to differences in time, such as the warmth of summer, the cold of winter, the dryness of autumn or the moisture of spring, and due to variations in the nature of places, like the heat or cold of the mine.[23] In general, there are many defects [which may affect the source].

When one of these defects predominates over [the source] during its journey as it evolves from one phase of development to another, leaving the property of one cycle for the property of another, and the power of that [new] abode is consolidated within it, then there appears within it a form

---

manifestation of their effects, and it is by this that both worlds are brought into being. See *Fut.*II.236–7, trans in *SPK*, 304–5.

20. Ar: *ma'ādin*, plural of *ma'din*, which means originally the place where mineral ores (*jawāhir*) are found, i.e. the mine or source from which they originate. It can be used metaphorically, as in English, to describe someone as a 'mine' of information or goodness. It also sometimes, as here, designates the mineral substance itself.

21. Perfection (*kamāl*) is associated with gold, both as a principle of perfection and as a completion – it is undifferentiated potentiality, and by journeying through the degrees it arrives at the point of its own fulfilment, which is goldenness. Gold is its fullest manifestation. The first two degrees, crucial to its further development through the phases, are sulphur and quicksilver, which act as catalysts for the other metals.

22. Both these terms refer to the 'sicknesses' of individuation: *'illa* (*pl. 'ilal*) = defect, deficiency, flaw, malady (or philosophically, cause); *maraḍ* (*pl. amrāḍ*) = sickness, ailment. We may note that elsewhere Ibn 'Arabi remarks that the existence of a thing is due to a combination of the self-subsisting quality of spiritual reality (its verticality), which is its inherent cause (*'illa*, or defect?), and the inclination to manifest (its horizontality), which is its ailment (*maraḍ*). See *Fut.*II.122 (trans in *Seven Days*, 164).

23. Ar: *ma'din*.

that translates [the source's] substance[24] into [the form's] reality. This [form] is called sulphur[25] or quicksilver.[26] These are [known as] the two progenitors, because on the one hand, other metals appear from their conjunction and union,[27] resulting from certain defects that can befall offspring. On the other hand, these two may unite together and conjoin with each other in such a way that there results from them a most noble substance, perfect in constitution, which is called 'gold', something by which the two progenitors are ennobled – this is the rank that each of them is seeking in terms of their own minerality.[28] That original source is a 'breath' in the divine [realm] and a 'vapour' in the [realm of] Nature.[29] Likewise, the two progenitors are both a spiritual principle and a natural element.[30]

The reason why we say that this matter [of becoming gold] is sought by the two progenitors by virtue of their substance, not by virtue of their form, is that the property in the primordial substance belongs only to the forms. When

24. Ar: *jawhar* (substance), which is contrasted with *ṣūra* (form).

25. Sulphur (*kibrīt*): regarded as hot and dry, the solid element of metals.

26. Quicksilver (*zi'baq* or *zaybaq*, metal mercury or *argentum vivum*): considered to be cold and moist, the liquid element of metals.

27. The conjunction of these two opposing principles, the masculine sulphur and the feminine quicksilver, is the 'chemical wedding' required to produce the philosopher's stone (often represented as the hermaphroditic offspring of this union). Cf. Ibn 'Arabī's alchemical description of his close companion Badr al-Ḥabashī: 'He was purified at the time of fusion like pure gold. His word is true, his promise sincere' (*Fut.*I.10).

28. Ar: *jawhariyya*.

29. Spiritual breath manifests as vapour, i.e. damp air, in the exterior. According to Aristotle, metals grew from seeds and were produced within the earth by the action of 'vapour'. The vapour of quicksilver was also known as 'spirit mercury', 'the spirit that moves upon the face of the waters', showing how the physical and spiritual substances were always considered together. The vapour was said to have noxious properties, causing tremors, fainting, madness and so on.

30. Ar: *amrun wa ṭabīʿatun*.

the defect that befalls [the source] occurs within its mine, it makes it into sulphur or quicksilver. We also know that it is in their inherent potentiality – when there is no defect which might remove them from the power of natural equilibrium and make them deviate from that [middle] path – that the product which results from [their union] is one that transmutes their two essences into itself. Then they reach the stage of completion, which is gold, the object of their quest from the very beginning.

So [the two progenitors] are conjoined and united in the mineral, with the natural property of that particular mineral and with the property of being receptive to the natural effects of time. Then it is *on a straight path,*[31] like the primordial nature according to which God has created humankind: *it is the parents who make the child a Jew or a Christian or a Zoroastrian.*[32] Likewise, if the quantity of one progenitor becomes more prevalent over [the substance] due to a mineral disease[33] that comes from the temporal side, causing one particular characteristic to predominate over the others, then [that characteristic] grows and flourishes, while the rest [of the characteristics] become too weak to resist the one that is dominant. As a result this determines over the substance,

31. Recalling the oft-repeated Quranic imagery of a 'straight path' upon which each creature walks, which symbolises its natural unfettered development in time. See for example: 'Whomsoever He wishes, He places upon a straight path' (Q.6.39), or: 'There is no creature that moves which He does not hold by the forelock, for indeed my Lord is upon a straight path' (11.56).

32. A hadith often quoted by Ibn 'Arabī: 'Every child is born according to primordial nature (*fiṭra*); then his parents make him into Jew, a Christian or a Zoroastrian.' See *Fut.*II.616, where Ibn 'Arabī defines 'original faith' as 'the primordial nature in accordance with which God created mankind, which is their testifying to His Oneness at the taking of the Covenant' (see *SPK*, 195).

33. Ar: *'araḍ*, literally something that befalls or happens to the substance, which is 'accidental' and not related to its inherent nature, i.e. through the effects of time, which involves change and development.

holding it back [from completion] due to what the reality of that [particular] character bestows, and making it deviate from the path of equilibrium – which is the goal – that brings you to the Virtuous City[34] of Gold and Perfect Fulfilment. The one who reaches [gold] will never again be subject to those transformations that lead to lesser levels. When that particular character dominates the substance, it alters its essential nature,[35] and then there appears the form of iron or copper or tin or lead or silver, depending on what predominates over it.

Then you will come to know God's Word in its deeper meaning[36] *perfectly formed and imperfectly formed*:[37] in other words, fully formed, which refers only to gold, and not fully formed, which refers to all the other metals.

34. Ar. *al-madīna al-fāḍila*, a phrase drawn originally from the 'Just City' of Plato's *Republic*, a book which was commented on by several Andalusian philosophers, including Ibn Rushd (d. 595/1198, whose commentary has survived in Hebrew). It was also made famous by the great philosopher and polymath Abū Naṣr Muḥammad al-Fārābī (d. 339/950) in his work *Fī mabādi' ārā' ahl al-madīna al-fāḍila*, where he wrote of how the city's inhabitants should co-operate in order to achieve happiness, i.e. the fulfilment of their potential. One may note that the idea of perfect social organisation found form in the physical layout of medieval Islamic cities, with the heart of the city being the mosque and the metal workers ranged according to their rank around it.

35. Ar: *qalaba ʿaynahu*, a phrase that can be interpreted in various ways. Literally, 'it inverts/overturns its essential nature'. In other words, the nature of the essence is to be in equilibrium or to be gold, while the nature of the particular characteristic is the inverse, i.e. to deviate and become a metallic form.

36. Ar: *al-iʿtibār*.

37. Q.22.5: 'O mankind! If you are in doubt concerning the resurrection, surely We created you of dust, then of a sperm-drop, then of a blood-clot, then of a lump of flesh, perfectly formed and imperfectly formed, that We may make clear to you'.

During that time[38] the spiritual entity[39] of one of the seven planets takes charge of it. This is one of the angels of that [particular] heaven, circulating with the planet which is subservient[40] in its movement – for it is God who directs it to an end intended by the command of the One who gave it its nature[41] – who maintains the nature of that substance. Thus the form of iron is ruled over by an angel whose steed is the planet traversing the heaven which is the seventh from here.[42] The form of tin and of other [metals] – and it is the same for all metallic forms – is ruled by an angel whose steed is a planet traversing the heaven and celestial sphere[43] that is specific to it and in which its Lord directs it.

38. In other words, when the particular metal is formed within the womb of the earth by the marriage of sulphur and quicksilver, it develops under the influence or dominance of one of the seven planets. As there were only seven metals known, there was a natural connection between the metals and the planets. This is also paralleled in the hadith quoted above, where it is the parents who make their child the follower of a specific religion other than primordial submission. Here we may note the contrast with the conception of Jesus at the moment of Mary's state of dilation when Gabriel announced himself to her.

39. Ar: *rūḥāniyya*.

40. Referring to Q.7:54: 'the sun and the moon and the stars have been made subservient by His command'.

41. Ar: *khāliqihi*, literally, 'its Creator' or 'the One who created it'. The two aspects of directing and creating (or giving something its created nature) here refer to Q.20:50, where Moses describes the Lord to the Pharaoh as 'the One who gave everything its nature (*khalqahu*) and then guided it'.

42. Iron (*ḥadīd*), which is the name of the 57th Sura (see Q.57.25), is traditionally associated with the planet Mars in the fifth heaven. However, here it appears that Ibn 'Arabī is associating it with the cold and dryness of Saturn and the spirituality of the seventh heaven, to emphasise iron's inherent hardness. My thanks to Abdel Baqi Miftah for pointing this out to me.

43. Ar: *falak*, which can mean both celestial 'sphere' and 'body', i.e. the planetary body. The root means 'to turn or be round'. The universe was conceived of as consisting of concentric spheres, in which the planets or other celestial bodies are carried at varying distances from the Earth.

When there comes one who is versed in alchemical procedure,[44] he investigates what will be the easiest operation for him. If what is simplest for him is the elimination of defect from the metallic body,[45] in order to bring it back into the natural course of equilibrium from which it had deviated, then this is the first way. An astronomer will observe the planet, now in its true position in the heavens and now deviating from it, either above or below that position, and then the alchemist will turn to the cause that has made it into iron or whatever metal it is. He knows that this element has only dominated the whole substance because of the quantity [of different elements] in it.[46] So he decreases the amount where it is too much and increases it where it is too little. This is [called] 'physic',[47] and the one who employs it and is knowledgeable of it is a 'physician'.

By means of such an operation he eliminates from [the mineral substance] the form of iron, for example, or whatever form it has taken. When he has brought it back to the path [of equilibrium], he seeks to preserve it in a state of good health so that it will remain in it. When it is cured of its ailment, it is convalescing, and so he is concerned about it, treating it with soothing nourishment and protecting it from draughts.[48] Thus it proceeds along the direct path of

44. Ar: *al-'ārif bi'l-tadbīr*. The alchemical procedure (*tadbīr*) refers to the processes used in transformation, i.e. solution (*taḥlīl*), distillation (*taṣ'īd*), sublimation (*taqṭīr*) and so on.

45. Ar: *jasad*.

46. The fact that a metal takes a particular form such as lead or iron was thought to be due to the balance of its constituent elements, i.e. the proportions of heat, cold, moisture and dryness that were in it.

47. Ar: *ṭibb*.

48. Ar: *ahwiya*, 'draughts', but related etymologically to the word *ahwā'* in the human realm, i.e. passions, earthly desires. Thus, the alchemist's role is to cure the metal of 'disease' and then provide the right elemental conditions, just as a doctor

health,[49] until that substance is clothed in the form of gold. When that has happened to it, it goes beyond the domain of the physician and beyond its illness, for after [reaching] that complete perfection it cannot regress to a degree that is one of lack, nor will it be subject to it. Even if the physician wished to, he would not be able to [make it return to its previous condition].

Equally, [in law] a judge[50] has no [textual] authority in such a case, that he could pass judgment in it according to what he sees. The reason for that in reality is that a judge is imbued with justice and impartiality. Therefore he can only pass judgment against someone who deviates from the path of truth.[51] But this person [of truth] is clothed in gold, and no judgment can be made against him, because no-one who contends against him possesses any right. This is the cause of it.[52] One who adheres to the path of truth goes beyond the level of being judged and becomes [himself] a judge of things.[53]

Such is the [alchemical] method of eliminating defects, and I have not seen anyone on that [path] who was aware of this, pointed it out or [even] alluded to it. Indeed you will not find it except in this chapter or in our discussions.

---

tends to a patient after an operation. Protecting a metal from 'draughts' is the equivalent of safeguarding a human being from the domination of earthly desires.

49. Ar: *al-ṣirāṭ al-qawīm*.

50. Ar: *qāḍī*.

51. Ar: *ḥaqq*. This can also be translated as 'the path of God'.

52. That is, the reason why there can be no case against the man of truth is that there is nothing else than truth by which to judge him or her. This could also be translated as. 'this [truth] is his road'. The syllogistic proof which Ibn 'Arabī adduces here shows an equivalence between the physician who treats the sick and the judge who judges the wrongdoer, and between health and acting rightly or justly. Illness or lack of health is then, logically, akin to a deviation from truth.

53. This could also be understood as: 'he becomes that by which things are judged'.

On the other hand, when the master of this Art wishes to produce the essence which is called an 'elixir', in order to apply it to those mineral bodies that he wishes [to treat], he will transpose it according to what is determined by the natural constitution of that receiving body. [In this case], there is only one remedy, and that is the Elixir. Among the mineral bodies there is one which the Elixir can bring back to its own property, so that it becomes an elixir doing the job of the Elixir, in which case it is called an 'agent'.[54] It rises up[55] within the other metallic bodies and governs [them] by virtue of [the Elixir's] own authority. For example, he may take a *dirham*'s weight,[56] or any other measure you like, of the elixir essence, and cast it upon 1000 measures of whichever metallic body you like. If it is tin or iron, it gives it the form of silver. If it is copper or black lead or silver, it gives it the form of gold. If the body is quicksilver, it gives it its own power and leaves it as an agent for it: it can govern over the bodies with [the Elixir's] authority, but this is done through a different measure to that used with the other bodies, and that measure is a *dirham*'s worth of elixir. So he casts it upon a portion[57] of the wisdom which is particular to quicksilver, making it all into elixir.[58] Then he casts a measure of that

54. Ar: *nā'ib*.

55. Ar: *yaqūmu*, a word which echoes ideas of standing up and resurrection. Ibn 'Arabī appears to be alluding to the fact that this 'agent' is equivalent to a prophetic heir.

56. Every weight was supposed to consist of a particular number of weight *dirhams* (not to be confused with the silver coin of the same name). When the French came to Egypt with Napoleon, they found one *dirham* to be just over 3g (the Syrian *dirham* was considered to be a little lighter).

57. Ar: *raṭl*, the most common weight in the Near East for weighing small quantities. The exact weight of a *raṭl* varied from city to city and from century to century: the Damascus *raṭl* was approximately 600 *dirhams*, i.e. 1.8kg.

58. This implies that quicksilver is not a simple substance like the others, but somehow ethereal or spiritual, a 'wisdom' since it is metamorphosed into the elixir

substitute upon a thousand measures of the other metallic bodies, just as he did with the elixir essence, so that it acts in the same manner in terms of governing. This is the mode of originating,[59] while the first [mode of alchemical work] is the art of eliminating ailment.

We have brought this up so as to explain to you how [spiritual] wisdom is connected to what is called 'the alchemy of the two ways'.[60] But why is it called the alchemy of [true] happiness? Because happiness inevitably lies within it, and in addition, according to some of the people of God, there is nothing better than it, for it brings you to the degree of complete perfection which belongs to the real human male.[61] Not everyone who has found happiness is accorded perfection, for while all who are perfect are happy, not every happy one is perfect. Perfection means reaching and joining with the highest degree, and that is assuming the likeness of the Source.[62] So do not imagine that when the Prophet said that 'there have been many men who attained perfection',[63]

---

itself. In other words, being utterly passive to the action of the elixir, it is enabled to become a substitute elixir.

59. Ar: *inshā'*, which carries the idea of forming and constituting as well as the form which is produced; in addition, it conveys a sense of natural development or growth. This is not simple transformation from one form to another, but the evolution from one form to another. The elixir transforms and causes evolution into a superior form, based on the potential inherent in the being.

60. These two ways of alchemy (elimination and original formation) correspond to two forms of spiritual teaching which Ibn 'Arabī received from his Andalusian masters, al-Martulī and al-'Uraybī: to 'concern yourself with your soul' (eliminating defects) and to 'concern yourself with God alone' (original formation). See *Rūḥ al-quds*, 126 (R.W.J. Austin, *Sufis of Andalusia* (London, 1971), 88–9).

61. Ar: *rajul*, a technical term in Ibn 'Arabī's teaching, indicating the spiritual 'male', one who is 'virile' through being completely open to the action of God. He stresses that this degree of true humanity is open to men and women equally.

62. This likeness (*tashabbuh*) is the image or form of God in which the human being is created.

63. 'There have been many men who attained perfection, but none were perfect

he meant the [sort of] perfection that ordinary people talk about – rather, it is what we have mentioned here, and this is as much as can be given to the knowing aptitude in this low world. Now, after this introduction we shall go on, if God wills, to speak of the alchemy of true happiness.

And God is the One who brings success,
and there is no lord but Him.

among women except 'Āsiya, the wife of Pharaoh, and Mary, the daughter of 'Imrān' (al-Bukhārī *anbiyā'*, 62). The word 'men' (*rijāl*) here picks up Ibn 'Arabī's earlier mention of 'male' (*rajul*).

Part II[1]

KNOW THAT the perfection for which the human being is created, which is the [ultimate] object of desire,[2] is really the rank of [divine] representation. It was obtained by Adam through divine providential Grace.[3] It is a more specialised station than [the degree of] messengerhood in the messengers,[4] since not every messenger is a [divine] representative.[5] The only specification for the rank

1. The original text here has: *waṣl fī faṣl*, literally 'link in a section'. It can also be interpreted as connecting together what has been separated, or arriving at the destination (union) after being in separation. In alchemical terms, this suggests the full marriage of sulphur and quicksilver.

2. The desire may be understood in human terms, as our seeking fulfilment, or in divine terms, as Him seeking or loving to be known.

3. Ar: *'ināya*. See the opening poem and n.4.

4. Ar: *rusul*, plural of *rasūl*, literally 'one who is sent', usually translated as a messenger or envoy. In Islamic doctrine, a messenger is not simply one who is sent with a message, but someone who establishes religious codes and practices for their community, such as prayer, fasting, pilgrimage etc, as well as oral or written scriptures. The messengers are a sub-class of prophets, chosen by God to receive a message, and they may explain the meaning of these scriptures or reform the religions established by previous messengers. The prophetic messages tend to focus on universal aspects of truth rather than concrete instructions. For example, Noah is regarded as the first messenger (even if most of his community rejected his message). Abraham was also a messenger, while Isaac, Ishmael, Jacob and Joseph are regarded as prophets. The first prophet was Adam, and the last Muhammad.

5. Ar: *khalīfa*; deriving from the root *kh-l-f*, meaning 'to come after, to succeed', it denotes someone who is appointed to act on behalf of someone else, as their representative, viceroy or successor. It implies rulership over others. There are two Quranic references to the term *khalīfa*; the first (Q.2.30: 'Then your Lord said to the angels: "I am about to place a representative upon earth"') describes the special position of Adam in regard to the angels and typifies the dignity of the true human

of messenger is announcement, as He says: *There is no obligation upon the messenger except to announce.*[6] It is not his task to exercise command over one who opposes [him]. Rather, his role is to simply promulgate the ruling that is enacted by God or according to what God causes him to see. If God should grant him the authority to judge those to whom he has been sent, then that means he has been appointed as, and has the position of representative, and the person is then a messenger–representative. But not everyone who is sent [by God] passes judgment. If he is given the sword and wields it, only then does he possess full perfection, for he manifests with the authority and power of [all] the divine Names: he bestows and prevents, honours and humbles, gives life and brings death, causes harm and brings benefit.[7] He appears with opposing Names, as well as prophethood – and that

---

being; the second (Q.38.26: 'We have made you a *khalīfa* on the earth; so judge between people with truth') is specifically addressed to the prophet David, and is taken to mean that he combined the role of king and prophet. A distinction was therefore made between those who hold the outward position of *khalīfa* (as kings and rulers) and those who hold the inward role (as spiritual leaders): only the first four caliphs (from Abū Bakr to 'Alī), the 'rightly guided caliphs' (*al-khulafā' al-rāshidūn*), are traditionally considered to have combined the two. Amongst spiritual leaders the term *khalīfa* came to mean either those who were the direct successor of a great master, or certain disciples who had reached a stage of development that enabled them to guide others. The spiritual *khalīfa* can be understood as equivalent to the perfect human being (*al-insān al-kāmil*) inasmuch as they are the representative of the Muhammadian Reality: this includes both one who realises the Adamic nature of their humanity, i.e. their perfection, and one who inherits the station of David, as judge over others, 'wielding the sword' as Ibn 'Arabī puts it in this passage. See also the chapter of David in the *Fuṣūṣ al-ḥikam*, where Ibn 'Arabī describes this spiritual representation in relation to prophethood in more detail.

6. Q.5.99: 'There is no obligation upon the messenger except to announce; and God knows all that you manifest and all that you conceal.'

7. We may note that Ibn 'Arabī here deliberately begins this succession of pairs with a positive term, and by reversing the final pair, also ends it with one. This reflects his understanding of the good, i.e. mercy, as being the source of things and as always having the final word.

is necessary, for if he manifested this power of judgment without being a prophet, he would be a[n earthly] king but not a [divine] representative.

No-one can be a representative except one whom God appoints as such over His servants. It is not someone whom the people set up over them, pledging allegiance to him, making him lead and giving him priority over themselves.[8] It is [the divine appointment that constitutes] the rank of perfection.

Ordinary people may legitimately work towards attaining the station of perfection, but it is not for them to try to be a prophet. For while [divine] representation may be earned,[9] prophethood cannot. Some people, however, having seen the way that leads to prophethood as the external condition of such a property, and that whoever God wishes is able to follow [such a path], imagine that prophethood is earned, but they have erred. There is no doubt that the path is a matter of acquisition,[10] but when someone arrives at the door [of the divine Presence], [what they receive] will be according to whatever is set out for them in their own authorisation,[11] and that is a

8. The majority of historians and modern scholars tend to the view that the first *khalīfas* of the Islamic community were appointed as such by the leading Companions giving the oath of allegiance (*bayʿa*), and that traditionally it was the oath of the Believers which conferred the right of succession. Whatever the truth of this in the political sphere, from a spiritual point of view as expressed here, the real *khalīfa* can only be appointed by God, and acceptance by the 'community' to whom he is sent is simply a subsequent ratification.

9. The idea of 'earning' the position of *khalīfa* is supported by the following verse (Q.24.55): 'God has promised those of you who have faith and act righteously that He will appoint them as His representative on earth (or: will make them successors in the land) just as He did with those who came before them'.

10. Acquisition or earning (*kasb* or *iktisāb*) is a term employed in the Quran to denote the fruit of carrying out an action, whether good or ill. For example, 'God has created the heavens and the earth in truth and so that each soul can be rewarded for what it has earned' (Q.45.22).

11. The Arabic word used here, *tawqīʿa*, means a ruler's edict, letter of appointment

matter of divine specification. There are some people who are invested with the authority of friendship,[12] while others are authorised as a prophet or a messenger, or as a messenger and representative; others again are authorised as representative alone. When an outsider[13] observes that this investiture is only given to such people after they have followed [the path], through actions, words and states, until they come to this door, then they imagine that this [appointment] is something earned by the servant, but they are mistaken.

Know that with regard to its essential nature, the soul is prepared to receive the aptitude for whatever it is given by divine authorisation.[14] There are some who possess the aptitude to be specifically authorised with friendship, and do not go beyond it. Others are endowed with an aptitude for what we have mentioned of the spiritual stations, for either all of them or just some of them (wholly or partially). The reason for this is that souls are created from a single source, exactly as He says: *He has created you all from one Soul,*[15] and He says that after the aptitude of the creation of the body, *And I blew into him of My Spirit.*[16] So from a single spirit there comes about the inbreathed mystery within that into which it

---

or signature. It recalls the way in which during medieval times people used to present their petitions in a special audience held by the caliph: when a person's case was heard, the caliph's decision was put into writing by the secretary.

12. Ar: *tawqīʿ al-wilāya*, a phrase which was used in diplomatic circles as the letter of appointment for a governor.

13. Literally, 'one who sees [from outside]' or 'one who considers/thinks'.

14. This complete aptitude is also alluded to in the following prayer from Ibn ʿArabī's *Awrād* (Friday Eve): 'Lord, grant me the gift of the most perfect aptitude to receive Your Most Holy Effusion that I may be appointed Your representative in Your lands' (*Seven Days*, 118).

15. Q.4.1, 7.189 and 39.6.

16. Q.15.29, referring to the divine command to the angels: 'And when I have formed him harmoniously and breathed into him [some] of My Spirit, fall down in prostration to him.'

is blown, and this is the soul.[17] When He says: *composing you in whatever form your Lord wished,*[18] [by 'form'] He means the aptitudes, since it is by virtue of the aptitude that the divine order is received.

The origin of these individual souls[19] is pure by virtue of their 'parents',[20] but an individual reality cannot appear for them except through the existence of this physical body. As a result, [Universal] Nature becomes the second 'father', and they come about as a mixed constitution. There appears in them neither the radiance of the pure Light that is detached from matter nor the deepest darkness which is the province of Nature.[21] Nature can be compared to the elemental mine, while the Universal Soul is similar to the celestial bodies, which have an active function and whose movements have direct effects upon the [various] elements.[22] The metallic body that is brought into being in the mine corresponds to the human body.[23] The specific characteristic that is the spirit of the metallic body corresponds to the individual soul belonging to the human body, and this is the inbreathed spirit.[24]

17. This sentence also suggests that the 'mystery' or 'inmost consciousness' (*sirr*) is pure, healthy and without defect when it is blown into the body. Note also that the 'soul' (*nafs*) is related etymologically to 'breath' (*nafas*).

18. See Q.82.7–8: '[your Generous Lord], who created you, formed you harmoniously and shaped you, composing you in whatever form He wished'.

19. Ar: *al-nufūs al-juz'iyya*, literally 'partial souls', i.e. particular or individual souls as opposed to the Universal Soul (*al-nafs al-kulliya*).

20. The parents of the individual or partial souls are the Universal Soul (f.) and the Spirit (m.).

21. The mixed constitution is both dark and light.

22. Ar: *'anāṣir*, which means both 'races' or 'families' (referring to humankind) and the elements from which all material substances are composed.

23. Ibn 'Arabī uses a different word for the human body (*jism*) in contrast to the metallic body (*jasad*).

24. Ar: *al-rūḥ al-manfūkh*, referring to the spirit which is breathed into the human form by God, as in Q.15.29: 'When I formed him harmoniously and breathed into him of My Spirit'.

Just as metallic bodies are graded in degrees because of the defects that befall them while they are being formed, and yet they [all] seek the rank of completion, for which their realities became manifest, likewise, the human being is created for perfection. Nothing can divert him from this completion except the defects and ailments that befall people, whether that is within the provenance of their own nature or due to accidental matters.[25] So be aware of this!

Now let us begin with what is necessary and appropriate to deal with in this particular chapter, by saying as follows. God has empowered the particular souls to have management of this body and appointed them to be in charge of it, making clear to them that they are a *khalīfa*[26] over it, so that they might become aware of the fact that they have a Creator who has put them in charge of it. Therefore it is incumbent upon them to seek out knowledge of the One who appointed them in such a way. Is He one of their own kind? or is He similar to them in some way? or does He have no likeness to them at all? In their search for knowledge of Him, questions abound of their own accord. They are in this situation, looking for the way that leads to that [knowledge], when there arises among the individual souls someone who has been given a greater rank in being than they have.[27] They feel comfortable in his company because he is just like them. They ask him: 'You have been given a higher dignity than us in this realm, so has what occurred to us also struck you?' He asks: 'And what is it that has occurred to you?' They reply:

25. In other words, defects may occur within them, interiorly, when they are developing, or outside them, exteriorly, as a result of the accidents that occur during life.

26. The term *khalīfa* here denotes that the 'self' or soul has been appointed by a higher power as the ruler of the body and in charge of all its faculties.

27. Ar: *taqaddama*, literally, 'has precedence or priority over'.

'To seek knowledge of the One who has appointed us as *khalīfa* over the management of this corporeal body.'[28] Then he says: 'On that subject I have completely sound knowledge, which I bring from the One who appointed you as *khalīfa*. He has made me a messenger to my own kind, to clarify for them the way of knowledge which leads to Him, wherein lies their true happiness.'

Then one of them[29] replies: 'That is exactly what I have been looking for. So do teach me knowledge of this path that I may follow it.' However, the other says: 'There is no difference between me and you, so I would like to discover the path to knowing Him by myself. I do not just want to follow you unconditionally in it. If you have obtained what you are and what you have brought through [the faculty of] reasoning,[30] which I also have, why should I be so lacking in aspiration as to simply imitate you? On the other hand, if it has resulted for you by virtue of some special favour from Him, just as He has favoured us [all] with the gift of existence after we were not, then that is a claim without any proper proof.' So [this person] will not heed his words, and he starts to think and theorise about that [question] with his intellect.

Such is the position of one who obtains their knowledge through intellectual proofs by rational thought. The former, on the other hand, typifies those who [consciously] follow the messenger and those who unquestioningly accept him with regard to what he explains about the knowledge of their

28. Ar: *haykal*.

29. That is to say, the mystic (*'ārif*) or follower of the prophet, while the 'other' is the rational philosopher (*nāẓir*), who together form the main protagonists of the rest of the chapter. There is a play on words here, where the mystic says 'teach me' or 'cause me to recognise or have inner knowledge of' (*'arrifnī*), which recalls the title of the chapter as an 'inner knowledge' (*ma'rifa*).

30. Ar: *naẓar*.

Maker. The person whom these two people are at variance about in their manner of following exemplifies the messenger who instructs. The revealed regulations[31] laid down by this instructor clarify the path that leads to the rank of Completion and Happiness, in accordance with what is required by the rational faculty of one of these two individuals who consider what the instructor offers[32] – that is, of the one who won't follow him. Agreement with the instructor only occurs in some of the different temperaments that are necessitated by the natural order of things. Each different temperament or character only comes about by virtue of a specific measure or a determined quantity. This is why [this knowledge] is called 'alchemy', because it introduces [principles of] quantification and measurement.

So when this particular individual sees that, he is delighted by it since he feels that he is doing it on his own, without having to copy the instructor. He reckons that he is better off than his companion who is [merely] imitating him, but in that he is mistaken. As for the 'imitator',[33] he remains simply engaged upon faithfully copying the instructor, while the 'non-imitator' augments [his teaching]. The latter is someone who refuses to follow such a person because he thinks he is [already] in conformity [with him], and isolates

31. Ar: *sharʿ*.

32. Ar: *shaʾn hādhā al-muʿallim*, literally 'the affair of this instructor', meaning the course that the instructor pursues or offers. We may note here Ibn ʿArabī's careful use of language: the 'instructor' (*muʿallim*) is a person of true and divine knowledge (*ʿālim*), one who has been given and teaches knowledge (*ʿilm*), while the one who is being instructed is a person of gnosis (*ʿārif*), one who has inner knowledge (*maʿrifa*).

33. Ar: *muqallid*. The kind of imitation that Ibn ʿArabī intends here is not slavish copying without any understanding, but a true exercise of open receptivity and imaginative identification, such as every human accomplishes when learning to speak a language, in other words a mimetic identification.

himself with his own thought-process on account of this [supposed] agreement.

So the two men – or rather two individuals, as they might be two women or one woman and one man – follow the path, one by virtue of using rational thought and the other by virtue of being a disciple. They both begin to engage in spiritual training,[34] which is the refining of character; spiritual endeavour,[35] which is enduring bodily hardship like hunger; and devotional acts[36] such as standing in prayer a long time and persevering tirelessly in it, fasting, going on pilgrimage, spiritual warfare and wandering. The one does this using his own rational intelligence, and the other through what is prescribed for him by his teacher and instructor, who is called a law-giver.[37] When they are free from the strength of the frame[38] of elemental nature, they are then able to take from the property of elemental nature only as much as is necessary to preserve the existence of the physical body. It is through the existence of this body, its equilibrium and continuation, that the individual soul obtains what she desires of the knowledge of God, who gave her the particular role of being *khalīfa*.

34. Ar: *riyāḍa*.
35. Ar: *mujāhada*.
36. Ar: *ʿibādāt*.
37. Ar: *shāriʿ*, from the same root as *sharʿ* and *sharīʿa* (revealed law).
38. See Q.76.28: 'It is We who have created them and made their frame (*asrahum*) strong.'

THE 1ST HEAVEN: ADAM & THE MOON

When they emerge from being dominated by the desires of elemental nature,[39] and the door to the nearest heaven is opened up to them, the 'imitator' meets Adam, who is delighted with him and seats him by his side. Meanwhile, the one who relies upon his own reason[40] meets the spiritual entity of the moon, which seats him at its side.

As the guest of the moon, which is in the service of Adam – for it is like his vizier, charged by the Real to be subject to him and serve him – the rational thinker sees all the knowledge that it possesses: how it cannot go beyond the elemental spheres[41] which lie below it, how it has no knowledge of what lies above it, and how its influence is restricted to what is beneath it. At the same time, he also sees how Adam possesses the knowledge of places beneath him and above him, and how he extends to his guest from what he has, which is not within the capacity of the moon to be aware of. He knows that [Adam] only reveals it to him as a blessing and grace from the instructor, who is the messenger. The rational thinker then becomes distressed, and regrets not

39. Ar: *al-shahawāt al-ṭabīʿiyya al-ʿunṣuriyya*. According to Ṣadr al-Dīn al-Qūnawī, those who are dominated by these low desires are in 'opacity, darkness and density', and are therefore 'wretched' because their spiritual faculties have been absorbed by their natural faculties (*Sharḥ al-ḥadīth*, no. 21, cited in Sachiko Murata, *The Tao of Islam* (Albany, NY, 1992), 101–2).

40. Ar: *ṣāḥib al-naẓar*, literally 'the one who possesses reason/intellectual observation', which we can also translate as 'the speculative thinker'. See the Introduction for more on this key term.

41. Ar: *al-ukar*, plural of *kura*, referring to the spheres in which each element (earth, water, air, fire) exists in pure form. For more on the four elements, see Murata, *Tao of Islam*, 135–9.

following the path of that messenger. He professes belief in him, affirming that when he returns from this journey of his, he will follow that messenger and set off again on another journey for his sake.

The disciple,[42] who is Adam's guest, is taught by his father as much about the divine Names as [Adam] sees that his temperament can bear. For the emergence of the elemental body has an influence over individual souls, so that they are not all at the same level of receptivity: one can receive what others do not. In the first of the heavens, he learns from Adam's knowledge by way of the private divine face,[43] which belongs to each existent other than God, who veils him from stopping with apparent causation.[44] The rational thinker has no knowledge of this face at all. The knowledge of the private face is the science of the elixir in natural alchemy, and it is the elixir of the mystics. I have not come across anyone

42. Ar: *al-tābiʿ*, literally 'follower', rather than the word *muqallid*, 'imitator', which was used up to this point. The change in terminology signifies that the person's rank of realisation is different once they have met Adam: they are no longer simply imitating, but are following the first human prophet. We may note that historically the 'Followers' (*tābiʿūn*) were the generation born after the Prophet Muhammad, who never met him directly but had contact with the 'Companions' (*ṣaḥāba*). There is, therefore, an equivalence between those who were Companions of the Prophet in this world and the prophets who represented the Reality of Muhammad to different peoples prior to the appearance of Muhammad himself. The mystic traveller joins the company of 'followers' through the meeting with Adam. Elsewhere Ibn 'Arabī connects *tābiʿ* to *walī* (friend of God, saint), stressing the difference between a saint who follows and a prophet or messenger who is charged with instructing, in terms of how they receive inspiration (see *Fut.*III.316).

43. Ar: *al-wajh al-ilāhī al-khāṣṣ*, one of the key terms in Ibn 'Arabī's teaching, referring to the direct interface between God and creature. For more, see the Introduction and *Unlimited Mercifier*, 98–103.

44. Ar: *sababihi wa ʿillatihi*, literally 'his direct cause and occasion'. That is to say, this essential connection between a being and God precludes being caught up with apparent causes. Here Ibn 'Arabī is deliberately using the word *ʿilla* in its causative sense, rather than the meaning of 'defect' which he discussed earlier in terms of alchemical treatment. See *SDG*,123–6 for more on *sabab* and *ʿilla*.

who has spoken of this apart from me, and I too would not have mentioned it were it not for the fact that I have been commanded to give counsel to this community, indeed to all the servants of God.[45]

So each of these two comes to know the ruling property belonging to this celestial sphere, which God has assigned to it over these four elements [of Nature] and engendered things,[46] and the command specific to it, which God has revealed in this heaven – as He says: *in each heaven He revealed its command*.[47] The rational thinker, who is the guest of the moon, only comes to know about the physical effects and transformations that take place in the bodily substances composed of natural elements. The disciple, on the other hand, receives what this celestial sphere specifically contains in terms of divine Knowledge, which individual souls may obtain, how that relates to the Being of the Real, what forms It takes in them, and in what sense [divine] representation really belongs to this human emergence, and in particular to Adam, who has been appointed as master of this heaven. The disciple comes to know the form that this appointment as *khalīfa* takes in the divine Knowledge, while the rational thinker only learns about the elemental appointment in the management of bodies, and what causes increase, growth and development in the bodies that receive that, and what causes decrease.

45. See the dream-vision that Ibn 'Arabī recounts in his *K. al-Mubashshirāt*, in which God said to him: 'O My servant, do not fear! I require nothing from you except that you counsel My servants' – see *Unlimited Mercifier*, 171.

46. Ar: *al-muwalladāt*, literally 'the things which are born', meaning everything in the world of the senses which is composed of various combinations of the four elements, i.e. the three kingdoms of mineral, plant and animal.

47. Q.41.12.

Everything that the rational thinker acquires is also acquired by the disciple, but not everything that the disciple obtains is obtained by the rational thinker. The rational thinker cannot grow and develop except in sadness and distress,[48] and they cannot confirm the truth until their journey comes to an end and they return to their body. They make this journey like someone asleep, who sees it all in their dream while knowing that they are asleep. They do not believe that they will ever wake up and be able to start daily life again, and be relieved of their distress. So they remain disturbed and fearful of what has happened to them during their journey, gripped by constriction, and they cannot progress after that. This is what upsets them. The disciple is not like this. He sees the constant progress[49] which accompanies him wherever he goes, because it comes from the private face, which is recognised only by the one who possesses it.

When they have both stayed in this heaven as long as God wishes, they set off again on the journey, bidding farewell to their respective hosts. They rise in their spiritual ascensions to the second heaven. In the first heaven it is the seventh divine agent[50] that has been put in charge of the sperm-drop[51] that comes into existence within the wombs,

48. Ar: *ghamm*, from a root which means 'to cover, conceal, veil'. See Q.22.22 in reference to those who cover up the Truth and are cast into the fire: 'Every time they try in their distress (*ghamm*) to come out of it, they are returned to it and [told] "Taste the torment of the fire."'

49. Ar: *taraqqī*, literally 'climbing', which Ibn 'Arabī defines as 'being transported through the spiritual states, stations and sciences (*ma'ārif*)' (*Iṣṭilāḥāt*, no. 121, in *Rasā'il*, 537).

50. Ar: *nā'ib*; this 'agent' is the spiritual or angelic counterpart of the alchemical elixir's agent that was mentioned before.

51. Ar: *nutfa*, an important Quranic term which applies to all the children of Adam and was much commentated upon (see Q.23.12–14, 35.11 and 80.25–7). Ibn 'Arabī is here pointing to a symbolic sevenfold relationship between the seven heavens, their characteristics and the stages of development of a human foetus. In the Quran

in which appears this human emergence; it takes on that responsibility in the seventh month from the depositing of the sperm, and the baby in this month is a foetus, growing and developing in the belly of its mother with the waxing of the moon, fading and decreasing in movement with the waning of the moon, which is a distinguishing mark – for if it is born in this month, it does not grow in strength in the same way as one born in the sixth.[52]

---

there is a sevenfold hierarchy of development to produce another separate human being: clay, sperm-drop, clot, tissue, bones, flesh and the inbreathing of the spirit. There are also seven different references to the creation of the Adamic human being from clay: dust (Q.3.54), clay (6.2), moulded mud (15.26ff.), clinging clay (37.11), ringing clay (15.26/33), potter's clay (55.14–15) and breath (55.14, 38.71–2). The Arabs tended to follow the teaching of Galen, who thought that all of the human being was contained within the man's sperm, and the woman only contributed the womb as a place for this sperm-drop to develop and mature. Given that it is usually considered one of the great contributions of Western science to have shown that men and women contribute equally to the development of the embryo, it is worth noting that Ibn 'Arabī specifically states such a view in chapter 298 in a discussion of the conception of Jesus: 'the natural scientists argue that nothing is created from the fluid of the woman at all, but that is incorrect. According to us, the human being is created from the fluid of the man and the fluid of the woman' (*Fut.*III.185).

52. It can be deduced from this that it was commonly believed that there were only seven months of pregnancy (presumably from when the mother's belly starts to visibly swell), corresponding to the seven planetary spheres. Thus a baby is born into the manifest world after passing through each of these heavenly spheres in turn. The observation that babies carried to term do not appear to grow as rapidly as those born early remains valid.

THE 2ND HEAVEN: JESUS, JOHN & MERCURY

When they knock on the door of the second heaven and it is opened up to them, they ascend together. The disciple halts with Jesus, who is accompanied by his cousin John,[53] while the rational thinker stops with Mercury.[54] When Mercury takes him in and gives him hospitality, it apologises to him, saying: 'Please do not wait for me, for I am in the service of Jesus and John, upon them be peace. Your companion has just stopped with them, and I must wait with them so that I can see if they want me to do anything for their guest. As soon as I have finished my duties for him, I shall return to you.' Then the rational thinker becomes more and more distressed and regretful that he has not followed the way of his companion or adhered to his creed.

Meanwhile the disciple stays with the two cousins as long as God wishes. They explain to him how the message of the instructor, who is the Messenger of God,[55] is confirmed by the sign of the miraculous nature[56] of the Quran – for it is the

53. Their mothers, Mary and Elizabeth, were cousins, and both were descended from the prophet Aaron.

54. Ar: *al-Kātib*, one of the Arabic names for the planet Mercury (it is also known as 'Uṭārid – see Appendix B). It also more literally means the 'writer, scribe or secretary', and it is this meaning which Ibn 'Arabī also has in mind here: the planets serve the prophets in a similar manner to the way various court functionaries served the caliph or sultan, as vizier (*wazīr*, like the moon towards Adam), or like the court scribe (*kātib*) towards Jesus. In addition, the 'scribe' suggests the notion of writing and the realm of words, a science which Ibn 'Arabī specifically places within this heavenly sphere.

55. That is, the Prophet Muhammad.

56. Ar: *i'jāz*. The miraculous nature of the Quran, which was given to and emerged from the Prophet, is regarded as the equivalent of the miraculous nature of Jesus,

presence of public speaking,[57] word forms and metrical measure,[58] the beauty that lies in the placement of words and the combining of subjects, and the appearance of one meaning in multiple forms. He obtains the ability to discriminate in the degree of miraculous happenings.[59] From this presence he comes to know the science of letter magic,[60] which is based on acting through the letters and names, not on incense, blood-offerings and other things. He recognises the high rank of words and how there are many meanings contained within a few words;[61] the reality of [the word] 'Be', how it is a specific word of [divine] Command, not a word of past, present or future,[62] and how [only] two letters appear in this

---

who was born to Mary. We may note the important distinction between this kind of 'miracle' and the graces (*karāmāt*) bestowed on God's friends.

57. Ar: *khiṭāba*, which also means eloquence, oratory, the science of rhetoric. It is from the same root as *khuṭba*, the sermon given in the mosque by the *khaṭīb*.

58. Ar: *awzān*, plural of *wazn*, which literally means the act of weighing. It can refer either to the forms of words (*fā'il*, *maf'ūl* etc.) or to poetic metricality.

59. Ar: *kharq al-'awā'id*, literally 'shattering of the ordinary or the habitual'. This meant the breaking of natural laws, which according to the Arabs were the normal, the ordinary, e.g. gravity. More specifically, it refers to the miracles of Jesus in healing the sick and reviving the dead, or to the more general changing of the apparent order through spiritual intervention. Here Ibn 'Arabī is referring to the question of the authorship of such miraculous acts of grace, whether they are human actions or divine.

60. Ar: *sīmiyā'*, derived from the Greek *σημεῖα* and Syriac *sīmya*, refers in general to 'natural magic', in the form of potions, perfumes etc., used to produce effects upon people and situations, but more specifically to the science of the secret properties of letters, which Ibn 'Arabī describes as the first knowledge given to God's friends (*awliyā'*). It is for this reason that Ibn 'Arabī dissociates it here from the first meaning of ordinary magic, and links it to the breaking of the natural order by virtue of the science of discrimination (*furqān*).

61. Ar: *jawāmi' al-kalim*, which could also be translated as 'the totality of the words', referring to the way that Muhammad's message unified all the messages that had come before. Here Ibn 'Arabī is emphasising the way that words convey multiple meanings.

62. That is to say, the word 'Be' (*kun*), as in Q.16.40: 'All We say to a thing when We desire it, is to say to it "Be" and it becomes', is an eternal word of command, not a word that denotes time. Ibn 'Arabī makes the same point when discussing the

word despite the fact that it is composed of three, and why the third letter, which is in the centre and in an intermediate position between the letter *kāf* and the letter *nūn*, has been left out of the word [*kun*] – this is the spiritual letter *wāw*, which bestows a mark of the King in the emergence of the created, despite its [actual] non-appearance [in the word *kun*].[63]

It is also in this heaven that he learns about the mystery of bringing into being,[64] how Jesus revived the dead, how he created the form of a bird and blew into the form and how the bird really became a flying bird.[65] Was this [becoming] by the permission of God, or was it Jesus' fashioning that created the bird and the blowing into it was by the permission of God? Which of the verbs that are mentioned [in the Quran] relate to His saying *by My permission* and *by the permission of*

---

meaning of the hadith that 'God is (*kāna*) and there is with Him no thing': 'what is meant here [by *kāna*] is existence (*kawn*), in the sense of being (*wujūd*), and so the true understanding of *kāna* here is that it acts as a letter indicating being, not as a verb requiring time' (*Fut.*II.56, 23rd question of al-Tirmidhī). The word *kun* only has two letters in writing, *kāf* and *nūn*, although the root of the word has three, *k-w-n*.

63. That is to say, the mark or sign, which is the letter *wāw* (English 'w'), appears (or is visible) in both the creation (*kawn*) and the Creator (*mukawwin*). The letter itself is invisible in the creative act (*kun*, the command 'Be'), appearing only in the form of the vowel *ḍamma* (English 'u'). This alludes to the mystery of the true human being as the instrument of God, appearing between the Creator and His creation, through whom the divine command and subsequent action takes place. For further details of Ibn 'Arabī's complex teachings on the letter *wāw*, see his treatise on the three special letters, *K. al-Mīm wa al-Wāw wa al-Nūn*, in *Rasā'il*, 106–16 (partial trans. in *Seven Days*, 165–70).

64. Ar: *takwīn*, from the same root as *kāna*, *kawn* and *kun*. It can be understood as the act of giving existence to things by saying 'Be', or in modern parlance, the creation of life.

65. Referring to Q.5.110, where God addresses Jesus: 'and how you shaped the form of a bird out of clay by My permission, and then blew into it so that it became a [real] bird by My permission; and how you healed the blind and the leper by My permission, and how you raised the dead by My permission'. See also Q.3.49, where Jesus refers to these actions as 'by the permission of God'.

God? Does it govern *it became* or *you blew*? According to the people of God, it governs *it became*, while those who establish the secondary causes and the people of [changing] states say it governs *you blew*. Knowledge of this is certainly gained by the one who enters this heaven and meets Jesus and John, although it is not attained by the rational thinker – I mean, it is gained [only] by direct experience.[66]

Jesus is the Spirit of God, and John possesses life. Just as spirit and life cannot be separated, neither can these two prophets Jesus and John [be separated], in respect of what they convey of this mystery. In fact Jesus possesses two branches of the science of alchemy: [firstly] the formation, as in his fashioning the bird from clay and blowing [into it], so that the form [of the bird] was manifested by his two hands, and its flight occurred by his blowing [into it], which is breath.[67] This is one way in the knowledge of alchemy, which we have already mentioned in the first part of this chapter [the way of originating]. The second way is by eliminating accidental defect or ailment: in the case of Jesus this was the curing of blindness and leprosy, which had come upon people while they were in the womb, which is the crucible of creation.

Thus the disciple obtains the knowledge of measure and balance, both natural and spiritual, from the way that Jesus combines the two orders. In the second heaven the disciple also obtains the life in knowledge through which hearts are revived, as in His saying: *or he who was dead, whom We have revived*.[68] This is a presence that gathers together everything

66. Ar: *dhawq*, literally 'tasting'.

67. Ar: *nafas*.

68. Q.6.122. See *Fuṣūṣ al-ḥikam*, chapter on Jesus, for a longer discussion of this key verse (128–9).

within itself. In it resides the angel who is responsible for the foetus in the sixth month. It is from this presence that help and support come for public speakers and [prose] writers, although not for poets. When Muhammad was given the 'totality of the Words',[69] he was addressed from this presence. It was said: *We have not taught him poetry*,[70] because he was sent to clarify and explain in distinctive detail. Poetry, on the other hand, comes from feeling:[71] its rightful role is not [logical] differentiation but [emotive] summation, which is the very opposite of clarification.

From here you will come to know how things are transmuted, and how spiritual states are bestowed upon those who possess them. From this heaven also come the theurgical properties of Names that manifest in the elemental world.[72]

69. Ar: *jawāmiʿ al-kalim*. See n.61 above.

70. Q.36.69–70: 'We have not taught him poetry. That is not proper for him. This is only a reminder and a recitation that is clear, that he might warn those who are alive and that the word may be proved true against the disbelievers.' As Ibn 'Arabī goes on to say, clarity of expression and detailed explanation is the most important quality of revelation as well as among ordinary speakers and writers of prose (see *Fut.* III.458, trans. *SDG*, 298, for further commentary). Also see for example Q.12.1: 'These are the verses of the Clear Book (*al-kitāb al-mubīn*)' and 6.114: 'It is He who has sent down to you all the Book in distinctive detail (*mufaṣṣal*)' (cf. 7.52). Differentiating meanings in detail (*tafṣīl*) is required in order to show the truth with clarity to all levels of understanding. In pre-Islamic Arabia poets were often viewed as possessed by a preternatural force and poetry as a kind of magic.

71. Ar: *al-shiʿr min al-shuʿūr*, a play on the root *sh-ʿ-r*, which means both to speak in verse and to know by feeling and sensory awareness. The ambiguous nature of poetry, which is allusive and evokes emotive forms within the imagination of the listener or reader, is being contrasted with the analytical quality of prose. See Cyrus Zargar, *Sufi Aesthetics* (Columbia, SC, 2011), 148ff., and Denis McAuley, *Ibn 'Arabī's Mystical Poetics* (Oxford, 2012), 37ff., for a discussion of this passage.

72. Ar: *al-nīranjiyyāt* (or *nayranjiyyāt*) *al-asmā'iyya*. *Nīranjiyyāt* (plural of *nīranj*, originally from the Persian *nayrang*) covers the whole field of white magic, but here is restricted to the magical properties of divine Names. According to Ibn Sīnā, the people of Mercury 'love the art of writing, the sciences of stars, theurgy, magic; they also have a taste for subtle and profound actions' (quoted in Nasr, *Three Muslim Sages* (Cambridge, MS, 1964), 271).

As for 'phylacteries',[73] they come from another presence than this: when they are given existence their spirits are from this heaven, but not the actual forms that are supports for those spirits. When he obtains knowledge of how these work and how quickly they bring about revivification, in contrast to the way in which changes normally occur over a long period of time, that comes from the knowledge of Jesus, not from the command which is revealed by Him in this sphere nor from the orbiting of its planetary body [Mercury]. It comes directly from the divine private face, which is outside the normal way [things are known] in the natural sciences, which requires a relational causal arrangement based upon the specific ordering.

Understanding this question is extremely difficult. The verifying knower[74] affirms the immediate cause, which one has to, but he does not maintain this specific ordering within the [realm of] immediate causes.[75] Now people who generally possess this science either deny everything or affirm everything, and I have not come across any of them who affirm the efficacy of the cause while at the same time denying its temporal succession.[76] It is a mighty science which

73. A phylactery referred originally to a small leather box containing four scriptural texts worn by Jews on every day except Sabbath as a reminder to keep the law. In the Islamic world it came to mean any kind of protective amulet that contained scriptural verses from the Quran, or written invocations dissolved in water, which was then drunk.

74. Ar: *al-'ālim al-muḥaqqiq*, a phrase referring to those whose knowledge is based on realisation of the truth, i.e. the highest grade of those who know reality.

75. One example of this understanding is given by Jalāl al-Dīn Rūmī: 'externally the branch is the origin of the fruit; intrinsically the branch came into existence for the sake of the fruit. Had there been no hope of the fruit, would the gardener have planted the tree? Therefore in reality, the tree is born of the fruit, though it appears to be produced by the tree.' (*Mathnawī*, Bk IV, 522, trans. R. A. Nicholson in *Rūmī, Poet and Mystic* (London, 1964), 124).

76. In other words, the true knower is able to maintain the principle of immediate

is known from this heaven. What [normally] comes about from a cause over a long period of time can take place from that cause *in the blinking of an eye or even shorter.*[77] This can be seen in what has been related concerning the way Jesus was brought into existence, as well as the way the bird created by Jesus came into being, and how he revived the dead man from his grave, prior to the earth undergoing birth-pangs in bringing forth engendered beings on the Day of Resurrection, which is in fact the day of their birth. So be mindful of this and hone your inner heart, so that your Lord may guide you on the right way! And from this heaven comes His saying regarding rising at night, that it *is most upright for speech.*[78]

When the disciple comes to these sciences, Mercury turns back to its guest [the rational thinker] and attends to him. It gives him some of the science that has been deposited within its mode of travelling,[79] in accordance with its

---

causality without denying the principle of divine causation. Elsewhere Ibn ʿArabī explains in connection with the Quranic verse 'O people, you are the one who are in need of God' (Q.35.15): 'So understand and realise the reliance that people have upon the forms of the immediate causes and the way they are in need of them. Yet God affirms that people are poor towards Him [alone], not towards anything else, in order that He may make clear to them that He is the One who reveals Himself in the forms of immediate causes and that the causes, which are the forms, are a veil over Him. This is known by those who know due to their knowledge of the degrees' (*Fut.*II.469).

77. Q.16.77: 'To God belongs the unseen of the heavens and the earth, and the matter of the Hour is but in the blinking of the eye, or even shorter.' According to Ibn ʿArabī as well as the Ashʿarites, creation takes place in an 'instant' we refer to as 'now', which can be described as the shortest possible unit of time, or better, the isthmus of zero-time between the past and the future. For Ibn ʿArabī's understanding of how creation is really a continuously fresh revelation, see *Fuṣūṣ al-ḥikam*, chapter on Solomon, where he discusses the miraculous transporting of Bilqis' throne (143).

78. Referring to Q.73.6–7: 'surely rising at night is firmest in tread, most upright for speech; during the day you have lengthy engagements.' The phrase 'most upright for speech' is usually understood to mean that the night is the best time for recitation of the Quran.

79. The planets were all considered as travelling (*jāriya*) through the heavens, i.e.

predisposition, regarding the ruling property it has over the bodies that lie below it in the elemental world, but not over their spirits.[80] When this is completed – for this is the way it hosts him– then the guest takes his leave and comes to his companion, the disciple.

They both depart in search of the third heaven, with the rational thinker going before the disciple, like a servant before his master – for he acknowledges his standing and his teacher's rank, and the blessing he has been given by following that teacher.

changing their position, retrograding etc., as opposed to the fixed stars which keep their position relative to each other.

80. In other words, philosophical knowledge is limited to the material realm, whereas the follower receives a total knowledge through the prophet.

THE 3RD HEAVEN: JOSEPH & VENUS

When they knock at [the door of] the third heaven, it is opened up to them and they ascend into it. There the disciple is welcomed by Joseph,[81] while the rational thinker finds the planet Venus,[82] which greets him and mentions to him what the previous subordinate planets have told him – this only serves to make him more distressed. Then the planet Venus comes to Joseph, who has his guest, the disciple, with him, as he is explaining to him the specific sciences God has bestowed upon him, which are connected to the forms of imagery and imagination – for he is one of the masters of the science of dream interpretation.[83] God spread before him the earth that He created from what was left over from Adam's clay,[84] and showed him the 'market

81. Ar: Yūsuf. Joseph was described by the Prophet as being so beautiful that he was blessed with half the beauty (*ḥusn*) of the entire world, while the other half was spread over the rest of it.

82. This Arabic name for Venus, *al-Zuhara*, comes from a root meaning 'to shine brightly', and also conveys ideas of beauty and splendour (*zahra*).

83. Ibn 'Arabī links dream interpretation to its prophetic exemplar, Joseph, whose ability to interpret dreams accurately enabled him to secure his freedom from prison and become a trusted adviser to the Pharaoh. In contrast, while Aristotle states: 'the most skilful interpreter of dreams is one who can see resemblances', Ibn Rushd defines a dream interpreter as 'someone whose soul is predisposed by nature to understand the semblances (*muḥākāt*) which occur in a dream-vision, someone who is benefited by the intellect with regard to the bodily realities that are imitated during sleep by spiritual realities' (quoted, with modifications, in Shlomo Pinés, *Studies in Arabic Versions of Greek Texts and in Medieval Science* (Leiden, 1986), 128).

84. This Earth is known as the 'earth of reality' (*arḍ al-ḥaqīqa*), which can only be entered by knowers of reality through their faculty of imagination. As Ibn 'Arabī explains elsewhere in chapter 8 of the *Futūḥāt*, 'when God had created Adam who was the first human body to come into being, and He had made him an origin and principle for the existence of all human bodies, a portion of the clay starter-dough was left over. From this surplus God created the palm tree (*nakhla, f.*), which is

of Paradise',[85] and the imaginal forms that are assumed by spirits of light and of fire[86] and by sublime meanings. He taught him their weights and measures, their relationships and origin. Thus He showed him years in the form of cattle, the years of plenty in the form of fat cows, and the lean years in the form of thin ones. He showed him knowledge as milk, and steadfastness in religion as a cord.[87] And He continued teaching him how meanings and relations are embodied in the form of sense-perception and what is perceived.[88]

---

therefore Adam's sister, and for us a paternal aunt... After the creation of the palm tree, there was still a tiny portion of clay left over, the size of a sesame seed, hidden away in secret. It was in this remainder that God laid out a vast unlimited Earth. When He had arranged in it the Throne and all it contains, the Footstool, the Heavens, the earths, all that is underground, and all the paradises and hells, everything could be found there like a ring lost in one of our deserts. In that Earth there are innumerable marvels and strange things, whose nature overwhelms and staggers the rational mind' (*Fut.*I.126; see partial trans. by Henry Corbin in *Spiritual Body and Celestial Earth* (London, 1990), 135–43). In the *Iṣṭilāḥāt*, no. 113, Ibn 'Arabī defines sesame as 'direct knowing (*ma'rifa*) which is too fine and subtle to be expressed' (*Rasā'il*, 537).

85. Ar: *sūq al-janna*, a phrase which occurs in various hadiths. For example, 'In Paradise there is a market to which the people will come every Friday (i.e. the day of gathering); then a wind will come from the north and blow on their faces and clothes, and they will increase in beauty. Then they will return to their wives who will also have increased in beauty. Their wives will say to them: "By God, you have increased in beauty since you left us", and they will reply: "And you also, by God, you have increased in beauty since we left"' (al-Tirmidhī, *Jāmi'* 41, Chapter 15).

86. That is, the angels and jinn, who are created of light and fire respectively.

87. Referring to the following hadiths: 'In a dream I was given a cup of milk. I drank it until I was full to the fingertips, then I gave the rest to 'Umar. He was asked, "What did you take it to mean, O Messenger of God?" "Knowledge", he replied' (al-Bukhārī, *'ilm* 82; Muslim, *faḍā'il 'Umar* 16); 'I love a cord [in dreams], for it is steadfastness in religion' (al-Bukhārī, *ta'bīr* 26; Muslim, *ru'yā* 6). The term *qayd* (cord or fetter) means something which binds or ties, whether made of rope or metal such as prison shackles. While these two relationships were mentioned by Muhammad, the knowledge of their meaning derives from Joseph, according to Ibn 'Arabī. See also *Fut.*III.361, trans. *SPK*, 122.

88. Ibn 'Arabī's wording here recalls the Arabic title (*Fī al-ḥiss wa al-maḥsūs*) for one of Aristotle's works, *Parva Naturalia*, on which his compatriot Ibn Rushd wrote a commentary. In particular, Aristotle's work was well known to the Islamic world for its discussion of dreams and their interpretation. For a discussion of the Arabic

He instructed him in how to interpret all that in terms of its original meaning,[89] for this is the heaven of complete representation[90] and harmonious arrangement.

It is from this [third] heaven that assistance is provided for poets.[91] From it also come the arts of composition and construction,[92] as well as geometrical forms within material bodies and the way they are imaged in the soul from the heaven from which [the disciple] has ascended. It is also from this heaven that he learns the meaning of strong construction and sound execution,[93] the beauty[94] that contains wisdom

---

recension of *Parva Naturalia*, as well as its links to Ibn Sīnā's *al-Risāla al-manāmiyya* ('Epistle on Dreams') and Ibn Rushd's *Summary*, see Pinés, *Studies in Arabic Versions of Greek Texts and in Medieval Science*, 96–145.

89. Ar: *ma'nā al-ta'wīl*. The literal meaning of *ta'wīl* is to take something back to its source, and hence to interpret. It is a word primarily associated in the Quran with the knowledge given to Joseph: for example, 'We gave Joseph a firm place on earth and so that We might teach him of how to interpret the true meaning (*ta'wīl*) of happenings' (Q.12.21).

90. Ar: *taṣwīr*, literally 'giving form to', or 'taking on of forms' (McAuley, *Ibn 'Arabī's Mystical Poetics*, 42).

91. The word Ibn 'Arabī uses here for what is given to poets, 'assistance' (*imdād*), indicates that it is an inspiration that derives from a lower level than the divine. In the pre-Islamic tradition, poetry was viewed as being given by a god or a jinn, similar to the Greek notion of the Muses. Here Ibn 'Arabī is suggesting that the power of poetry really comes from the universal level of the imagination and is directly linked to the polished perfection of its verbal arrangement and symmetry. Poetry in all its musicality comes before writing in every tradition. We should note that classical Arabic poetry had very strict rules of composition in terms of rhyme (*qāfiya*) and metre (*wazn*).

92. Ar: *al-naẓm wa al-itqān*, terms which could apply equally to poetry or physical substances and objects, since both suggest harmonious arrangement and beauty of form.

93. Ar: *al-itqān wa al-iḥkām*. An allusion to Q.27.88 '[on the day when the Trumpet is blown] you will see the mountains, which you considered to be so fixed, pass away as clouds pass away – the handiwork of God, who has created everything firmly and perfectly (*atqana kulla shay'in*)'. *Iḥkām* can also be understood as 'good organisation' (McAuley, *Ibn 'Arabī's Mystical Poetics*, 43).

94. Ar: *ḥusn*, which means both 'beauty' and 'goodliness'. See Q.3.195: 'And God, with Him is the most beautiful reward (*ḥusn al-thawāb*)', and the Prophet's saying 'I was sent to complete the beauty of character (*ḥusn al-akhlāq*).' It is the word used to

by its very existence, and the beauty which is desired by and suitable to a particular temperament.

In this heaven there is the fifth agent, who looks after the human embryo in the womb during the fifth month. Part of the command which God has inspired in this heaven is the arrangement of the [four] elements,[95] which lie below the bottom of the lunar sphere. Thus He placed the element of air between fire and water, and the element of water between air and earth.[96] Had there not been such an arrangement, then transformations could not have taken place within them, nor could engendered beings have come into existence from them, nor would there have appeared within these beings the changes that do occur. Where then would the sperm-drop have been, given the way it is transformed into flesh and blood and bone, veins and nerves?

It is from this heaven that God created the arrangement of the four humours[97] within this corporeal formation in the

---

describe the beauty of Joseph. As Ibn ʿArabī states in his *K. al-Isfār*, 'when God bestowed honour on the beauty of Joseph, he was tried with the humiliation of being a slave' (*Secrets of Voyaging*, 99).

95. According to this form of holistic thinking, all things are composed of four elements (*arkān*): fire, air, water and earth. These elements also appear within the human constitution in the form of four humours (see below).

96. This alludes to the wisdom that Joseph embodies: just as fire and water are two opposites that cannot mix without extinguishing each other, so are meaning and form opposed to each other – the medium of air represents the action of 'crossing-over' through correct interpretation from one realm to another, just as fire needs air to burn and transform water into steam or moisture. Air and earth are also opposites that cannot interact and are arid, as in a desert landscape – only water brings about life. There is also a hidden allusion to the miraculous graces of Jesus walking on water and of Muhammad travelling through the air. For the traditional Islamic understanding of the arrangement of the elements, see Jābir b. Ḥayyān in his *K. Ikhrāj mā fī al-quwwa ilā al-fiʿl* (*Essai sur l'histoire des idées scientifiques dans l'Islam*), vol. 1, ed. Paul Kraus (Paris 1935), 3.

97. Ar: *akhlāṭ*: yellow bile, blood, phlegm and black bile. The correspondence between the inner world of humours and the outer world of elements is as follows: yellow bile = choleric = Fire, dry + hot; blood = sanguine = Air, moist + hot; phlegm

most beautiful way and with the most scientific skill. He has placed yellow bile under the control of the governing soul, followed by blood, phlegm and finally black bile, which is the characteristic of death. If it were not for this astounding arrangement within the humours, there would have been no support for the doctor when he wants to remove a defect that has befallen the body or when he wants to maintain it in health.

From this heaven also manifest the four principles upon which poetic verse is based, just as the body is based upon four humours. These both comprise two 'cords' and two 'pegs':[98] a light cord and a heavy cord, a divided peg and a connected peg.[99] The divided peg produces dissolution, while the connected one gives composition; the light cord presents spirit, while the heavy one gives body. It is with totality that the human being comes into existence, so observe how well constructed is the existence of this world, macrocosm and microcosm!

When these two people have obtained these sciences, with the disciple gaining more than the rational thinker

---

= phlegmatic = Water, moist + cold; black bile = melancholic = Earth, dry + cold. See *Fut.*I.124 and Appendix B.

98. Ar: *al-sababān wa al-watadān*. The precise term for a Bedouin dwelling is *bayt sha'r*, 'a hair tent', indicating the material used in making it, which is cognate with *bayt shi'r*, 'a verse tent'. Thus the single line of the poem came to be known as a verse (*bayt*), and there is a parallel between the form and structure of a poem and that of a human dwelling. In the case of human habitation, *bayt* signifies a tent which is held up by cords (tying two elements together) and tent-pegs. In the case of poetry, the constituent parts of a metric foot are called a 'cord' (*sabab*, consisting of two letters) and a 'peg' (*watad*, consisting of three letters).

99. In the technical vocabulary of poetry, the light cord (*sabab khafīf*) is a movent letter followed by a quiescent letter, while the heavy cord (*sabab thaqīl*) means two movent letters; and the connected peg (*maqrūn* or here *majmū'*) means two movent letters followed by a quiescent, while the divided peg (*mafrūq*) indicates one movent, one quiescent, one movent. See Wright, *A Grammar of the Arabic Language*, 2/358.

through what the private face gives him of divine knowledge – as happened to them both in each [previous] heaven – then they travel on in search of the central heaven, which is the heart of all the heavens.[100]

100. That is to say, the fourth heaven lies at the centre of the celestial hierarchy, not only as the middle of the seven heavens but also as the very centre of all the 28 degrees of existence. It thus symbolises the 'heart' (*qalb*) of existence. See Appendix A, p.171.

When they arrive there, the disciple is met by Idrīs (Enoch), while the rational thinker is met by the planet of the sun. Exactly the same thing happens to the rational thinker with the sun as has happened before, which only makes him more distressed. Meanwhile, the disciple halts with Idrīs, and learns about the constant transformation[101] of the divine realities: he grasps the meaning of the Prophet's words, *the heart is between two of the fingers of the Compassionate*,[102] and how it is turned by them. In this heaven he sees how night envelops day and day envelops night, and how each of them is masculine towards its companion at one moment and feminine at another: thus [he sees] the mystery of their marriage and their union, what is born in them as children of the night and the day, and the difference between the children of the night and the children of the day – for each of them [night and day] is 'father' to what is born in its opposite and 'mother' to what is born within itself.[103]

101. Ar: *taqlīb*, 'turning, fluctuating, changing', from the same root as *qalb* (heart). 'Transformation (*taqlīb*) from one state to another state belongs to the heart, and this is why it is called 'heart' (*qalb*)' (*Fut*.III.198).

102. With regard to this hadith, Ibn 'Arabī explains elsewhere: 'the heart is between two of the fingers of its Creator, who is the Compassionate… in the hadith of the fingers there are divine good tidings in the fact that the two fingers are attributed to the Compassionate (*Raḥmān*): He only turns the heart from one mercy to another, even though there is affliction in the various kinds of fluctuation. For concealed within [affliction] lies a mercy hidden from the human being and known to the Real, for the two fingers belong to the Compassionate One' (*Fut*.III.199).

103. As the next sentence indicates, night and day here represent the non-manifest and the manifest, leading Michel Chodkiewicz to observe that the children of the day describe those whose spiritual perfection is visible, and the children of the night

He also learns in this heaven the science of the unseen and the seen, the science of the veil and revelation, and the science of life and death, intimacy and ease, friendship and compassion.[104] He learns what appears of the Name Manifest in the interior places of manifestation by virtue of the private face, and what appears of the Name Hidden in the exterior, due to the aptitudes of the places of manifestation. For the Names vary in manifestation because the essential realities are different.

---

are those whose sainthood is hidden from other people's eyes (the *malāmiyya*). See *Seal of Saints*, 161.

104. This alludes to the following verses in Sūrat al-Rūm (Q.30.19–21): 'He it is who brings forth the living out of the dead and brings forth the dead out of that which is alive, and gives life to the earth after it has been lifeless… And among His signs is the fact that He creates for you partners out of your own kind so that you may find ease and familiarity (*taskunū*) with them, and He engenders friendship (*mawadda*) and tender compassion (*raḥma*) between you.' 'Partners' are elsewhere described as a 'garment' (*libās*, hence translated here as 'intimacy') for each other in the act of lovemaking: 'It is permitted to you to enter in to your wives on the night before the fast: they are a garment for you, and you are a garment for them' (Q.2:187). This connects to the idea of coupling in order to produce 'children', which was already mentioned. We might also note two further possible contrasts: between clothing (the ordinary meaning of *libās*), which covers the individual, and housing (another meaning of *sakan*, here translated as ease), which covers the family or society; and between loving friendship among individuals and compassion to all creatures.

THE 5TH HEAVEN: AARON & MARS

Then they journey on in search of the fifth heaven, where the disciple lodges with Aaron, and the rational thinker stays with Mars.[105] Then Mars makes its excuses to its companion and guest for not being [able to be] with him while it is occupied with serving Aaron for the sake of his guest. When Mars calls on Aaron, he finds his guest with him, being received most openly and warmly. Mars is most surprised at such an expansive welcome and asks about it, to which [Aaron] replies: 'This is the heaven of awe, fear, severity and affliction, all attributes which necessitate a state of constriction.[106] Now this visitor has just arrived through following the Messenger, which makes it necessary that he should be treated with proper consideration and respect. He has come in search of knowledge and looking for a divine authority, which he can turn to for help against the thoughts that assail him, in fear of overstepping the limits set down by his master.[107] So I unveil for him the underlying features of these limits, and welcome him with expansiveness so that he

105. Ar: *al-Aḥmar*, literally 'the Red', a word that has associations with anger and blood, as well as excellence (the planet is also known in Arabic as *al-Mirrīkh* – see Appendix B). Traditionally Mars was not only associated with martial qualities but also considered (with Saturn) to be one of the two planets of misfortune.

106. That is to say, these qualities both stem from a state of constriction (*qabḍ*) and cause that in others: forcefulness or severity (*shidda*) implies harshness towards others, like a very severe teacher, and affliction (*ba's*) can mean the inner misery produced by divine punishment as well as the strength that causes affliction in others. This condition of constriction, normally associated with Mars, is being contrasted with the expansiveness of Aaron's welcome and teaching.

107. See Q.65.1: 'Whoever oversteps the limits set down by God has surely wronged their own soul.'

may receive what he is looking for, with an openness of soul, by means of a holy spirit.'

Then [Aaron] turns back to [the disciple] and says: 'This is the heaven of being a representative for humankind:[108] such a leader is weak in authority, even though the origin of this [representation] has been made of the strongest construction, and he is ordered to be gentle towards tyrants and oppressors. So we were told: *Speak to [the Pharaoh] with words of gentleness.*[109] Nobody is ordered to speak with gentleness except one whose strength is greater than that of the one he is sent to, whose power is *mightier.*'[110] Since the Real made known that He has set a seal upon every heart that manifests almightiness and self-exaltation,[111] and that [the Pharaoh] was within himself the most humble of the humble, [Moses and Aaron] were ordered to treat him with mercy and gentleness, so as to suit his interior and so that his exterior might be forced to give up its aura of omnipotence and self-importance, *...that perhaps he may be mindful or be afraid.* Now 'perhaps' and 'maybe', when coming from God, are [actually] two necessities. So through the gentleness and submissiveness he received, [the Pharaoh] was reminded of the way that he was in his interior, so that exterior and interior might become alike.

108. Ar: *khilāfat al-bashar*, since Aaron was appointed to be both a prophet and Moses' representative in his absence. Aaron typifies the priestly leader, who acts as the representative of God's representative to his people.

109. Q.20.44: God said to Moses and Aaron: 'Go to the Pharaoh, for he has become tyrannical; yet speak to him with gentleness, that perhaps he may be mindful or be afraid.'

110. Ar: *baṭshahu ashaddu*, an implicit reference to Q.50.36: 'How many a generation have We destroyed before them, who were mightier in power.'

111. See Q.40.35: 'Those who engage in disputes concerning God's Sign, without any authority that comes to them [their action] is of grievous hatefulness with God and with those who believe. Thus God sets a seal on every arrogant, tyrannical heart (*qalbin mutakabbirin jabbārin*).

This leaven continued to work within his interior, with the divine expectation, which necessitates the actual occurrence of what is hoped for. The power of this leaven grew stronger and stronger until he gave up all hope of his followers, and death by drowning intervened between him and his ambitions. It was then that he had recourse to the submissiveness and neediness that had been hidden within his interior, so that the divine expectation might be realised in the eyes of those who have faith. [The Pharaoh] said: *I believe in the One in whom the children of Israel believe, and I am one of those who submit.*[112] So he manifested the real condition of his interior, as well as the true knowledge of God that was in his heart. He uttered the words *the One in whom the children of Israel believe*, to remove any ambiguity in his difficulties, just as the magicians said when they professed their faith: *We believe in the Lord of the worlds, the Lord of Moses and Aaron,*[113] that is, the One to whom the latter summoned them. They came out with that in order to dispel any doubt. And the Pharaoh's words *I am one of those who submit* were an address from him to the Real because he knew that the Exalted One heard and saw him. Then the Real addressed him in the language of rebuke, and made him hear: *Only now* are you manifesting what you knew [in your heart], *when you resisted before and were one of those who spread corruption*[114]

112. Q.10.90: 'And when he was about to drown, he exclaimed: "I believe that there is no deity except the One in whom the children of Israel believe, and I am one of those who submit."' The slightly abbreviated version given here can also be found in *Fuṣūṣ al-ḥikam*, chapter on Solomon (144).

113. Q.7.122: 'The magicians fell down in prostration and said: "We believe in the Lord of the worlds, the Lord of Aaron and Moses."'

114. Q.10.91: 'Now? When you resisted before and were one of those who spread corruption?'

among your followers. [The Real] did not say to him 'you are one of those who spread corruption', and that is a saying of good news for him, by which He teaches us to hope for His Mercy despite our exceeding the bounds and our culpability.

Then He said: *Today We shall deliver you*, giving him good news prior to seizing his spirit, *with your body that you may be a Sign to those who succeed you,*[115] meaning that the deliverance may be a mark of proof, *an evident Sign*, for those who come after you. Since he said what you [the reader also] say, there will be salvation for him, just as there is for you.[116] There is nothing in this verse saying that the affliction of the hereafter will not be lifted or that his faith will not be accepted. Rather, what this verse shows is that the affliction of this world is not lifted from those upon whom it falls, when they believe at the moment they see [the truth], except for the people of Jonah.[117] His saying *Today We shall deliver you with your body* shows that punishment is only connected to your exterior and that I [God] have demonstrated to the creation that he was delivered from punishment. The beginning of drowning was a punishment, and then death in [the drowning] became pure and guiltless testimony, unadulterated by opposition.

115. Q.10.92: 'Today We shall deliver you with your body that you may be an evident Sign (*āya*) to those who come after you – indeed many people are ignorant of Our Signs.'

116. In other words, the reader, who has accepted submission to God (*islām*) in this world, has been assured of salvation in the next through his faith, and it is in the same manner that the Pharaoh will be saved.

117. See Q.10.97–100. Unlike other peoples who were destroyed for their lack of faith, the people of Jonah were saved in this world and the next because they turned to God in prayer and the divine punishment was averted. In contrast, the Pharaoh only came to faith at the end, and professed his belief, still thinking that he would be saved in this world. This contentious interpretation of the Pharaoh story may be contrasted with the story of Faust, who never believed that the Mercy of God is all-embracing or that he could be forgiven.

Then you were seized[118] in the midst of the best action, which is the profession of faith. All of that was done so that no-one should despair of God's [infinite] mercy. The judgment of deeds depends on how they are completed. Faith in God never ceased passing through [the Pharaoh's] interior. The divine essential seal on creatures intervenes between pride and the human subtle faculties, so that haughtiness never enters into them.

When He says *But their coming to faith when they saw Our affliction could not possibly benefit them,*[119] it is a truthful statement of the utmost clarity, for the One who gives benefit is God and nothing could benefit them except God. His [subsequent] Word *the way of God which has always applied to His servants* means the faith that comes at the moment of seeing exceptional affliction.

[The Real] has also said: *All that is in the heavens and all that is upon the earth prostrate to God, willingly and unwillingly.*[120] The lowest form of this faith is where it occurs under duress, and yet the Truth has attached it directly to Himself. The place of unwillingness is the heart, just as the place of faith is also the heart. God never imposes on the servant actions that are onerous to him simply because he finds them troublesome – on the contrary, [if it is something he finds difficult] He doubles the recompense he will receive for them.

118. Alternatively, 'I seized [his spirit]'.

119. This refers to previous generations who ridiculed divine messengers and only changed their view when they saw disastrous consequences. See Q.40.84–5: 'Then when they saw Our affliction, they said: "We believe in God as the One alone, and we renounce all belief in what we used to associate with Him." But their coming to faith when they saw Our affliction could not possibly benefit them – that is the way of God that has always applied to His servants – thus those that disbelieved were lost' (Q.40.85).

120. Q.13.15.

In this particular case, it was not so difficult for [the Pharaoh] – rather, he came willingly into his faith, even though he did not go on living after that. Likewise, He says of those who travel by sea, when it is very rough: *whoever you invoke apart from Him vanishes, forgotten,*[121] and then He rescues them. If He were to take [someone's soul] at the moment they were rescued, they would die professing His Unity, and would have obtained deliverance. So He took the Pharaoh's soul and did not delay the moment of his death because he was in a state of faith, in case he should [change his mind and] return to what he had been claiming.

Then to complete [the Pharaoh's] story He says: *And many people are ignorant of Our Signs.*[122] In other words, your deliverance has been manifested as a Sign, that is, a mark[123] indicating that you have achieved salvation, but most people are unaware of this Sign, condemning the person of faith to suffering. As for His saying *and he led them down to the Fire,*[124] there is no mention here that [the Pharaoh] actually entered the Fire [of Hell] with them. On the contrary, [elsewhere] God says: *Bring in the Pharaoh's people*![125] He does not say: 'Bring in the Pharaoh and his people.'

The Mercy of God is more all-encompassing than to be unable to embrace the faith of one who is constrained by need.[126] What greater constraint could there be than the

121. Q.17.67: 'When adversity befalls you at sea, whoever you invoke apart from Him vanishes, forgotten. As soon as He brings you safe onto dry land, you turn away [and forget Him] – indeed the human being is most ungrateful.'

122. See n.115 above.

123. Ar: *'alāma*.

124. Q.11.98: 'He shall go before his people on the Day of Resurrection; he led them down to the Fire – evil the watering-place to be led down to!'

125. Q.40.46: 'On the day when the Last Hour dawns, [He will say] "bring in the people of the Pharaoh!"'

126. Ar: *mudṭarr*, one who is forced or compelled by need. Being constrained is

plight of the Pharaoh at the moment of drowning? And God says: *who is it that answers the constrained when he calls unto Him, removing the ill?*,[127] directly linking together [His] response to the one in need when he calls upon Him, and removing ill from him. Such a person has secure faith in God alone, for he did not just call to Him in order to remain in the life of this world, out of fear of what might happen to him later, or such a request would have come between him and the true devotion which he reached at that moment. [The Pharaoh] preferred meeting with God to remaining [in this world] by his pronouncing the [words of] faith, and He made that drowning *the warning sign of the hereafter and this world.*[128] His punishment was no more than the affliction of the salty water,[129] and He took him with the best quality. This is what the words state literally. This is the meaning of His saying: *surely in that there is a lesson for anyone who experiences reverent fear*,[130] that is to say, in His seizing [him] was *the warning sign of the hereafter and this world.* He put the mention of the hereafter first and this world last, so that it might be known that such a punishment, i.e. that of drowning, is the warning sign of the next world, which is why He mentioned it first before this world. This is *the great bounty.*[131]

---

usually contrasted with being free to make choices.

127. Q.27.62: 'Who is it that answers the constrained when he calls unto Him, removing the ill and appointing you as representatives of the earth? Is there a god with God? Little do you remember.'

128. Q.79.25: 'So [Moses] showed [the Pharaoh] the great sign, and he cried lies and rebelled, then he turned away hastily, then he mustered and proclaimed, and he said "I am your lord, the most high!" So God seized him with the warning sign of the next world and this one. Surely in that is a lesson for him who fears.'

129. Ar: *al-mā' al-ajāj*. The word translated as 'salty' here, *ajāj*, means anything that burns the mouth, whether salty or hot, suggesting the fiery nature of punishment.

130. Q.79.26.

131. Ar: *al-faḍl al-ʿaẓīm*, perhaps referring to Q.8.29: 'O you who have faith, if

So observe, o saintly friend, what speaking gently results in and how it bears such fruit. And may you, o follower, be gentle in your dealings, for proud souls can be won over by gentle persuasion.

Then [Aaron] orders him to be kind towards his companion, the rational thinker. The reason why Aaron tells him to do this is that this is what happened to him as a matter of his own direct experience, when Moses took hold of his head and pulled it towards him. [Moses] made him experience humiliation by grabbing him by the beard and hair.[132] So [Aaron] appealed to him by invoking the more tender-hearted of their parents, saying *O son of my mother, do not pull me by my beard or my hair* and *do not let my enemies gloat over me*,[133] when his brother Moses dominated him with the attribute of superior force.[134] Aaron was forced to experience ignominy,[135] despite his being innocent of what he was humiliated for, and his humiliation was doubled. So he had to call upon [his brother] through their maternal relationship. This is the cause of his advice to the follower [to be kind to the rational thinker].

---

you are mindful of God, He will assign you a salvation, and acquit you of your evil deeds and forgive you; and God is possessor of great bounty.'

132. The root of the word *liḥya* (beard) also means insult.

133. See Q.20.94: 'Son of my mother, do not grab me by my beard or my head! For I feared that you would say "You have divided the Israelites, and did not regard my word."' Also Q.7.150: 'And he threw down the tablets, grabbed his brother by the hair, drew him to him, and [Aaron] said "Son of my mother, the people have abased me and nearly killed me. Do not let my enemies gloat over me, and do not put me with unjust people."'

134. Ar: *qahr*. Note that Mars is also known as the planet of all-conquering force (*al-Qāhir*).

135. Ar: *dhillat al-khuluq* (or *al-khalq*), literally 'lowness and humility of nature'. That is to say, Aaron had to endure being subject to Moses' anger, even though he was the elder brother and a prophet, and should therefore have been treated with respect. Instead of deferring to him, Moses publicly humiliated him in front of their people.

If Moses had not thrown down the tablets, he would not have grabbed his brother by the head, for written upon them was guidance and mercy as a reminder to Moses.[136] He would have treated his brother with mercy, and his question regarding his people would have been clarified through the guidance. In fact *when his anger abated in him, he took up the tablets*, and the only thing his eye fell on that was written there were [the words] 'guidance' and 'mercy'. Then he cried out: *O my Lord, forgive me and my brother, and enter us into Your Mercy, for You are the Most Merciful of the mercifiers.*

[Aaron] also instructs [the follower] to put the bloodshed required by his heaven into offerings and animal sacrifice, so that animals may attain the degree of the human – for only at this degree is there completion with regard to the sacred Trust.[137] Then the one who is with him [the rational thinker] leaves with the robe of [Mars], who has been hosting him, and takes his companion by the hand, having been apprised as far as he can of those sciences which lie within Mars' compass and no further.

136. See Q.7.151–4: '[Moses] said: "O my Lord, forgive me and my brother and enter us into Your Mercy; for You are the Most Merciful of the mercifiers"... And when Moses' anger abated in him, he took up the tablets; and inscribed upon them was guidance and mercy to those who stand in awe of their Lord.'

137. Ar: *amāna*, referring to Q.33.72: 'We offered the Trust to the heavens and the earth and the mountains, but they refused to carry it and were afraid of it. And man carried it. Surely he is unjust, ignorant.' Ibn 'Arabī often speaks of the Trust in the context of the human as God's representative: 'He created Adam in His own form, and designated him with all His most beautiful Names. Through the power of the [divine] form he was able to bear the Trust that was offered to him. The reality of the form did not allow him to reject the Trust in the way that the heavens and earth refused it' (*Fut.*II.170). 'He created the human being and He enabled him to carry out the Trust by giving him vision over all existent things and the power of dispensing over them through the Trust' (*Fut.*II.267).

THE 6TH HEAVEN: MOSES & JUPITER

They both depart in search of the sixth heaven, where Moses receives him, and with Moses is his minister, Jupiter.[138] The rational thinker does not recognise Moses, and so Jupiter takes him and looks after him. Meanwhile, the follower stays with Moses, who instructs him in 12,000 divine sciences,[139] in addition to explaining to him the sciences of rotation and periodicity.[140] He teaches him that the divine self-disclosure[141] only occurs in the forms of beliefs and needs, so he is vigilant. Then [Moses] explains to him how he was looking for fire for his family,[142] and how God only revealed Himself

138. Ar: *Birjīs* or *Barjīs*, one of the names for the planet Jupiter which appears in hadiths. Here again Ibn ʿArabī uses courtly imagery to refer to the planet by referring to it as Moses' *wazīr* (vizier). It is also known as *al-Mushtarī* (see Appendix B), and called 'the larger star of good fortune' (*al-saʿd al-akbar*), that is to say, greater than the 'lesser' planet of good fortune, Venus.

139. This number implicitly refers to Q.2.60: 'And remember when Moses sought water for his people and We said: "Strike the rock with your staff", at which twelve rivers gushed forth from it so that all the people knew their place of drinking.' As Chodkiewicz remarks, these twelve rivers correspond not only to the twelve tribes of Israel but also to 'so many aspects of the *walāya mūsawiyya*' (*Seal of Saints*, 162). The fact that the number is here multiplied by a thousand indicates that these are sciences which appear in manifestation.

140. Ar: *al-dawr wa al-kawr*. These terms were often coupled together to explain the motions of the planets (*dawr*, literally 'revolution') and the longer periods of time within which these take place (*kawr*, literally 'turning'). See *Risāla* 35, *fī al-adwār wa al-akwār*, of the *Rasāʾil Ikhwān al-Ṣafā*. It is also possible to understand this as referring to the proverbial pair *al-ḥawr wa al-kawr*, which are mentioned in a prophetic hadith 'We take refuge in God from a bad state of affairs (deficiency, bad fortune) coming after a good state (abundance, prosperity).'

141. Ar: *tajallī*.

142. A reference to the story of how Moses came upon the Burning Bush: 'Then when Moses had fulfilled the term, and was travelling with his family, he perceived a fire by Sinai. He said to his family: "Stay here, for I perceive a fire. Maybe I can bring you some information from there or a burning coal from the fire, so that you

to him in that [fire] because it was the same as his need – so he did not see [the revelation] except through his own neediness. For everyone who seeks is necessarily in need of what he is seeking.

In this heaven [Moses] also instructs him in how [apparent] forms can be removed from the substance and other forms can clothe it, teaching him that the individual essences,[143] which are the essences of forms, are unalterable. Otherwise it would mean that the realities themselves could be altered. On the other hand, perceptions are directly linked to objects of perception, which are in themselves indisputably true.[144] One who does not have knowledge of realities imagines that the actual essences have changed, but they have not altered [in fact]. From this he comes to know how the Real reveals Himself on the Day of Resurrection in a form which those who have stopped [with a particular understanding] take refuge from: they take the Real to be transcendent of that form and seek refuge in God from it.[145] Yet He is the Real, and there is nothing other than Him. That is how they see it, in their perception – for the Real cannot be subject to alteration or change.

ʿUlaym al-Aswad[146] once said to someone: 'Stop.' Then ʿUlaym put his hand on a column in the Sacred Precinct [in

---

may warm yourselves." Then when he got there, he was called from the right side of the valley, from a tree on blessed ground, "Moses! It is I, God, Lord of the universes"' (Q.28.29–30). See also Q.20.10–14.

143. Ar: *al-aʿyān*, referring to the potential realities of things as established in God's knowledge (*al-aʿyān al-thābita*).

144. That is, they are 'true' insofar as the forms of perceptible objects are what they seem to be. Even a mirage is predicated on some kind of perception. The error, therefore, lies in the understanding, not in the perception.

145. Referring to a well-known *ḥadīth qudsī* regarding one group on the Day of Resurrection. See Ibn ʿArabī's *Mishkāt al-anwār*, 26th hadith (*Divine Sayings*, 45).

146. Possibly to be identified with the man known as ʿUlaym al-Majnūn (the

Mecca], and the man saw it as made of gold. 'Ulaym said to him: 'Listen, the essential realities are unalterable, but this is the way you will see Him because of your reality with your Lord', pointing to the revelation of the Real on the Day of Resurrection and His transmutation in forms in the eye of the beholder.

From this heaven he learns the wondrous science that few people are privy to. In fact it is better that most do not know it. It is the inner meaning of what He asked Moses – and no-one knows what God intended except Moses and whoever God has favoured – *'And what is that in your right hand, Moses?', to which he replied: 'It is my staff.'*[147] Now questions about self-evident truths are hardly going to be put to someone who knows the answer to them, unless it is for the sake of a concealed meaning. Moses answered by explaining that it was a staff *upon which I lean and with which I beat down leaves for my livestock, and it has other uses for me too*, all of which derives from its being a staff. Do you really think that he could inform the Real of something that the Real did not already know? This is a reply that states the obvious, responding to a question about something known which is perceived as obvious. Then God said to him: *Throw it down*, meaning from your hand along with the conviction that it is a staff. So Moses *threw it down, and behold, it* – that is, the staff – *was a slithering serpent.* When God gave the staff – I mean its substance – the form of a snake, He also made it

mad or love-struck), who is mentioned by al-Qushayrī in his *Risāla* (see *Epistle on Sufism*, trans. Alexander Knysh (Reading, 2007), 148).

147. Q.20.17 21: '"And what is that in your right hand, Moses?", to which he replied: "It is my staff: I lean on it and beat down leaves for my livestock with it, and it has other uses for me also." He said: "Throw it down, Moses." So he threw it down and behold, it was a slithering serpent. He said: "Pick it up without fear; We will restore it to its original state."'

have the characteristic of a snake, which is sliding, so that it was clear to Moses because of its slithering that it was a serpent. If his fear of it were not the general terror mankind has of snakes, then we could say that God created life within the staff, so that the staff became alive from life,[148] slithering upon its belly due to its being alive and having no legs and feet to move with. It had the form of a snake because of its outward appearance as a staff.

When Moses took fright at it because of its form, God said to him: *Pick it up without fear* – and this is the fear that occurs when something totally unexpected happens. Then He said to him: *We will restore it*, referring to the staff, *to its original state*. The substances of things are alike, but different in terms of form and accident, for [actually] the substance is one. In other words, it became a staff again as it was in its essence[149] and as your eye perceived it, just as it was a snake in its essence and as your eye perceived it. This was in order that Moses might know who it is that sees, what is seen and through whom he sees. This was divine instruction for him and for us. It is equally what ʿUlaym said, namely that the essences do not alter. The staff did not become a snake, nor did the snake become a staff. Rather, the substance, having assumed the form of the staff, then took on the form of the serpent. These are forms which God, the All-Powerful Creator, removes from the substance when He wishes, conferring another form upon it.

148. Ar: *ḥayya min al-ḥayāh*, an untranslateable play on words. The root *ḥ-y-y* carries both the meaning of life (*ḥayāh*) and snake (*ḥayya*, pl. *ḥayyāt*).

149. Ar: *dhāt*, a word that in Islamic philosophy can have several meanings. It can mean simply the self of a thing, but it can also designate the underlying substance and essence, as contrasted with its inherent qualities, or essential qualities as opposed to accidental attributes. Ibn ʿArabī here indicates that the single substance has both possibilities of staff and snake inherent within it.

If you are discerning, then I have informed you of the science regarding those forms of existent things that you see. You will affirm it as necessary, because you are unable to deny it, for it has become clear to you that 'transformations' are in fact unreal.[150] God has 'eyes'[151] in some of His servants, with which they can perceive the staff as a snake in its very state of being a staff, and that is a divine perception, which in us is imaginal. And this is the same for all existents.

Consider then: if it were not for these sensory faculties, you could not say that this is a mineral that does not feel or speak or possess life, and this a plant, and this an animal, which can feel and perceive, and this a human being possessed of intelligence and reason. All of this is what you get from rational observation. Now someone else might come and stand by you, and he can actually see and hear the salutations proffered to him by the minerals, plants and animals. Both experiences are valid, and the faculty that you use to judge the non-validity of what he says is the very same faculty by which this person is guided. The [objective] evidence employed by each of them is exactly the same, but their [subjective] conclusions are different. By God, the staff of Moses was always a snake and it was always a staff! All of this is how it is experienced, and neither of these two people is mistaken in terms of how things actually are in reality.[152]

But we have seen that and verified it with our own eye: the former and the latter [points of view] come from a single

150. Ar: *al-istiḥālāt muḥāl*, another untranslateable pun. Both words come from the same root, *ḥ-w-l*.

151. Cf. Q.7.195, referring to that which is invoked apart from God, which are but 'servants like you': 'Or do they have eyes with which they can see?'

152. Alternatively, 'neither of these two people is mistaken in terms of how things are in themselves.' In other words, they are both right about what they have seen, the same object possessing apparently opposing characteristics.

source.[153] In the first revelation it is no other than itself, and in the second revelation it is also no other than itself. So say 'God' or say 'the world'; say 'I'; say 'You'; say 'He' – all [being] in the presence of pronouns, continuously and unceasingly. Thus Zayd says about you 'he', while 'Amr says of you 'you', and you say of yourself 'I'. But [that] 'I' is the same as the 'you' and the 'he' – and yet 'I' am not the same as 'you' nor the same as 'he'! It is [simply] the relations that vary. And herein lie infinitely vast oceans, fathomless and shoreless. By the Exalted Might of my Lord, were you aware of what I have said in these pearls [of wisdom], you would be transported with eternal rapture and you would experience the fear from which there is no security for anyone. For the crushing of the mountain is the same as its establishment, and Moses' regaining consciousness is the same as his losing it!

Observe His Face in every happening of existence,
And do not try to tell anyone else about It

O you Muhammadian follower! Be not unmindful of what I have just told you, and go on seeing Him[154] in every form. For the place of [His] self-revelation is most evident.[155]

153. Ar: *'ayn wāḥida*. Here Ibn 'Arabī is playing on the meanings inherent in the word *'ayn*, i.e. 'eye', 'source', 'essential reality'. The sentence is also ambiguous as the subject could also refer to God, i.e. 'He is the First and the Last from a single source'. The following lines then refer also to God as being no other than Himself in each revelation.

154. That is to say, His Face (the pronoun here could refer to either Him or His Face).

155. Ar: *al-majlā ajlā*, a very elegant word-play as both words are from the same root *j-l-w*, which has meanings of being clear, disclosing, being manifest or uncovered. *Majlā* also means the forehead which displays the first signs of baldness, while *ajlā* can indicate the beauty that is displayed in the disclosing of the forehead. Elsewhere Ibn 'Arabī comments that the world is preserved in existence, not out of divine concern for it, but only to be the place of His self-revelation, so that the properties of His Names can be manifest (see *Fut.*III.120).

Then Jupiter takes him by the hand and brings him to the rational thinker, teaching him as much as is appropriate for him of what the follower was taught from Moses' knowledge – this is the knowledge that it specifically possesses regarding the influences of celestial movement upon elemental formation, and nothing more. The two travellers then depart [from the sixth heaven], the Muhammadian upon the litter of divine Grace[156] and the rational thinker upon the steed of reflective thinking.

156. The distinction between the two travellers is here emphasised by the contrast between the effortlessness of being carried upon a litter or carriage (*rafraf*) and the active attention and concentration demanded by riding a steed (*burāq*).

THE 7TH HEAVEN: ABRAHAM & SATURN

Then the seventh heaven is opened up to them, which from there is actually the first [of the heavens].[157] Here Abraham, the intimate friend,[158] comes to greet him, while the rational thinker is met by the planet Saturn.[159] Saturn installs him in a dark, deserted and desolate house, and says to him: 'This is the house of your brother,' meaning his own soul,[160] 'stay in it until I come to you, for I am in the service of this Muhammadian follower because of the one with whom he is staying, who is the intimate friend of God.'

Then Saturn goes off to Abraham, and finds him resting his back against the Visited House,[161] with the follower seated before him as a son sitting in front of his father, and Abraham

157. That is to say, this heaven is seventh in ascending order from earth, and first in descending order.

158. Ar: *khalīl.* This epithet is given to Abraham in the Quran (4.125).

159. Ar: Kaywān, the Persian word for Saturn, which derives from an Akkadian word meaning 'the steady one'. Its other name, Zuḥal (see Appendix B), was used as a metaphor for exaltedness and might explain why Ibn 'Arabī chose not to use it. In some texts the planet was also known as *al-Muqātil* (the warlike).

160. Ar: *nafs.* The soul or self here denotes the lower soul unrefined by the light of faith and gnosis. Ibn 'Arabī also uses it in other contexts to describe more refined dimensions of the self, leading to its fullest receptivity as the perfected or complete soul (*nafs kāmila*).

161. Ar: *al-bayt al-ma'mūr.* This celestial site and its identification with Abraham is attested in various hadith (see A.J. Wensinck, *Concordance* (Leiden, 1992), 4/353–4). According to Anas b. Mālik, '70,000 angels enter it each day, and they do not return there' (Muslim, *īmān* 259). The root of *ma'mūr* (*'-m-r*) has meanings of 'to cultivate (the earth), make sure that the house is not deserted, frequent, visit, inhabit, be inhabited and live long'. *Ma'mūr* could be translated as both peopled or oft-visited and frequented. As the House of the Heart, it is viewed as being visited or peopled by the angels who are constantly coming and going, a place of constant movement where guests are welcomed, standing in stark contrast to the deserted and lonely house of the soul.

is saying to him: 'What an excellent and devoted child.' The follower asks him about the three lights,[162] to which Abraham replies: 'They were my proof against my people: God gave them to me out of sheer grace from Him to me. I did not speak of them as being associations [with God], but I placed them as a hunter's snare with which to catch the wandering thoughts[163] of my people.' Then Abraham says to him: 'O you who follow [the prophet], distinguish the levels[164] and recognise the various creeds.[165] Stand upon clear proof from your Lord[166] in your affairs, and do not neglect your tradition,[167] for you are not neglected nor is a legacy bequeathed in vain.

162. Referring to the star, moon and sun mentioned in Q.6.76–9: 'When night fell over Abraham, he saw a star and said: "This is my Lord." But when it set, he said: "I love not that which goes down." When he saw the moon rising, he said: "This is my Lord." But when it set, he said: "If my Lord does not guide me, I will be among those who go astray." When he saw the sun rising, he said: "This is my Lord. This is the greatest!" But when it set, he said: "O my people, surely I am quit of what you associate. I have turned my face to the One who originated the heavens and the earth, a man of pure faith (*ḥanīf*). I am not one of those who cover up."'

163. Or: 'errant intelligences'.

164. The levels (*marātib*) of existence are an integral part of the cosmos, and therefore must be distinguished. 'The levels make known that which is ranked higher and that over which it is ranked. The levels distinguish between God and the world, and they manifest the realities of the divine Names in terms of their more or less inclusive connections [with the creatures]' (*Fut.*II.469, trans. *SPK*, 48). 'He who knows that excellence pertains to the levels (*rutab*), not to his own entity (*'ayn*), will never deceive himself into thinking that he is more excellent than anyone else, although he may say that one level is more excellent than another level' (*Fut.*III.225, trans. *SPK*, 48).

165. The creeds (*madhāhib*, plural of *madhhab*) would usually be taken to refer to the four schools of Islamic law, Hanafi, Hanbali, Maliki and Shafi'i. But it is more common for Ibn 'Arabī, as here, to take it in its most universal and literal sense as 'the ways of going' to God, or individual forms of belief and practice. Note also that the word *madhhab* comes from the same root as *dhahab*, 'gold', and could be understood as the golden path.

166. Alluding to Q.11.17: 'And what of him who stands upon clear proof from his Lord, and a witness from Him recites it, and before him is the Book of Moses as guide and mercy?' According to Wehr (Wiesbaden, 1979), 107, to 'stand upon clear proof' means to 'be fully aware'.

167. Ar: *ḥadīthaka*, which may refer to the Tradition of the Prophet Muhammad.

Make your heart like this Visited House, by being present with God in every state. Know that of all that you see, nothing is large enough for the Real God except the heart of the believer,[168] and that is you!'

When the rational thinker hears this address, he says: '*Woe is me for what I have squandered of what is due to God, for indeed I was one of those who mock.*'[169] He realises how he has failed to have faith in that messenger and follow his teaching and example,[170] and he says: 'If only I had not taken my intellect as a guide, and followed it on the path of thinking!'[171]

Each of these two people perceives what the high spiritual beings bestow and what the Highest Assembly[172] glorifies and praises, each according to the purity and freeing of their soul from the captivity of the natural constitution.[173] Within the essential nature of the soul of each of them is imprinted everything that exists in the universe, so that they can only come to know what they observe of their own self in the mirror of their essential nature.

168. Alluding to the frequently cited *ḥadīth qudsī*: 'Neither My heavens nor My earth can contain Me, but only the heart of My faithful servant is large enough to contain Me.'

169. See Q.39.55–6: 'Follow the best of what has been revealed to you from your Lord, before there comes to you the agony, suddenly, while you are unawares. Lest a soul might say, "Ah me! Woe is me for what I have squandered of what is due to God, for indeed I was one of those who mock."' Ibn 'Arabī is here making a sharp distinction between the heart of the servant, which is faithful and in a state of rapture with God, and the soul, which is full of regret and self-absorption.

170. Ar: *sunan*.

171. Ar: *fikr*, meaning speculative thought and opinion, employing the mind alone to attain meaning. This phrase echoes Q.25.28–9: 'If only I had taken a way along with the messenger! Woe is me, if only I had not taken so-and-so as a friend (*khalīl*)!' The use of the term *khalīl*, which is associated particularly with Abraham, is a telling example of Ibn 'Arabī's fidelity to the meaning of each word of this Quranic text.

172. Ar: *al-mala' al-a'lā*, referring to the heavenly host of angels.

173. Ar: *asr al-ṭabī'a*. This can also be read as 'from the strength of natural disposition'.

Now there is a story[174] about a wise man who wanted to demonstrate this spiritual station to the king: while a master painter occupied himself with painting a picture of the most exceptional composition and the most perfect workmanship, the sage devoted himself to burnishing the [opposite] wall, which was facing the painting. Between the two of them there was a curtain hanging down. When they had both finished their work, and done their very best as far as they were each concerned, the king came and stood in front of what the artist had painted: he saw marvellous pictures, with such beauty of composition and excellence of painting as would dazzle the mind. He looked at the colours in this beautiful composition, and it was just like looking at a wonderful view.

Then [the king] looked at what the other [the sage] had done in burnishing that surface, but he saw nothing. Then the sage said to him: 'O king, my work is more full of grace and loveliness than his, and my wisdom more recondite and difficult to comprehend than his. Raise now the curtain between me and him, so that you may see at one glance my work and his.'

So the king lifted the curtain, and upon that burnished surface was displayed all that the other man had painted, in an even more beautiful form than it was in itself. And the king was astonished. Then the king also saw his own form and the form of the sage–polisher in that surface, at which he was [even more] bewildered and astounded.

'How can this be?' he asked, to which the sage replied: 'O king, I did this for you as an example of your own self in

174. Compare this with the story in Rumi's *Mathnawī* about the Greeks (who are called Sufis) and the Chinese (Bk I, 3480ff.). The source for the story would appear to be al-Ghazālī (*Sharḥ ʿajāʾib al-qalb*, chapter 8 of Bk. XXI of *Iḥyāʾ ʿulūm al-dīn*).

relation to the forms of the world: if you were to polish the mirror of your soul with spiritual practices and exercises, until you were pure of heart and you had removed the rust of nature from your soul, then you would receive the forms of the world in the mirror of your essence, wherein everything that is in the whole world is portrayed.'

It is at this limit that the rational thinker and the follower of the messengers come to a stop. For this comprehensive presence belongs to both of them. Yet the follower goes beyond the rational thinker in [knowing about] certain matters which have not been wholly depicted in the world – this is by virtue of that private face which belongs to God within every possibility that arises from that which cannot be limited, grasped or depicted. It is by that [knowledge of the private face] that the disciple is distinguished from the rational thinker.

And from this [seventh] heaven may come the enticement, which one does not know about,[175] the hidden trickery which one is not aware of,[176] the *secure guile*[177] and the veil,[178] and being steadfast amidst one's affairs and proceeding in an unhurried fashion in them.[179]

175. See Q.7.182: 'We will draw them on/entice them whence they know not.'

176. See Q.27.50: 'And they devised a trick; and We devised a trick while they were not aware.'

177. See Q.7.182–3: 'We will draw them on, whence they know not; and I respite them – assuredly My guile is secure.' Also Q.68.45. It could also be translated as 'powerful stratagem'.

178. See for example Q.41.5: 'They say: "Our hearts are veiled from what you call us to, and in our ears is a heaviness, and between us and you is a veil; so act; we are acting!"'

179. This passage seems to refer most particularly to the example of Abraham when commanded to sacrifice his son, and how he remained true to what he was told to do, a steadfastness that is reflected in the earthy gravitas associated with the saturnine disposition.

From here he will also know the meaning of His saying: *the creation of the heavens and the earth is greater than the creation of mankind.*[180] For both of them occupy the rank of parenthood[181] in relation to mankind, who never attain to them. The Exalted One says: *Be grateful to Me, and to your parents.*[182]

From this heaven he also comes to know that everything else apart from humans and jinn is blessed,[183] and does not enter into the misery of the other world. He knows that among men and jinn there are those who are wretched and those who are blessed. The miserable one only remains among the wretched for a determined period, since Mercy and Compassion is precedent to Anger, whereas the blessed are such indefinitely, without time restriction.

It is here that he also comes to know the high esteem accorded to the creation of the human being[184] and the special employment of the two divine Hands in creating Adam, unlike any other creature.[185] He knows, moreover, that all

180. Q.40.57: 'the creation of the heavens and the earth is greater than the creation of mankind, but most of humankind do not know.'

181. Literally, 'fatherhood'. The parentage of the heavens and the earth echoes the Quranic description of Abraham as 'the father of you all' (Q.22.78), as in the Semitic tradition that Abraham is our father in faith. Ibn 'Arabī calls Abraham 'our second father' (*Fut.*I.5), since Adam is our first father in bodily terms.

182. Q.31.14.

183. The terms *sa'īd* (happy, blessed, felicitous) and *shaqī* (unhappy, miserable, wretched) are Quranic expressions applied to the people who inhabit the Gardens of Paradise and the Fire of Hell, respectively.

184. Ar: *insān*.

185. Alluding to Q.38.75, where God says to Iblīs: 'What prevented you from prostrating yourself to him [Adam] whom I created with My two Hands?' Ibn 'Arabī explains the meaning of the two Hands not in terms of blessing and power, since that is true of every existent, but rather in terms of incomparability (*tanzīh*) and similarity (*tashbīh*). Only in Adamic Man can God manifest all His attributes, both transcendent and immanent. 'His words [in the above Quranic verse] point out Adam's eminence' (*Fut.*II.4). From a different point of view, human beings also manifest *tanzīh* and *tashbīh*, in that they are part of nature and also different in terms of their inner capacity.

species of creatures possess a single way of being created, without having the diversity of ways of creation that has been bestowed upon the human. For the human being there are different ways of being created: the creation of Adam differs from the creation of Eve, and the creation of Eve differs from the creation of Jesus, and the creation of Jesus is not the same as the creation of the rest of the children of Adam, and yet all of them are human beings.

It is for this reason that for human beings the badness of one's action may be presented in a favourable light, so that one takes it to be good. Following the disclosure of [the reality of] this illusory embellishment, the follower gives thanks to God for delivering him from such a thing. As for the rational thinker, he only experiences joy in this revelation, which bestows good upon him in that which is [actually] bad, and this comes from the divine trickery.[186] Thus the realities of the forms, which lie below this sphere all the way down to the earth, are established within the essential substance.[187]

In this way the creed[188] of Abraham is recognised – it is a tolerant creed,[189] with no sense of restriction in it.[190] When

186. Ibn 'Arabī devotes chapter 231 of the *Futūḥāt* to the various forms of divine trickery or deception (*makr*). 'In our own view, God's deceiving the servant is that He should provide him with knowledge that demands practice, and then deprive him of the practice; or that He should provide him with practice, and then deprive him of sincerity in the practice' (*Fut.*II.529, trans. *SPK*, 267). Ultimately, 'trickery' is a mercy that is educational, and brings the servant to the realisation of true indigence.

187. Ar: *jawhar*.

188. *Milla* may mean either religion/creed or the community which follows that creed.

189. Ar: *milla samḥā'*, recalling the saying of the Prophet Muhammad: 'the religion that is most beloved to God is pure, generously tolerant faith (*al-ḥanīfa al-samḥā'*)' (al-Bukhārī, *Ṣaḥīḥ*, trans. Muhammad Muhsin Khan, 1/34, modified trans.). For a full discussion of the principle of tolerance within Islam, see Reza Shah Kazemi, *The Spirit of Tolerance in Islam* (London, 2012).

190. See Q.22.78: 'Struggle for God as is His due, for He has chosen you and has laid upon you no restriction in religion, being the creed of your father Abraham

the rational thinker knows of these spiritual realities, and becomes acquainted with the fatherhood of Islam, he desires to be close to Abraham. Abraham then asks the follower: 'Who is this stranger with you?' and the follower replies: 'He is my brother.'

'Your milk-brother or your blood-brother?' Abraham asks.

'My water-brother', the follower replies.

'You are right. This is why I do not recognise him. Do not keep company with anyone except your milk-brother, just as I am your milk-father. The presence of Supreme Happiness[191] only admits milk-brothers, milk-fathers and milk-mothers, for they are suitable in the sight of God. Do you not see that knowledge manifests as milk in the presence of Imagination? This comes from suckling at the breast.'[192]

The rational thinker's means of support is removed,[193] when the relationship with the fatherhood of Abraham is cut off from him. Abraham then bids the follower enter the Visited House, and he goes into it without his companion. His companion [the thinker] hangs his head low, and then leaves through the door by which he came in. He cannot leave through the door of the angels, which is the second

– he/He named you muslims before and in this that the Messenger might be a witness over you and you be witnesses over mankind.'

191. Ar: *al-ḥaḍra al-saʿādiyya*, the presence of supreme bliss and fulfilment referred to in the title of this chapter, 'the alchemy of happiness' (*al-saʿāda*).

192. In ancient Arab culture, as in many societies, suckling (*raḍāʿ*) was not only a relationship between a baby and its natural mother but also with a foster-mother. It was common for families in the towns to send their baby sons to be suckled and weaned among the Bedouin tribes, as happened in the case of the Prophet Muhammad (see Martin Lings, *Muhammad* (London, 1983), chapter 8). This led to the prohibition on marriage between foster relatives as well as blood relatives (see Q.4.23).

193. That is to say, it is the last straw for him.

door, because of a special quality in it – which is that the one who leaves by it will never return.

Then [the follower] departs from the presence of [Abraham], seeking to rise again, and he embraces his companion, the rational thinker, there. To the latter it is said: 'Wait here until your companion returns – you cannot go on, as this is the end of the [realm of] smoke.'[194] Then the thinker says: 'I will submit, and put myself under the authority of that which my companion has entered.' But he is told: 'This is not the right place to receive Islam. When you return to your own home, from which you and your companion [first] came, that is [the proper place]: once you have submitted [there] and believed [in your heart] and followed the way of those who turn again and again to God, with the repentance of the messengers who bring news from God,[195] only then can you be received in the way that your companion has been accepted.'

194. Smoke (*dukhān*) is a way of describing the arena of celestial nature. As the following passage explains, smoke is the heavenly aspect of nature, which rises by itself, and within which non-material forms (angels and jinn) arise. 'The angels belong to the world of nature: they are the inhabitants of the spheres and the heavens. God has instructed you that *He went straight to the heaven when it was smoke* (Q.41.11) and then *He proportioned them as seven heavens* (2.29), making its folk [angels] from them, which is what is meant by His words *and He revealed in each heaven its command/order* (41.12). No-one denies that smoke is from nature, even if the angels are luminous bodies, just as the jinn are fiery bodies' (*Fut.*II.650, trans. *SDG*, 306).

195. The word Ibn 'Arabī uses for turning to God in repentance, *anāba/ināba*, also has the meaning of being appointed as a deputy. As the Prophet says, 'Follow me that God may love you.'

So while the rational thinker is left behind [in the seventh heaven], the follower goes on further [alone] and comes to the lote-tree of the furthest limit.[196] There he sees the forms of the actions of those who are blessed[197] through the prophets and those who follow the messengers, and he sees his own action amidst all their actions. Then he gives thanks to God for having granted him success in following the messenger who gives instruction.[198]

He sees with his own eyes four rivers there: one of them a magnificent, great river from which come [numerous] small streams,[199] and from that vast river [also] flow forth three [other] large rivers. When the follower asks about these rivers and streams, he is told: 'This is a symbolic example for you: the great river is the Quran, and the three [other] rivers are the three Sacred Books of the Torah, the Psalms and the Gospel. The small streams are the scriptures that were revealed to the prophets. Whoever drinks from any of these

196. Ar: *sidrat al-muntahā*, mentioned in Q.53.14–16: '[And he saw him on another descent] by the lote-tree of the furthest limit, near to which is the garden of refuge, when the lote-tree was covered by that which enveloped [it].' According to legend, this heavenly tree 'of the furthest limit' is said to grow in Paradise and provide shade, and to have as many leaves as there are human beings, each leaf bearing the names of a particular person and their parents. Every year, the tree is shaken, and those leaves that fall indicate those who face death in the coming year. No angel can pass beyond it, so it indicates the boundary of the known universe.

197. Ar. *al-suʿadā'*, literally 'those who are happy', indicating those who have reached true happiness and fulfilment (*saʿāda*).

198. Ar: *muʿallim*.

199. The imagery here is the inverse of what takes place in this world, where side streams and tributaries flow into a large river, which in turn flows into the sea.

rivers or streams is an heir to the one from whom he has drunk. And each of them is true, for it is the Word of God. *The people of knowledge are the heirs of the prophets*[200] by virtue of what they have drunk from these rivers and streams. So plunge[201] into the river of Quran and you shall succeed in every path that leads to happiness – for it is the river of Muhammad, who is authenticated as possessing prophethood *while Adam was between water and clay*;[202] who was given concise comprehensive speech;[203] who was sent to all people; through whom the branches of religious rulings[204] were abrogated, but no judgment of his was revoked by anyone else.'[205]

200. A hadith (al-Bukhārī, *ʿilm*, 10, Abū Dāwūd, *ʿilm*, 1, etc.) often quoted by Ibn ʿArabī: see, for example, *Fut.*I.223.

201. Ar: *ishraʿ*, from the same root as *sharʿ* meaning the divinely revealed law. Hence this plunging carries also the meaning of being open to the entire weight of the Quranic revelation.

202. Ibn ʿArabī clarifies this in the following passage: 'The first human being that God brought about, Adam, was a prophet. Whoever walks in his path afterwards is undoubtedly an heir through this earthly emergence. In terms of station, Adam and those apart from him are heirs of Muhammad, because he 'was a prophet while Adam was between water and clay', i.e. when Adam was not yet an existent thing. Hence prophethood belongs to Muhammad, but not to Adam; the Adamic, natural human form belongs to Adam, while Muhammad has no form – may God bless him, Adam and all the prophets and give them peace. So Adam is the father of human bodies, and Muhammad is the father of the heirs, from Adam to the one who seals the matter among the heirs' (*Fut.*III.456–7, chapter 373, also translated in *SDG*, 296).

203. Ar: *jawāmiʿ al-kalim*, literally 'bringing together of the words', which can be understood in various ways: concise pithy expression containing many meanings; unifying different religious revelations and points of view in a single message.

204. Ar: *furūʿ al-aḥkām*. These refer to rules and legislation given to earlier communities, religious rules covering prayer, fasting and so on, as well as social matters such as marriage, buying and selling, corporal punishment etc. Those that were no longer regarded as valid were revoked in the Islamic revelation. Islamic jurisprudence recognises two categories, roots (*uṣūl*) and branches (*furūʿ*), which cover the various legal principles and applications of those principles.

205. This is a classical restatement of the unique character of Muhammad: his prophethood, his unifying capacity, his bringing a message for all humankind, and the unchanging nature of his message. It is not clear from the text whether this should all be considered part of the (divine?) address to the follower, as there are no quotation

He gazes at the beauty of the light which covers this lote-tree, and sees that that which envelops [it] has [completely] veiled it from him. It is utterly indescribable because of its luminous covering, which cannot be penetrated by sight or even perceived. Then he is told: 'This is the tree of purification, wherein lies the good-pleasure of God – this is why lote-tree leaves[206] are prescribed for washing the dead for the meeting with God – water and leaves – so that the cleansing power of that [heavenly] lote-tree might reach [the dead person]. This is where the blessed actions of the children of Adam end up and where they are stored until the Day of Reckoning. This is the first of the rungs of the blessed. The seventh heaven at which your companion came to a halt is the furthest limit of smoke: that [heaven] and whoever is under its authority are inevitably subject to the transmutation of form, [forms] with which it is endowed or likenesses prior to it becoming a heaven.'

---

marks in Arabic, but given the pronoun 'you', I have chosen to translate it as if it is one statement.

206. While the lote-tree is sometimes considered to be a mythical tree that grows at the uppermost boundary of human experience, it also refers to an actual tree whose leaves were used in the washing of the dead, possibly the nettle-tree or hackberry (*Celtis australis*). Much favoured by the Romans for its shade, the nettle-tree is supposed to have been the lotus (*lotos*) of the ancients, as described by Homer (Odyssey, Book IX), Herodotus and Dioscorides, and whose dark purple berries were said to be so delicious that those who eat them forget their own country. The identification is by no means certain, and other suggestions have been made for the *lotos*, such as the tropical evergreen Christ-thorn jujube (*Zizyphus spina-christi*, an important source of medicine and fruit), *Zizyphus lotus* (the Libyan lotus) or *Nitraria tridentata*. See Mary Stieber, *The Poetics of Appearance in the Attic Korai* (Austin, 2004), 164.

THE LUNAR MANSIONS

Then the follower is told to rise up, and he ascends to the sphere of the lunar mansions,[207] where he is received by stellar angels and spirits numbering more than a thousand, and scores of presences in which these spirits reside. He beholds the way-stations[208] of those who journey to God by means of prescribed devotional acts. This has been described by al-Harawī in a work of his called 'The Way-Stations of the Spiritual Travellers',[209] which includes a hundred stations, each of which comprises ten stations or abodes. As for us, we have discussed these abodes in our book entitled 'The Pathways of Ascent' (*Manāhij al-irtiqā'*),[210] which contains 300 stations, each comprising ten way-stations, making a total of 3,000 way-stations. [The follower] continues to traverse them, degree by degree, through seven realities that

207. Ar: *falak al-manāzil*, the sphere of the lunar mansions, which number 28 stars or groups of stars near which the moon is to be found during its monthly revolution. This sphere forms a kind of backdrop not only to the lunar phases but also to all planetary movements, and was also sometimes known as the sphere of the fixed stars (*al-kawākib al-thābita*).

208. Ar: *manāzil*, plural of *manzil*, meaning a place one stops at or goes through during a journey, a temporary abode or residence, as well as a lunar mansion (which the moon passes through in its cycle). Bearing in mind the Arabic root *n-z-l*, it literally means 'a place of descending or alighting and lodging'. It became a technical term in Sufism for describing the various stages of the spiritual journey or ascent. Here it is contrasted with the term *maqām*, 'station', or more literally 'a place of standing'.

209. *Manāzil al-sā'irīn*, a famous book by Abū Ismā'īl 'Abdullāh al-Anṣārī al-Harawī (396/1006–481/1089), which was commented upon by one of Ibn 'Arabī's later followers, 'Abd al-Razzāq al-Kāshānī (d. 730/1329).

210. Although this work is mentioned in the *Fihris* (13) and *Ijāza* (13) as well as *al-Tadbīrāt al-ilāhiyya*, it does not appear to have survived. Existing copies that carry this title do not match this description of 3,000 way-stations (see Osman Yahia, *Histoire et classification de l'oeuvre d'Ibn 'Arabī* (Damascus, 1964), *RG* 405).

he follows – just like the way the seven planets pass through the mansions, although he accomplishes it in a much shorter time – until he comprehends their realities in their entirety, which is what he was enjoined to do by Idrīs.

When he has beheld every one of these way-stations, he sees them and all the stars that are within them traversing yet another sphere lying beyond them. So he desires to ascend into [this higher sphere], so that he might see what signs and wonders, demonstrating God's Omnipotence and Knowledge, He has placed within it. When he reaches its surface, he finds himself in the dark-green Garden,[211] and he sees what it contains, which God has described in His Book when talking about the Gardens of Paradise. He beholds its [sublime] levels and its [lofty] chambers, and what God has prepared there for its people. He sees his own paradise set aside specifically for him, and comes to know the [various] Gardens of Inheritance, Gardens of Distinction and Favour, and Gardens of Good Works.[212] He tastes as much delight in each of them as he can be given to experience of the place of heavenly bliss.[213]

211. Ar: *al-janna al-dahmā'*, which could also be translated as 'the dark or black paradise'. The idea of Paradise as a 'garden' meant to the Arab Bedouin mind an oasis of trees, providing shade, refuge from the heat and tranquillity. The blackness is associated with lush foliage and intense greenery, like the forests of date-palm and other trees that used to characterise Iraq. It also suggests a throng of people or a multitude of possible heavenly gardens. This is a reference to Q.55.62: 'And nearer than these shall be two [other] gardens – which of your Lord's bounties will you two deny? – with dark-green foliage (*mudhāmmatān*).' The following Quranic verses describe their contents: fountains, fruits, palm-trees, pomegranates, beautiful women and so on, i.e. all the best of good things.

212. These three paradises convey succinctly three different kinds of heavenly abode: the bliss associated with being heir to a prophet (*mīrāth*); the bliss of being specially favoured by God (*ikhtiṣāṣ*); and the bliss derived from acting in accordance with the sacred laws (*a'māl*).

213. This can also be read as: 'as much delight as the place of heavenly bliss can give him as experience'.

When he has attained there all that he wishes, he is led up to the most radiant level and the most brilliant veil. He sees the [heavenly] forms of Adam and his children, the blessed ones, from behind these veils, and comes to know their spiritual reality and the wisdom that God has placed within them, and the robes of honour that are upon them, with which the children of Adam are invested. Then these forms greet him with salutations of peace, and he sees his own form among them: they embrace each other, and hurry off together to the position of Nearness.[214]

214. See Q.34.37: 'Neither your wealth nor your children are what brings you close (*zulfā*) to Us. It is only those who have faith and do good [that will draw near]. These will have a double reward for what they did, and they will be secure in high rooms.'

THE CONSTELLATIONS & GARDENS

He enters the sphere of the zodiacal constellations,[215] of which God speaks and by which He swears: *By the heaven that holds the constellations.*[216] He then comes to know that the creations that exist in the Gardens of Paradise arise from the motion of this sphere. The motion of the day in the temporal world occurs because of it, just as the movement of the night and the day takes place within the sphere containing the heavenly body of the sun. On the other hand, the formations that are found in the Inferno of Hell[217] come from the movement of the sphere of the fixed stars, which is the roof of Hell – actually I mean its concave underside, as its upper surface is the earth of Paradise. The stars that fall and whose light is scattered[218] remain dark, but their action, with which they

215. Ar: *falak al-burūj*, which is the Arabic name for the ecliptic or zodiacal belt that represents the path of the sun through the heavens in the annual revolution. Just as the previous sphere is related to the moon, this sphere is determined by the passage of the sun. The twelve divisions of the ecliptic are the zodiacal signs and constellations (*burūj*), from Aries to Pisces. This is also known as the starless sphere (*al-falak al-aṭlas*).

216. Q.85.1. There are two further mentions of *burūj* in the Quran: 'We have set constellations in the sky and made it beautiful for those who behold it' (15.16); and 'Blessed is He who has set constellations in the sky and has placed among them a lamp – a moon that gives light' (25.61). The context of these passages gives the textual basis for some of Ibn 'Arabī's following remarks.

217. Ar: *jahannam*, Gehenna, which etymologically evokes the idea of 'depth' (infernus, inferno). The term is used in connection with two recording angels (Riḍwān and Malik), who mete out reward and punishment on the Day of Reckoning: 'You two, cast into Jahannam every rebellious man of ingratitude, hinderer of good, transgressor, doubter, who adopts another god along with God. Throw him into the severe punishment... the day when We shall say to Jahannam, "Have you been filled?" and it will say, "Are there still more?"' (Q.50.24–30). I am using both Inferno and Hell as a translation for *jahannam* in this passage, although some translators simply use the term Jahannam or Gehenna.

218. This refers to the falling of meteors or meteorites in the physical realm, but

are endowed, endures. All this is the cause of the exchanging that occurs in the Inferno: *every time their skins are consumed, We shall give them other skins,*[219] all of that by permission of God, who arranges things in their [proper] degrees.

This is like what happens when the sun passes through the sign of Aries, and the season of spring arrives. The finery of the earth[220] appears: trees burst into leaf and are bedecked with beauty – *it brings out growth of every beauteous kind.*[221] And when the sun passes through the sign of Capricorn, then the opposite appears. The receptacles[222] receive [only] as much as their natural constitution allows; however different they may be in terms of constitution, they receive what God brings about in these celestial motions in accordance with how they are.

Similarly, in the Gardens of Paradise there is a new creation[223] at every moment and a new delight, so that boredom never sets in. For if each thing in the natural world were to be continuously affected by something without it being

---

also symbolically to the Last Hour mentioned in Q.82.1–2: 'When the heaven is rent asunder, when the stars are scattered.'

219. Q.4.56: 'every time their skins are consumed, We shall give them [new] skins in exchange, that they may taste the torment. God is Mighty and Wise.'

220. Ar: *zīnat al-arḍ*, meaning all the various forms of vegetation, including plants and flowers.

221. Q.22.5.

222. Ar: *al-qawābil*. Elsewhere Ibn 'Arabī explains the way that things 'receive' the activity of the divine: 'the realities (*a'yān*) of the possibilities are receptacles for the manifesting of the Being of the Real (*wujūd al-ḥaqq*)' (*Fut.*II.69).

223. Ar: *khalq jadīd*, a Quranic term which Ibn 'Arabī often employs to indicate the fact that each moment is unique and different, as each thing undergoes constant change and transformation. Commenting on the verse 'Were We worn out by the first creation? No, but they are in doubt about the new creation' (Q.50.15), he writes: 'The reality (*'ayn*) of every person is renewed at each breath, and this has to be the case since the Real never ceases to be the active agent in the possibilities of Being. This is indicated by the diversity of properties that flow over the [multiple] realities in each state' (*Fut.*IV.320).

subject to change, a human being would inevitably succumb to boredom with that. In that case boredom would be an essential part of his condition. Then God would not be able to replenish him with something new at each instant, and prolong pleasure in that for him. [Were that the case], boredom would overtake [people in Paradise]. However, every time they contemplate what they possess,[224] the people of Paradise perceive an order and a form which they have not seen before – and they are delighted by this new appearance. In the same way, in every mouthful they eat and every drop they drink, they come across a delicious new taste which they have never encountered before in previous meals, and they are delighted by that and their appetite grows greater.

The reason why this transformation is so rapid and constant is that the origin[225] is like that. His bounty towards the created world is in accordance with what the reality of His level[226] entails, so that He is constantly creating and the creation is perpetually in need. The whole of existence is perpetually in movement, both in this world and the hereafter, because the creative act[227] does not happen from non-movement. From God's side there are constant facings[228] and inexhaustible words, which is His saying: *what is with*

224. Literally: 'in each glance which they direct at their property'.

225. Ar: *aṣl*.

226. Ar: *martaba*. Ibn 'Arabī means here the level of God in respect of the Names, which demand the existence of universe as the place in which to manifest their effects. He uses the analogy of the family to clarify different levels of closeness and dependence: 'the Names are to Him like a family that depends on Him, where the head of the family strives to support them. Created beings are the extended family of God, and the Names are close family. The universe asks of Him due to its existence as mere possibility while the Names ask of Him in order for their effects to be manifest' (*Fut.* III.316–17).

227. Ar: *takwīn*.

228. Ar: *tawajjuhāt*, literally, the turning of the face towards something, facing towards something else. In the case of the divine, this refers to the facing of God

God remains.[229] Thus with God is the facing [towards a thing], which is His saying: *when We desire it*, and the word of Presence, which is His saying to each thing that He desires: *Be*, with the meaning that is appropriate to His Majesty.[230] 'Be' is a word of existence:[231] nothing comes into being from it except existence. Non-existence cannot come into being from it, since non-existence does not exist. What does come into being is existence.[232]

These facings and words in the treasuries of Generosity belong to each thing as it receives existence.[233] The Exalted One says: *And there is nothing whose treasuries are not with Us,*[234] and that is what we have mentioned. His saying: *and We send it down only in a known measure* is from His Name the Wise,[235] since it is Wisdom that governs this divine bringing-down.[236] This occurs when these things are brought out

---

towards His own possibilities of expression, so that 'all We say to a thing, when We desire it, is to say to it "Be" and it becomes' (Q.16.40).

229. Q.16.96.

230. Ar: *jalāl*.

231. Ar: *ḥarf wujūdī*, literally 'a letter of existence'. The word *ḥarf* has not only a grammatical meaning as letter or consonant or particle, but it also indicates a word or mode of expression. See *Fut*.III.46.

232. Ar: *al-kawn wujūd*. The Arabic here is pithy and allusive: that which accepts the command 'Be' (*kun*) and comes into being or existence (*wujūd*), is the created world (*al-kawn*, from the same root as *kun*). Non-existence (*'adam*) is merely hypothetical, as by definition it cannot receive the command 'Be'.

233. The notion of divine Generosity (*jūd*) is related etymologically and cosmologically to the coming about of existence itself (*wujūd*). As Ibn 'Arabī's friend and teacher in Tunis, 'Abd al-'Azīz al-Mahdawī, put it, the Arabic language itself points to the progression (by the addition of a single letter) from unseen generosity (*jūd*) to existence (*wu-jūd*) to the existent thing (*ma-w-jūd*). See Pablo Beneito and Stephen Hirtenstein, 'The Prayer of Blessing by 'Abd al-'Azīz al-Mahdawī', *JMIAS* 34 (2003), 27.

234. Q.15.21: 'And there is nothing whose treasuries are not with Us, and We send it down only in a known measure.'

235. Ar: *al-ḥakīm*.

236. Ar: *inzāl*. It is often used in connection with the bringing-down of the

of the treasuries [of potentiality in the Unseen] into the existence of their realities [in the world of manifestation].

This is something we mentioned at the beginning of the Preface to this book: 'All praise belongs to God who has brought things into existence from non-existence and its non-existence.'[237] The non-existence of non-existence is existence. It is the relation of the being[238] of things [at the level where they are] preserved[239] within these treasuries [of Generosity], existent in God,[240] established in their potential realities[241] without being existent in their own selves. In consideration of their own realities, they become existent from non-existence; and with respect to their being with God in these treasuries, they become existent from the non-existence of non-existence, which is existence. If you like, you may give preponderance to the side of their being in the treasuries. So we say: '[who] has brought things into existence' from their existence in the treasuries to their existence in their individual entities, for the sake of the pleasure and blessing in them or something other than that. Alternatively, once you have understood the meaning of what I have just mentioned to you, you can say: '[who] has brought things into existence from non-existence'. Say whichever you like,

---

Quranic revelation. See for example, 'Praise be to God, who sent down the Book to His servant' (Q.18.1) and 'We brought it down on the Night of Power' (Q.97.1).

237. These are the opening words of the Preface (*khuṭba*) (*Fut.*I.2).

238. Ar: *kawn*, which means both being and existence. It is used here in contrast to the term *wujūd* because *wujūd* belongs to God, and *kawn* is used of things which have been commanded to 'be' (*kun*).

239. Alluding to the Preserved Tablet (*lawḥ maḥfūẓ*), the pure receptivity upon which the divine Pen writes.

240. Literally, 'existent for God' (*mawjūdatun lillāh*). That is, their existence belongs to God, since they are His possibilities.

241. Referring to *al-aʿyān al-thābita*, the realities which are established in God's knowledge.

for He is the One who gives them existence in any case, in the arena where they manifest due to their potential realities.

As for His saying: *what is with you comes to an end,*[242] that is self-evidently true in terms of knowledge, because the address here is to the reality of the individuated essence,[243] and all that is with it, that is to say, every existent [thing] that is with that essence. Or rather, it designates all those qualities, accidents and created things that God brought into being in its place of receptivity, these being at the second stage or in the second state, however you like to put it. You can say either 'at the moment of their existence' or 'in the state of their existence'. [Either way], these things become non-existent in relation to us – this is what is meant by His saying: *what is with you comes to an end.* He is constantly renewing likenesses or opposites for the individuated substance from these treasuries. This is what theologians mean when they say: 'an accident does not last for two moments'. This is a true statement, something incontrovertible, since it is the actual situation that characterises the possibilities. While these [appearances] are always being renewed with regard to the substance, its essential reality always remains as God wishes. He has wished that it should not pass away, and therefore it must remain [in existence].

242. Q.16.96: 'what is with you comes to an end, and what is with God remains'.

243. Ar: *'ayn al-jawhar*, which can also be translated as 'the essence of the substance'. Here *jawhar* refers primarily to the intrinsic essence of a thing that receives existence insofar as it is differentiated from other 'essences'. It is part of a fundamental threefold categorisation, contrasted by Ibn 'Arabī with the physical body (*jism*), which he views as an instrument, and the accident (*'araḍ*), which he describes as a 'place' in which to manifest – 'there is nothing except substance or body or accident. Each category is specialised by things that are not possessed by others, and glorifies God with these qualities and from that station. Only the Perfect Human glorifies God with every form of glorification in the universe because he is a direct copy (*nuskha*) of Him' (*Fut.*III.77).

From this Presence the follower learns about the formations of Paradise and all that we have mentioned. As for the rational thinker, the follower's companion, he has no information about any of this, because it is a prophetic instruction, not a matter of intellectual observation. The rational thinker is restricted to being dominated by his thought process,[244] and thinking can only operate within its own specific arena, which is something known among the fields. Each faculty within the human being has a domain within which it roams, and which it should not exceed. Whenever it exceeds this field, it falls into error and fault, and is qualified by deviation from its straight way. For example, the unveiling of the inner eye may be able to witness things where intellectual proofs slip up, and that [slip] is because the intellect has left its proper domain. The intellects that are described as misguided are led astray only by their own thought processes, and these reflections have been led astray only because of operating outside their rightful sphere. The fact that some thought processes operate outside their proper domain and roam beyond their own field simply happens in order that the superiority of certain people over others can be made manifest. Superiority appears in the world so that it may be known that the Real takes special care of some of His servants, while forsaking other servants of His, and so that it may be known that the possible cannot leave its condition of possibility. The One who favours one over another has a special regard[245] for whichever of these

244. Ar: *fikr*, which can also be translated as 'thinking, reflection', the power of mind that leads to understanding the world and one's place in it.

245. Ar: *naẓar*, here referring to the divine regard as contrasted with the all too fallible human faculty of rational consideration (also *naẓar*).

abilities He wishes, in whatever way He wishes – *and He is the All-Knowing, the All-Powerful.*[246]

246. Q.30.54: 'He creates what He wishes; He is the Knowing and the Powerful.'

THE FOOTSTOOL & THE SUPREME LIGHT

Then the follower is taken with his mount[247] to the Footstool,[248] where he sees the dividing of the Word, which prior to its arrival at this station is qualified by unity.[249] He sees the Two Feet that are placed upon [the Footstool], and at once he throws himself down to kiss them: the one Foot which establishes the people of Paradise in their Gardens, which is the Foot of Confirming Truth; and the other Foot which installs the people of Hell in the Inferno in whatever condition He wishes, which is the Foot of All-Compelling Power.[250] This is why He says regarding the people of Paradise: *a gift uninterrupted*,[251] and does not ascribe an end to it. On the other hand, He says regarding the people of Hell, who are

247. That is, the litter of divine Grace mentioned above at the entry to the seventh heaven.

248. Ar: *kursī*.

249. In Ibn 'Arabī's understanding, the Footstool, upon which the divine Feet rest, is a symbol of the all-embracing knowledge by which all the high and low are distinguished. 'His Footstool – which is His Knowledge – embraces the heavens and the earth' (*Fut.*IV.256, trans. *SDG*, 329). It is also the highest of the treasuries with God: 'The treasuries with God are high and low: the highest of them is the Footstool, which is His Knowledge, and His Knowledge is His Essence. The lowest of the treasuries is what reflective thoughts store up in mortal man' (*Fut.*IV.248, trans. *SDG*, 256). The divine Word (*kalima*), which is single ('Be'), here divides into two possible orders, the affirmative do and the negative don't, command and prohibition, which are mirrored in obedience and disobedience (see *Fut.*II.257, trans. *SDG*, 172).

250. Ar: *jabarūt*. These people are compelled to recognise the Source, i.e. against their will, instead of confirming the truth of their accord (*ṣidq*).

251. The whole passage refers to Q.11.106–8: 'As for those who are wretched, they will be in the Fire, in which there will be sighing and sobbing for them, remaining there as long as the heavens and the earth last, except as your Lord wishes; surely your Lord carries out all that He wishes. As for those who are happy, they will be in the Garden, remaining there as long as the heavens and the earth last, except as your Lord wishes – a gift uninterrupted.'

wretched because the Foot of Power has total dominion: *indeed your Lord carries out all that He wishes.* He does not say that the condition they are in will not cease, as He does for the blessed ones. What prevents that is His saying: *My Mercy embraces everything* and His saying: *Indeed My Mercy precedes My Wrath* in this emergence.[252] For existence is mercy with respect to every existent, even though some of them suffer at the hands of others. Hence their remaining in the state of blessing is without end, while their remaining in the state of having vengeance inflicted upon them depends upon [the divine] will.[253] The vengeance exacted from them may simply result in punishment for them, and nothing more, and then vengeance comes to an end.

This is how He explains it in passages that mention the pain which is suffered, where He says: *a painful punishment* or *the painful punishment*,[254] and in passages where He does not tie the punishment to pain but [rather] removes the link. For example, He says: *the punishment will not be lightened for them*,[255] meaning [this will be the case] even though the pain has been removed. He speaks of *the torment of the Inferno*, without specifying it as painful, and says: *it will not be abated for them*[256] since it is punishment, and *they are in it*, i.e. in the punishment, *afflicted with despair*,[257] i.e. distanced from

252. See Q.7.156: 'My Mercy embraces everything. I shall ordain it for those who are mindful and who pay the alms-tax and who believe in Our Signs.' The second is a hadith, a saying transmitted by the Prophet (see *Fut.*II.157).

253. Thus blessing (*na'īm*) equates to Mercy (*raḥma*) and being, while vengeance (*intiqām*) equates to Anger (*ghaḍab*).

254. For example, see Q.2.10, 104, 174 or 178 for 'a punishment'; and Q.10.88, 97 or 15.50 for 'the punishment'. Most passages use the indefinite.

255. Q.2.86, 162 or 3.88.

256. Q.43.74–5: 'the evildoers will remain in the torment of Hell: it will not be abated for them, and they are in it, afflicted with despair (*mublisūn*).'

257. Ar: *mublisūn*. The root *b-l-s* means according to Ibn 'Arabī 'to be far from',

the happiness that can occur in this abode. Despair is an expression specific to the people of Hell, as regards their remoteness. This is why He mentions despair, causing this linguistic term to appear in its [proper] place along with its people, so that they may come to know it. There are [various] terms that belong to the abode of Hell, rather than to the people of the Paradises, and despair is one of them. So the follower comes to know from this station [of the Footstool] what belongs to each abode.

Then he leaves this place and is plunged into the supreme light, where love-ecstasy[258] overcomes him. This light is the presence of [spiritual] states, whose power is manifest in human individuals. People are usually overwhelmed when they listen to music: when these [states] descend upon them, they pass through the spheres. The movements of the spheres have sweet happy melodies that enrapture the ears, something like the music of the water-wheel. The melodies clothe the states, descending with them upon living souls during sessions of audition.[259] Whatever 'thing' the soul is taken with, be it an attachment to a slave-girl or -boy, or to one of the people of God, that linkage is [really] a love of divine beauty[260] clothed in imaginal form. They acquire

hence 'to be sad, in despair, or be prevented from accomplishing the pilgrimage' (see Kazimirski, 1/159). From the same root comes 'Iblīs', the name for Satan.

258. Ar: *wajd*, a term that is cognate with *wujūd*, finding or being. It signifies an experience of mystical self-transcendence, an overwhelming and heightened state of awareness and various responses, usually of joyful intoxication and wonderment, but sometimes of grief, to the direct encounter with the divine. See Aladdin, 'The Unity of Being', 3–26.

259. Ar: *majālis al-samāʿ*, referring to spiritual sessions, in which listening to music or recitation of the Quran or of poetry became an accepted way of experiencing ecstasy within various ritual or social settings. It often resulted in physical movements such as dance, as in the *samāʿ* sessions originated by Rūmī.

260. This can also be read as 'a divine love of beauty'.

this from what the Prophet mentioned, as is reported in the *Ṣaḥīḥ*: *Indeed God is beautiful and loves beauty* and in the *Tajrīd*: *worship God as if you see Him.*[261] Thus loving ecstasy seizes a person according to what they have created in their imagination.

The state pervades some of them without it being from the presence of imagination – rather, they experience something that is unconditioned and does not come under some kind of limitation or measure. For others perfumes waft towards them from the states that bring ecstasy, because their souls are only able to love in a partial manner, not total. These scents bestow upon such a person part of the ruling property [of ecstasy], which is why this is referred to by the term 'summoning up ecstasy'.[262]

261. Muslim, *Ṣaḥīḥ*, Īmān 147; Aḥmad al-Zabīdī, *al-Tajrīd al-ṣarīḥ* (abridgement of al-Bukhārī's *Ṣaḥīḥ*), Īmān, 13–14.

262. Ar: *tawājud*, attempting to summon up ecstasy. It is defined as 'seeking to gain and achieve for oneself the experience of ecstasy' (*Fut.*II.535), which as Ibn 'Arabī makes clear here, is already the effect of ecstasy. For a discussion of this, see *SPK*, 212.

THE THRONE & ITS BEARERS

Then [the follower] departs from that light to the place of Universal Mercy and Compassion which embraces everything – this is depicted as the Throne.[263] There among the angelic realities, he finds Israfil (Isrāfīl), Gabriel (Jibrīl), Michael (Mīkā'īl), Riḍwān and Mālik.[264] Among the angelic human realities he finds Adam, Abraham and Muhammad.[265]

With Adam and Israfil he finds the knowledge of the forms manifesting in the world, which are called *jism*, *jasad*

263. Ar: *al-ʿarsh*. The link between the divine Throne and Mercy is specified in Q.20.4–5: 'A revelation from Him who created the earth and the high heavens, the Compassionate (*al-Raḥmān*) who seated Himself upon the Throne.' In an earlier treatise (*ʿUqlat al-mustawfiz*), Ibn ʿArabī distinguishes five kinds or degrees of the throne which he draws from the Quran: Life (*ḥayāh*), which is the divine identity (*huwiyya*); Glory (*majīd*), which is the Pen or Intellect; Grandeur (*ʿaẓīm*), which is the Tablet or Soul; Mercy (*raḥmān*); and Noble Generosity (*karīm*), which is the Footstool (see Carullah MS 2111, fols. 73b–76a). See Appendix A under *Qāf*.

264. The five angels mentioned here are associated with: the horn of light or trumpet (*ṣūr*), within which manifestation takes place and which is blown on the Day of Resurrection (Israfil, sometimes identified with Seraphiel, Uriel or Raphael); inspiration and revelation (Gabriel); sustenance and nourishment (Michael); the promise of paradise (Riḍwān); and the threat of hell (Mālik). Gabriel and Michael are specifically named in the Quran (2.97–8), as is Mālik (43.77).

265. '[On the Day of Judgment] The angels will be on its borders, and above them eight will carry the throne of your Lord' (Q.69.17). According to the Prophet, there are four bearers in this world, and eight in the Hereafter. In chapter 13 of the *Futūḥāt al-Makkiyya*, Ibn ʿArabī expands Ibn Masarra's comment that 'the Throne which is carried is the kingdom [of creation], and it is restricted to body, spirit, nourishment and degree (*martaba*)', saying: 'Adam and Israfil are related to form, Gabriel and Muhammad to spirit, Michael and Abraham to nourishment, and Mālik and Riḍwān to promise and threat… the carriers of the Throne is an expression for those who are in charge of directing [the kingdom]' (*Fut.*I.148). We may note that the human figures listed here represent the three fathers of humankind, and the middle figures (Michael and Abraham) in each list are associated with the elixir.

and *haykal*,[266] according to whether they are luminous or non-luminous [forms]. With Gabriel and Muhammad, he finds the knowledge of the spirits blown into the forms that are with Adam and Israfil. He comes to know the meanings of all this, seeing how these spirits are related to these forms and their governance of them, and how one [spirit] is superior to another despite their coming from a single source, and likewise for the forms. He knows all of that from this Presence.

He also comes to know from this Presence the knowledge of elixirs, which transmute the forms of bodies[267] by means of the spirit that the elixir possesses. He faces towards Michael and Abraham, and finds with them the knowledge of nourishment, how bodies and spirits are fed and how they continue [in existence]. He learns how the elixir becomes nourishment specific to that metallic body, and restores it to [the condition of] gold or silver after it had been iron or copper – this is the true health of that body, and the disappearance of its malady which had come upon it while it was in its mine, and caused it to become iron or something else. All this is made known to him from this Presence.

Then he looks towards Riḍwān and Mālik, and finds with them the knowledge of happiness and misery, of Paradise and its heights and of Hell and its depths. It is the knowledge of the degrees in [divine] promise and threat, and he comes

266. These three terms, which could all be translated as 'body', often have specific meanings for Ibn 'Arabī. For example, *jism* is the physical body composed of elements (animals, plants and minerals); *jasad* designates the imaginal or subtle body of intermediate realities such as jinn or angels, and metallic bodies within the earth; *haykal* is the temple or framework of the governing spirit. See *SDG*, 279ff. for passages regarding the different bodies.

267. Ar: *ajsād*, which can be taken to mean not only metallic bodies in the external sense, but (more likely) the inner imaginal body which is composed of intermediate realities and which can be purified (as silver and gold).

to know what it really is that causes each of them. When he knows all this, he knows the Throne and its bearers, and what lies within its compass. This is the furthest limit of bodily forms, beyond which there is no composite body with any form or dimension.

When he knows all this, then he rises up in a further ascension, spiritually without any imaginal form, to the level of the Measures.[268] Here he comes to know the quantities and weights of bodily things in the bodies that have been appointed, from the All-Encompassing [Throne] to the earth, and all the species and genera of the universe that lie within them and between them and inhabit these realms.

268. Ar: *maqādīr*. The 'measure' (sing. *miqdār*) means not only the measurable amount or quantity of a thing, in terms of time, space etc. (for example the length of a person's life), but also the means by which it can be measured or proportioned. It corresponds to the level of what he calls elsewhere Universal Body and Shape (see *Fut.*II.433–5).

Then he passes on to knowledge of the Universal Dark Substance,[269] which does not consist of parts and in which there is no form. This is the non-visibility of everything in the universe that lies behind It.[270] It is from It that all these lights and illuminations[271] appear in the realm of bodies. They are composite lights, which have been detached from this Substance so that It remains dark, in the same way that day is detached from night so that darkness becomes distinct.[272] This is the principle of darkness in the world and the principle of the world in divine laws.[273]

269. Ar: *al-jawhar al-muẓlim al-kull.* This notion is rather different to the distinction made between substance and accident (by Islamic theologians) or primary and secondary qualities in metaphysics and epistemology (for example, by Locke and Descartes), since it privileges darkness over light. It is like the non-visible side of the lote-tree enveloped in light. There is a distinct similarity between this Dark Substance and what physicists describe as dark matter and dark energy, which are hypothesised to permeate all space in the physical universe. Elsewhere this degree is called the Dust or the Dust Substance, 'in which are manifest the forms of bodies and whatever is similar to this Substance in the world of compound things' (see *Fut.*II.431–3 and *SDG*, xxix). It is worth noting that the degrees from here are all described by pairs of terms (Dark Substance, Bountiful Nature, Preserved Tablet, Supreme Pen) until the Cloud is reached.

270. The universe is 'behind It' in terms of what the mystic has left behind in his ascension through all the degrees to this point.

271. The distinction between the light (*nūr*) of the moon and the illumination (*ḍiyā'*) of the sun is given in the Quran (10:5): 'It is He who made the sun an illumination and the moon a light, and decreed for it mansions, that you might know the number of years and the reckoning [of time].'

272. See Q.36.37: 'A Sign for them is the night: We detach the daytime from it, and they are in darkness.'

273. Ar: *al-aḥkām al-nāmūsiyya*. The Arabic *nāmūs* derives from the Greek *nomos*, meaning humanly established law, but its primary meaning is divine law revealed through the prophets. 'The great human beings set down limits and firmly established laws (*nawāmīs*)... ensuring protection for people's property and families and so on.

Then he leaves this station and passes on to the Presence of Bountiful Nature.[274] He comes to know Her rulership over bodies, [which is exercised] unrestrictedly with respect to their various compositions and states. He also understands the reason why certain naturalists[275] are mistaken in knowing Her ruling properties, due to their ignorance of the knowledge of Her true nature, whereas the one who possesses such an insight is aware of all this.

They were called laws, a word that means "the causes of good", since *nāmūs* in technical usage is that which brings good' (*Fut.*I.324). In its greatest form, the term refers to the divine laws brought by inspiration by the Archangel Gabriel, known as *al-nāmūs al-akbar*, the light of whose divine inspiration reveals the world as dark. See Plessner, 'Nāmūs', *EI2*, 7/953.

274. Ar: *al-ṭabī'a al-basīṭa*. The word *basīṭ* was used in philosophy to denote 'simple' or 'uncompounded' as opposed to 'compound' or 'made up of parts', but here I take the epithet to suggest more of the original meaning of *basīṭ* as 'liberal, bountiful, spreading beneficence over everything'. Nature is thus not only the root of all composition (bodies and states), but also inherently bountiful. According to Islamic cosmology, derived from the Greeks, Nature is the Great Mother and contains four 'natures', heat, cold, wetness and dryness. We may note a similar contrast made by later Western thinkers such as the German philosopher Schelling, between Nature as productivity or subject (*natura naturans*) and Nature as product or object (*natura naturata*). According to Ibn 'Arabī, Nature is the child of the Universal Intellect/Pen and the Universal Soul/Tablet (see *SDG*, *xxix*, for Chittick's summary of chapter 198 in the *Futūḥāt*).

275. Ar: *ba'd al-ṭabī'iyyīn*. It is unclear exactly who Ibn 'Arabī has in mind here, although he mentions the naturalists (*ahl al-ṭab'iyya*) in other contexts, especially when discussing the birth of Jesus: he quotes a scientific view of the time (one that he disagrees with) that the woman plays no part in the formation of the foetus (see *Fut.* I.125). See also a category of philosophers mentioned in a passage in al-Ghazālī's *al-Munqidh min al-ḍalāl* (Beirut, 1959), 96–7. According to al-Ghazālī, there are three major categories of philosophers: firstly, the 'materialists' (*dahriyyūn*), who deny the existence of an omniscient and omnipotent Creator–Regulator; secondly, the 'naturalists' (*ṭabī'iyyūn*), who accept the existence of a wise Creator but believe that man's intellectual faculty is dependent on the constitution and perishes along with the soul at death – hence they reject any idea of the Afterlife or of heaven and hell; and thirdly, the theists (*ilāhiyyūn*), who include later Greek philosophers such as Socrates and Plato – Aristotle is then credited with refuting the doctrines of the materialists and the naturalists, and is said to have dissociated himself from the theists.

Then he passes on from observing that to witnessing the Preserved Tablet,[276] which is the existent that originates [directly] from the Pen. God has inscribed upon it whatever created things He wishes to come about in the world. The one who can read what is [written] on this Tablet comes to know the knowledge of two powers, i.e. the science of knowledge and the science of actions, and he knows the effects that are brought about [by them]. From the existence of this spirit as a tablet, he discovers what the One who named it 'tablet' has recorded upon it with the divine Pen, from that which the Real dictated to it.[277] His writing upon it is the engraving of the forms of every knowable thing, which God sets in motion[278] in the universe of this world right up to the Day of Resurrection – these are sciences that are limited and written in form, like the forms of the letters inscribed upon tablets and in books, which are called 'words'.[279] The number of their 'mothers' is what results from squaring the degrees of the celestial sphere, neither more nor less.[280]

276. Ar: *al-lawḥ al-maḥfūẓ*, the Tablet which is the record of the decisions of the divine Will and is preserved from erasure. The idea that all that takes place on earth is written on heavenly tablets, either as the originals of revelation or the tablets of fate, is present both in the Quran (85.22) and in earlier Jewish texts (e.g. Jubilees, 5.13; Enoch, 43.2). In Ibn 'Arabī's cosmology it is identified with the Universal Soul, the primary receptive substance.

277. That is to say, this is a two-step process in which the Pen writes upon the Tablet only what the Real has dictated should be written.

278. The original text is unclear here as there is no pointing. I am reading *yujrīhā* rather than *yuḥdithuhā* (Mansoub edn.).

279. Ar: *kalimāt*. These 'words' can refer in a general way to the spoken word, but here it seems that apart from the obvious meaning that letters are formed into words on a page of writing, Ibn 'Arabī is pointing to the realised Word of God. 'There is no changing the words of God' (Q.10.64). As he says elsewhere, the words of God are 'nothing other than the essences (*a'yān*) of all existing things, which are eternal by virtue of their immutability and contingent by virtue of their concrete existence and manifestation' (*Fuṣūṣ*, 198).

280. That is to say, 360 × 360 = 129,600. This is curiously similar to the number

Thus God placed 360 degrees in the sphere through which the stars traverse in their motion, constituting a year in earthly terms through the movement of the sun and moon. The Exalted One says: *the sun and the moon [run their course] according to a fixed reckoning.*[281] Every year they recur – although it is not in fact a repetition – from the beginning of their existence until the number that results from the multiplication of 360 by itself in years has been completed – for that will be the lifespan of the universe of this world.

Then He will dictate another order [of reality] and sciences that concern the Resurrection and the Scales,[282] until there is reached *a stated term,*[283] which is differentiated in the two realms – this entails the ending of the period of [divine] Vengeance suffered by the people of the realm of Wretchedness. Then He will begin writing the punishment [that is to be meted out] in this realm, along with the everlasting duration in the two abodes [of Heaven and Hell] encountered by their peoples. However, whatever is written can only take its course for a stated term, since it is impossible for that which is endless to enter into existence.[284]

Then this follower passes on from this station to witnessing the Supreme Pen. From this place of witnessing

---

of prophets (Words) who have been sent to humankind. According to most Islamic scholars, there have been some 124,000 prophets, but their precise number is not known.

281. Q.55.5.

282. 'We shall set up the scales of justice on the Day of Resurrection, and no soul will be wronged in any way' (Q.21.47). See *Fut.*III.6, trans. *SPK*, 173.

283. Ar: *ajalin musamman*, referring to Q.11.3: 'Ask forgiveness of your Lord and turn to Him in repentance; [If you do so] He will give you fair compensation until a stated term, and He will give Grace to everyone possessed of grace.'

284. And hence be written on the Tablet. That is to say, Mercy has no end and everything existent comes from Mercy. What exists must have a beginning and an end – so Punishment, which is subsequent to Mercy, must also have a beginning and an end.

he attains to the knowledge of friendship.[285] It is from here that the degree of caliphate and acting as representative[286] begins. This is also where the divine councils are held [and appointments are made], and where the authority of the divine Name the Director–Distinguisher appears. As He says, *He directs everything, making the Signs distinct,*[287] and this is the Pen's knowledge. He witnesses the activation of the Right [Hand], which is the operation of spiritual Benevolence, and from where it derives. He sees that it is from his own essence that he has knowledge of summation and differentiating.[288] The differentiation appears by being recorded in writing, and that is the same as his inherent realities.[289]

285. Ar: *walāya*, the condition of being friend to God and His being the Friend.

286. Ar: *al-khilāfa wa al-niyāba*. The degree of being *khalīfa* was discussed earlier.

287. See Q.13.2: 'It is God who raised up the heavens without any support that you can see; then He settled upon the Throne and subjected the sun and the moon to His command, each to run its course for a stated term. He directs everything, making [His] Signs distinct, so that you may have certainty that you will meet your Lord.' The divine Name which Ibn 'Arabī derives from this Quranic passage is a 2-in-1 Name: *al-mudabbir* (the Director) *al-mufaṣṣil* (the Distinguisher). This passage can also be translated as 'He directs the command (*amr*)', which he explains as meaning: 'He is the Creator of the universe and its Director… He directs the command from the heaven to the earth' (see *K. al-Ifāda*, Manisa 1183, fol. 114a).

288. Ar: *al-ijmāl wa al-tafṣīl*. By 'summation' (*ijmāl*) Ibn 'Arabī alludes to the fact that in the Quranic text quoted in the previous note, regulating or directing only has one object (*al-amr*, literally 'the affair', meaning everything) while the making distinct or differentiating involves plurality (*āyāt*, His multiple Signs in the universe). The regulating is summative since it concerns the whole, while the distinctive detail concerns the parts or aspects. See also the second heaven of Jesus, where the same two terms are used in connection with the emotive quality of poetry (summation) and the analytical distinction of prose (differentiation).

289. Ar: *dhawāt*, the plural form of *dhāt*, 'essence' just mentioned. Here Ibn 'Arabī is pointing to the possible realities or multiple aspects inherent in the nature of individuated being. Commenting on the Quranic verse 'There is nothing whose treasuries are not with Us' (15:21), he says: 'Things can never reach sheer non-existence. On the contrary, the apparent situation is that their non-existence is a relative non-existence. In the state of their non-existence, things are witnessed by God. He distinguishes them by their essential realities, differentiating some of them

So he has no need of a teacher upon whom he can rely apart from his Creator. Its writing is engraving,[290] which is why it is 'established' [eternally] and cannot be erased. This is also why the Tablet is called 'preserved', that is, it is preserved from erasure. If the divine Pen's writing were like writing with ink, then it could be removed, just as a tablet can be erased in the created world by the pen which is particular to it, being held *between two of the fingers of the Compassionate.*[291]

From this contemplation he will be able to distinguish between pens, tablets and different kinds of writing. He comes to know the science of judgment and wise execution.[292] From here he also learns that whatever is required to be a signifier of God cannot remain in the realm of possibility without being manifest as a signifier; even though the signifiers are numerous, they are united in each perfectly signifying [Him].

---

from others. He does not see in them non-differentiation (*ijmāl*)' (*Fut.*III.193, trans. *SPK*, 87).

290. Ar: *naqsh*. This term means something engraved or inscribed, as on a signet-ring, and therefore a permanent mark. It also means decoration or variegation, in terms of different forms or colours, and making a discovery by scrutinising a thing very carefully, and so suggests a plurality of aspects which the mark has.

291. Alluding to the hadith: 'The hearts of the children of Adam are like a single heart between two of the fingers of the Compassionate. He turns it wherever He desires. O God, Turner of hearts, turn our hearts towards obeying You!' (Muslim, *Qadar* 17).

292. Ar: *al-aḥkām wa al-iḥkām*, both words from the same root *ḥ-k-m*.

Then [the follower] looks to the right of this place of witnessing, and observes the world of being lost in love, which is the world that was created out of the Cloud.[293] Then he passes on to the Cloud [itself], which is the seat of the Name Lord,[294] just as the Throne is the seat of the Compassionate. The Cloud is the first degree of 'where'.[295] From it manifest the spatial relations[296] and degrees within That which cannot be conditioned by place or location but does recognise position or rank.[297] From it manifest the receptacles

293. Ar: *al-'amā'*, literally, 'clouds', signifying a place of non-distinction, in which vision is impossible. It is related etymologically to the word *'amā*, meaning 'blindness'. Ibn 'Arabī describes those angels who are lost in love (*al-haymān*) as being in a world derived from this Cloud, since they have been blinded by love and can no longer see or know anything but God. The Cloud 'is the first place of divine manifestation in which He manifests Himself: within it the essential Light flows in secret... and when the Cloud was dyed with light, He opened up within it the forms of angels lost in love, who are above the world of natural bodies, and no throne or created thing preceded them... He revealed Himself to them in His Name the Beautiful, and they lost themselves in the Majesty of His Beauty – they never regain consciousness' (*Fut.*I.148).

294. Ar: *al-rabb*. This refers to the following hadith (al-Tirmidhī, *al-Jāmi'*, *tafsīr al-Qur'ān*, Sūra 11.1): 'The Prophet was asked: "where was our Lord before He created the creatures?" He replied: "He was in a cloud, neither above which nor below which was there any air."' See *Secrets of Voyaging*, 182–4.

295. Ar: *ayniyyāt*, literally, 'wherenesses' or 'ubieties'. That is to say, the Cloud is the first degree that can be described by where.

296. Ar: *ẓurūf* (sing. *ẓarf*). In grammar, *ẓarf al-makān* means a preposition of place: i.e. above it no air, below it no air.

297. Place/location (*makān*) and position/rank (*makāna*) are related etymologically in Arabic. Ibn 'Arabi writes: 'God created position before He created places. Then He stretched subtle links (*raqā'iq*) from position to specific places within the seven heavens and the earth. Then He brought into existence the spatially determined things in their places according to their position/rank' (*Fut.*II.582). See the chapter of Idrīs in *Fuṣūṣ al-ḥikam* for further discussion of the two in terms of height.

that are open to meanings embodied in sensory and imaginal form. It is a most noble existent, whose meaning is the Real – this is the Real through whom every existent other than God is created.[298] It is the meaning within which the essential realities of possible things are established and reside. It can accept locational reality, spatial relationship and positional rank, and the term 'receptacle'. From the world of the earth up to this Cloud there are no Names of God at all except the Names of Acts – no other Names than these have effect on any being from the intelligible or sensory world that may lie between them [the earth and the Cloud].

However, when the follower's companion, the rational thinker, was left behind in the seventh heaven as the follower travelled on, a subtle link[299] extended itself out of him in a different manner to the follower's ascension. This thread appears to the follower at the sphere of [fixed] stars, but then he loses sight of it in the Garden of Paradise; then it appears to him [again] in the sphere of zodiacal constellations, but he loses sight of it again at the Footstool and the Throne; it reappears to him at the degree of the Measures and in the Dark Substance, only to disappear from view in Nature; it appears again in the [Universal] Soul insofar as It is Soul, not in respect of It being Tablet, and also appears to him in the

298. Alluding to Q.10.5: 'God created that only with the truth (*bi'l-ḥaqq*)'. This idea is reminiscent of the technical term coined by Ibn Barrajān, 'the truth by which [everything] is created' (*al-ḥaqq al-makhlūq bihi*) – see, for example, *Fut.*I.297; II.60, 104, 577; III.77.

299. Ar: *raqīqa*. This technical term in Ibn 'Arabī's thought describes the subtle linkages between the viewer and what he observes (see *Fut.*II.582). Here he is using it to show how a follower can see the limitations of philosophy in terms of these deepest levels of Reality: for example, a philosopher knows the idea of the Universal Soul but does not comprehend the experiential reality of the Tablet, and likewise he understands the First Intellect but not the Pen. Equally, a philosopher is unable to comprehend at all the stage 'beyond' transcendence, which the mystic enjoys.

creative Intellect insofar as It is Intellect, not in respect of It being Pen. After that [the thread] separates from him, and it cannot be seen at all.

From this Cloud [the follower] begins to progress upwards and ascend in the Names of transcendence, until he arrives at the Presence in which he witnesses that transcendence limits Him, [merely] indicating and confining Him. He looks out over the world in its entirety, from meaning and spirituality to body and physicality. In his vision he finds nothing that the One who manifests there could be transcended from: he sees [everything's] connection to Him as the relationship of a degree to the One who possesses it. So he can no longer maintain the kind of transcendence that he used to imagine, nor can he maintain immanence, for there is no-one there [to do so].

There is then naught but God, nothing other than He –
And there is naught but a Oneness of onenesses

Then he parts from the Names of actions, and the Names of transcendence welcome him. He sees his companion, the rational thinker, concurring with him until he arrives at the Presence which admits neither transcendence nor immanence. Then he is free from limitability by negating transcendence, and from measurability by negating immanence,[300] and this is where he loses his fellow-traveller, the rational thinker.

300. Just as God cannot be grasped by concepts in the intelligible realm or by measurements in the sensible realm, so the mystic here is liberated from these two aspects in his self-knowledge.

THE RETURN

At this point he returns [from his journey],[301] looking for where he has come from. Then God the Exalted makes him travel a different path to the one he first followed.[302] This is a way that just cannot be talked about.[303] Nor can it be known, except by someone who directly witnesses it through experiential taste.[304]

His companion also returns, but in the same way that he ascended, since he cannot become a follower until he reaches his bodily existence again. There he re-joins his fellow-traveller [the follower]. From then on the rational thinker promptly goes to the messenger, if he is present, or to his heir, and pledges allegiance to him, sealing the pledge of faith and good-pleasure, in accordance with what has come as clear proof from his Lord and as a sign from his soul.[305] A witness from Him follows him,[306] and this [witness] is the

301. Ar: *inqalaba*, which also carries the meaning that he is now in an altered state of being.

302. Once the alchemical process of integration and fusion has been completed, and the gold of perfection has been reached, there is no return to prior states of disintegration.

303. Ar: *lā yatamakkan an yanqāl*. Here Ibn 'Arabī is lapsing into the Andalusian vernacular!

304. Ar: *dhawq*.

305. The language Ibn 'Arabī uses here is highly reminiscent of the way the people pledged allegiance to the Prophet at Ḥudaybiyya, a pact which is referred to in Q.48.18: 'God was pleased with the people of faith when they swore allegiance to you [Muhammad] under the tree, and He knew what was in their hearts. And so He sent down peace upon them and rewarded them with a victory near at hand.'

306. This phrase is somewhat ambiguous. Quoting the words of Q.11.17: 'And what of those who take their stand on clear proof from their Lord, when a witness from Him recites it.' The word 'recites it' (*yatlūhu*) can mean either 'follow it/him' or 'recite it', and is usually understood by the commentators as referring to the

follower [of the messenger]. Thus [the rational thinker] has faith in God due to the faith He has prescribed for him, not because of his own reasoned proof. He finds with Him and in his heart a light which he had not experienced before: he sees at one glance, by standing in that light, all that he saw with the follower in his first ascension, but [this time] he does not stop. Rather, he ascends in the manner of a follower, until he arrives at the Cloud and the utmost destination. He perceives the true nature of things.[307] He sees that what he had previously judged impossible through rational thought and intellect actually has to be so, and how it cannot be otherwise.

He is given the elixir of bringing into existence,[308] and he sees how bodies are gathered,[309] going forth from one stage to another, exhibiting different properties as the cycle turns. Forms undergo change; states are turned about.[310] He perceives directly what we have described [in the following poem] regarding such things:

---

revelation of the Quran by Gabriel to Muhammad, then conveyed by the latter to the world. The word particularly means to follow the divine Scriptures either by reading, reciting or acting in accordance with them. Here Ibn 'Arabī is alluding to his teaching on the witness (*shāhid*), which remains in the heart after the encounter with the divine: 'it is what the heart retains of the vision of the One that is contemplated' (*Fut.*II.132).

307. Ar: *al-shay' fī al-ashyā'*, literally 'the thing in the things', that is, the relationship between the One and the Many. The word *shay'* (thing) seems to be used here in order to make this as general a statement as possible. Cf. al-Qūnawī's famous dictum: 'every thing is in everything' (*kullu shay'in fī kulli shay'in. al-Nafaḥāt al-ilāhiyya*, 126).

308. Ar: *takwīn*, 'creation or bringing into being'. This is akin to the breath of Jesus, animating the bodies and giving them life, but here seems to be referring to the second 'creation' in the next world, when there will be true vision of forms in Reality.

309. Ar: *ḥashr*, which is used in the Quran (19.85) to describe the gathering of people on the Day of Resurrection (*yawm al-ḥashr*): 'on the Day when We gather together the mindful to the Compassionate'.

310. Ar: *taqallaba*, suggesting an oscillation from one state to its opposite. See: 'They fear a day when hearts and eyes will be turned about' (Q.24.37).

When the heaven is rent asunder,[311] Reality[312] is given form
Whoever belongs to Her through Her is [truly] Hers;
when the stars are thrown down,
seeking in their scattering; and rocky *mountains are set moving,*
germinating in their erupting; and the fire of *Hell is set ablaze,*
its furnace kindling it; and *the Garden of Paradise is brought close,*
a company entering it from their *grave which has been overturned;*
I ask Her: 'What is it You desire?' And She replies:
'*Wild beasts driven together*'[313]
And then my soul sees *all that it has sent before and all that it has held back.*

---

311. This extraordinary poem is an intriguing interweaving of two Quranic suras (81 and 82) with commentary, describing how enormously powerful forces are unleashed in true awakening and each human soul sees directly all their actions and their consequences. The italics demarcate the parts which Ibn 'Arabī is quoting: '*When the heaven is rent asunder*, when the stars are scattered, when the seas pour forth, *when the graves are overturned*, then *a soul will know what it has sent before and what it has held back*' (Q.82); 'When the sun is enveloped, *when the stars are thrown down, when the mountains are set moving*, when the pregnant camels are untended, *when the wild beasts are driven together*, when the seas are made to boil, when the souls are paired, when the baby girl that was slain is asked for what sin she was killed, when the scrolls are unrolled, when the sky is stripped, *when Hell is set ablaze, when Paradise is brought near*, then a soul will know what it has produced' (Q.81). While Sura 82 uses imagery about the breaking of limits, Sura 81 emphasises the disruption of normal activity (the sun no longer shines, the stars are no longer fixed in their place, the mountains are no longer stable etc.).

312. Note the use of the feminine for Reality (*ḥaqīqa*), which also alludes to the primary attribute of Mercy (*raḥma*) and the Essence (*dhāt*).

313. A powerful image of the alchemical fusion, in which energies that have been disparate ('wild') are aligned with each other and become creative.

When the rational thinker has surrendered and accepted faith[314] in his heart, and seen from his station all that the follower saw during his ascension in a direct vision of the eye, he asks to see the station of those who have earned punishment.[315] They are people who merit this abode [of Hell], entering it by virtue of their just desert, and they know that knowledge is the noblest vestment, and ignorance the basest ornament,[316] and that Hell has no room in it for anything good, just as Paradise has no space for anything bad. Then he sees that faith has been established in the heart of someone who has no knowledge of what really belongs to the Majesty of God,[317] while knowledge about God's Majesty and what is proper to it has been established in [the mind of] someone who has no faith at all. Someone who knows their own lack of faith[318] has surely deserved the abode of misery.

314. Ar: *aslama wa āmana*, i.e. accepted *islām* and embraced *īmān*.

315. Ar: *al-mujrimīn*, usually translated as 'sinners' or 'wrongdoers', a term used in the Quran for those whose actions have earned (*jarama*) the retribution of hell. See, for example, Q.19.85–6: 'On the Day when We gather together the mindful to the All-Compassionate, in throngs, and drive the wrongdoers (*mujrimīn*) to Hell like animals to water.' See also the discussion of the people of Hūd in the *Fuṣūṣ al-ḥikam*.

316. Ibn 'Arabī is here making a word-play on the same root, contrasting an intrinsic quality which clothes a person (*ḥulla*), i.e. knowledge, and a quality which is additional to one's true nature (*ḥilya*), i.e. ignorance.

317. The best way to act in this case is to refrain from trying to know. Elsewhere, Ibn 'Arabī notes that 'the spiritual courtesy (*adab*) proper to His Majesty is that they should make no judgments concerning Him' (*Fut.*IV.170). This *adab* forms the subject-matter of the next chapter, 168, on 'the inner knowledge of the station of spiritual courtesy and its mysteries'. See Denis Gril, '*Adab* and Revelation', in *Muhyiddin Ibn 'Arabi*, ed. S. Hirtenstein and M. Tiernan (Shaftesbury, 1993).

318. This could also be read as 'someone who knows but has no faith'.

Someone who is not a person of knowledge but has faith has merited, through [their] faith, the abode of true happiness and levels of ascent instead of descent.[319] The knowledgeable person who has merited the abode of misery, on the other hand, has his knowledge taken away, until it is as if he never knew it or is unable to know anything. Then because of his ignorance he suffers more intensely than any pain he ever experienced in the sensory realm, and this is a most intense suffering for him. At the same time, his knowledge is bestowed upon the unknowing faithful one, who has entered Paradise through his faith. With the knowledge that has been taken away from the other, whose desert is to dwell in the abode of misery, the person of faith attains the degree that this knowledge pertains to: he enjoys it psychically and sensorily, and on the Dune[320] at the degree of vision [of God].

Then the disbeliever[321] is given the ignorance of the unknowing person of faith, and with this ignorance he comes down to the lowliness of that in the Fire [of Hell]: such a grievous affliction passes over him, as he recalls the knowledge that he had before and how he no longer possesses it, and he realises what he has lost. Then God uncovers his sight so that he sees the level of knowledge that he would have had in Paradise, and he sees the garment of his knowledge

319. The levels of ascent (*darajāt*), as opposed to levels of descent (*darakāt*), are often referred to in the Quran: for example, 'These are in truth the people of faith, who have levels of ascension with their Lord, receiving forgiveness and generous provision' (8.4).

320. The Dune of White Musk (*kathīb al-misk al-abyaḍ*), according to Ibn 'Arabī who bases himself on various hadiths, is a place in the Garden of Eden, where people gather for the direct vision of God. He describes various degrees of vision, as determined by knowledge, faith and belief (see *Fut.*II.84–5). For further references in the *Futūḥāt*, see *SDG*, 393, n.16.

321. Ar: *kāfir*, literally 'one who covers up the Truth', meaning the person who has no faith in their heart.

upon another, someone who did not work hard to obtain it – he looks for some of it in himself but he cannot find any. Meanwhile, the person of faith looks and becomes aware of the affliction of hellfire: he sees the badness of his ignorance upon that knowledgeable one who had no faith, and his happiness and joy increase. How much greater and more wonderful that is than sorrow!

Something amazing happened to me personally in connection with this matter, when one of the doctors of philosophy heard me give this explanation. Maybe in his own mind he thought it absurd or he was scornful of my views on this. Then God informed him through an insight[322] in which he had no doubt regarding his own soul, and he realised that the matter was exactly as I had said. He came to me weeping for his soul and for being so remiss. I had a conversation[323] with him and he told me what had happened. He repented, sought to rectify the error, and had true faith. He told me: 'I have seen no greater sorrow than this', and he realised the truth of His saying: *I counsel you not to be one of the ignorant*[324] and His saying: *Do not be one of the ignorant.*[325] For

322. Ar: *kashf.*

323. Ar: *suḥba*, suggesting that the relation between Ibn 'Arabī and this man was one of spiritual converse, as between a shaykh and his disciple.

324. Q.11.46: 'Do not ask Me for that of which you have no knowledge. I counsel you not to be one of the ignorant.' This was the divine address to Noah, when he asked his Lord why his son had not been saved in the Ark, which seemed contrary to the divine justice and promise. It is noteworthy that Noah's response (11.47: 'My Lord, I seek refuge in You from asking You for that of which I have no knowledge') was to unquestioningly accept the divine Will and rely on His forgiveness and mercy.

325. Q.6.35: 'Had God wished, He would have brought them together to the guidance; so do not be one of the ignorant.' This divine address to Muhammad came in response to his feeling distressed at being rejected by those he was addressing. Note how Ibn 'Arabī goes on to contrast the divine imperative here ('Do not…'), which is emphatic, with the previous recommendation to Noah ('I counsel you not to…').

these bring together an address of gentle kindness with one of forceful severity: the first was to an elderly person [Noah] with whom He spoke in a kindly manner, while the second was to a young man [Muhammad] whom He addressed with a powerful imperative.

May God benefit us with knowledge and place us among His own people.[326] And may He never let us be one of those who do a disservice to His goodness towards that which is other than Him and who are miserable![327]

Amen, by His Might and Glory.

326. Ar: *ahlihi*, literally 'His family'. It can be read as referring to God's family or Muhammad's family. According to a prophetic hadith (see Wensinck, 5/346), 'the people of the Quran are the people of God and His elite'. This refers, in Ibn 'Arabī's view, to the greatest friends of God, a special group of the 'people of blame' (*malāmiyya*), whose only quality is that of the Essence Itself (*Fut.*II.20).

327. The text here is ambiguous and could equally be read as: 'May He never let us be one of those who strive for their own benefit in respect of others and remain miserable!'

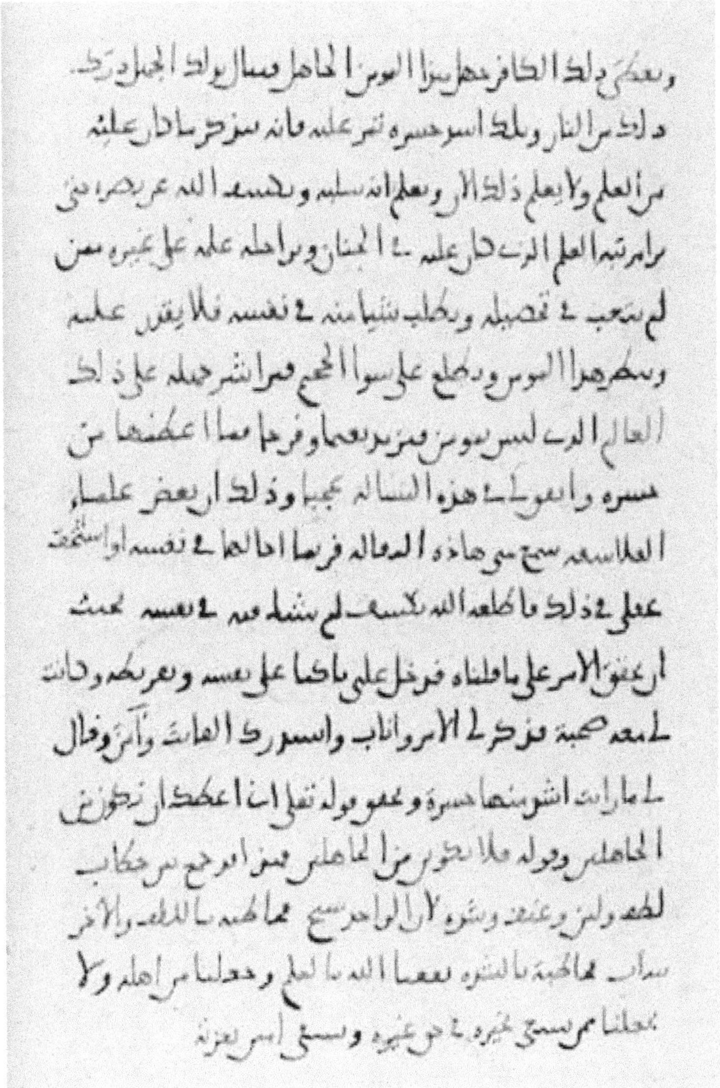

The final page of the chapter in Evkaf Müzesi MS 1859, fol. 43b, in the author's own hand. Courtesy of the Turkish and Islamic Arts Museum, Istanbul, Turkey.

APPENDIX A

The Cycle of Creation according to Ibn ʿArabī

The following table represents the degrees of existence which Ibn ʿArabī formulates in chapter 198 of the *Futūḥāt*.[1] The 28 degrees correspond to the 28 mansions of the moon and the 28 letters of the alphabet, and are linked to 28 divine Names. This cycle of 28[2] represents the whole universe in distinctive form.

The journey of 'descent' begins from the degree of the Supreme Pen, as the starting point of the creative process. The journey of 'ascension' begins from the 'lowest of the low' (*asfal al-sāfilīn*), which is the 27th degree, that of the human being: the ascension through each degree consists of contemplating the 'signs' of the divine Presence at each level, until each degree has been re-integrated within the human consciousness. The exteriorising journey of creation is re-enacted in the interior of the human being. The full re-assimilation of the 27 degrees is summarised in the 28th degree, which represents the level of the perfect human being.

1. *Fut.*II.397–9, and *SDG*, xxix–xxii.

2. The number 28 is noteworthy not simply because it is the number of the lunar mansions, but because it is the second 'perfect' number – this is a positive integer that is the sum of its divisors (excluding the number itself). The number 6 is the first perfect number (1 + 2 + 3 = 6) and represents the Perfect Human, created in the image of God; the number 28 is the second perfect number (1 + 2 + 4 + 7 + 14 = 28) and represents the macrocosmic image, the universe.

However, at the same time this schema should properly be regarded as a circle, according to Ibn ʿArabī:

> existence (*wujūd*) is a cycle, and the beginning of the circle is the existence of the First Intellect… and creation ends with the human being, thus completing the cycle. The human being is attached to the Intellect, as the last degree of the circle is joined to the first.[3]

As he goes on to explain, this means that each degree is like the spoke of a wheel, every part of the circumference being directly attached to the centre, because

> the relationship of the Real to all existent things is a single relation, in which there is never any change – everything contemplates Him and receives from Him what He lavishes upon it, the parts of the circumference [each] looking to the central point.'

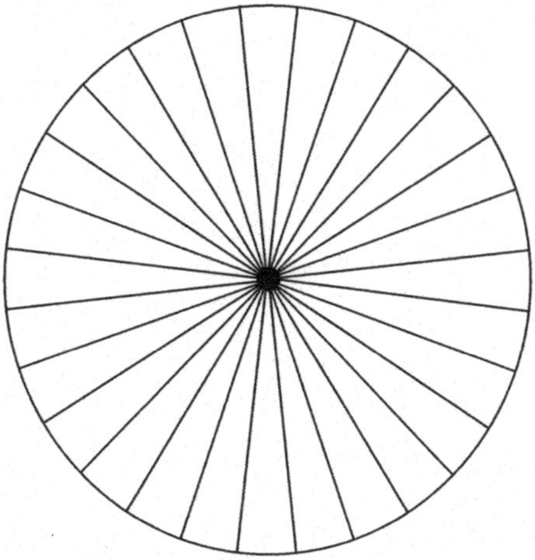

3. *Fut.*I.125.

This is another way of expressing the centrality of the 'private face' (*al-wajh al-khāṣṣ*, see Introduction). It also has a very important implication: these degrees of existence are no longer a simple hierarchical series stretching from the One to the many, but are places of divine revelation, in which God is wholly present. The journey of ascension is not to Him, but in Him.[4] Ibn 'Arabī is alluding to a fundamental teaching: each person or thing is connected to Reality in two ways: directly, without intermediary through the private face, and indirectly, via intermediaries through the chain of causation. In addition, the chain of secondary causation is somewhat ambiguous, because in itself each degree is never anything other than a direct manifestation of Reality. This is why he can say that some of those who know are aware that everything comes to them through the private face.

So representing this cycle as a table is a way of viewing the flow from interior to exterior, of focusing on the relationship of one degree to another. However, it should not obscure the fact that each degree is really a form of contemplation, of relationship with the Real. This explains Ibn 'Arabī's insistence on the subservience of the planetary spheres to the rulership of specific prophets, i.e. those who have realised all 28 degrees within themselves and return under divine orders to instruct others in a particular way. As representatives of the centre on the circumference, they act as *khalīfa* on earth in their lifetime and in heaven in their spiritual reality.

4. See *Fut.*III.340: 'I only make him travel to see the signs, not [to come] to Me, for no place can contain Me and the relation of all places to Me is a single relation.'

Letter	Degree	Divine Name
Hamza	Intellect and intellects, the Supreme Pen, the divine self-extension and support, its degrees both essential and additional	He who originates, the Inventor *al-Badīʿ*
Hāʾ	The Preserved Tablet, the Universal Soul, the Spirit blown into forms, the first thing to be given existence	He who raises up, the Sender *al-Bāʿith*
ʿAyn	[Universal] Nature, the breaths of the world contained in four realities, their differentiation and their synthesis	The Non-manifest, the Interior *al-Bāṭin*
Ḥāʾ	The Dust Substance in which bodily forms arise, and what resembles this substance in the world of composition	The Last *al-Ākhir*
Ghayn	The Universal Body	The Manifest, the Exterior *al-Ẓāhir*
Khāʾ	Configuration, particularity, likeness	The Wise *al-Ḥakīm*
Qāf	The Throne and the thrones of Grandeur, Nobility and Glory	The All-encompassing *al-Muḥīṭ*
Kāf	The Pedestal/Footstool and the Two Feet	The Grateful *al-Shakūr*
Jīm	The starless sphere and of the constellations, the occurrence of the days through its movement and its having recourse to the Name Time	The Rich, the Independent *al-Ghanī*
Shīn	The sphere of fixed stars and paradises, the apportioning of the stars in this sphere's hollow, earth of Paradise and roof of Hell	He who ordains and determines *al-Muqaddir*

Yāʾ	The first heaven (Saturn), the Visited House and the Lote-tree of the Furthest Limit, House of Abraham the Intimate Friend, Saturday	The Lord *al-Rabb*
Ḍād	The second heaven and its planet (Jupiter), and House of Moses, Thursday	The All-Knowing *al-ʿAlīm*
Lām	The third heaven and its planet (Mars) and House of Aaron, Tuesday	He who subjugates and overpowers *al-Qāhir*
Nūn	The fourth heaven, which is the heart of the body of the composite world, the Sun, the occurrence of night and day in the world of elements, the spirit of Idrīs and his Polehood, Sunday, the blowing of the partial spirit in the perfect forming of sperm	The Light *al-Nūr*
Rāʾ	The fifth heaven and its planet (Venus), fashioning, beautifying and beauty, House of Joseph, Friday	He who gives the form, the Fashioner *al-Muṣawwir*
Ṭāʾ	The sixth heaven and its planet (Mercury), House of Jesus, equilibrium, Wednesday	He who takes account of everything, the Enumerator *al-Muḥṣī*
Dāl	The heaven of this world, the Moon, ebb and flow, House of Adam, Monday	He who clarifies, the Illuminator *al-Mubīn*
Tāʾ	The Ether and what appears in it of meteors and burning fires	He who grasps and causes contraction *al-Qābiḍ*
Zāy	What appears in the element of Air	The Living *al-Ḥayy*

Letter	Degree	Divine Name
Sīn	What appears in the element of Water	He who gives life *al-Muḥyī*
Ṣād	Earth	He who brings death *al-Mumīt*
Ẓā'	Minerals	The Mighty, the Cherished *al-ʿAzīz*
Thā'	Plants	He who bestows provision and nourishes *al-Razzāq*
Dhāl	Animals	He who abases and makes tractable *al-Mudhill*
Fā'	Angels	The Strong *al-Qawī*
Bā'	Jinn	The Subtle *al-Laṭīf*
Mīm	Human (*insān*)	He who reunites and synthesises *al-Jāmiʿ*
Wāw	Appointment of the degrees (*rutab*), stations (*maqāmāt*) and abodes (*manāzil*)	He who elevates the degrees *Rafīʿ al-darajāt*

The text in the three columns is based on the printed text of chapter 198 in the *Futūḥāt* (*Fut.*II.397ff.) and the original in Ibn ʿArabī's hand (see Mansoub edn., pp.5/481–508).

APPENDIX B

Macrocosmic and Microcosmic Correspondences

The correspondences that Ibn ʿArabī draws between the macrocosm and the microcosm are summarised in the following two tables: the first gives the correspondence between the heavenly realm of planets and the earthly realm of metals; the second gives the relation between the external universe and the human being.

Heaven	Prophet	Planetary Sphere	Metal
First	Adam	Moon	silver
Second	Jesus	Mercury	quicksilver
Third	Joseph	Venus	copper
Fourth	Idrīs	Sun	gold
Fifth	Aaron	Mars	iron
Sixth	Moses	Jupiter	tin
Seventh	Abraham	Saturn	lead

Higher world, permanence (baqāʾ)[1]	*Macrocosm: universe*	*Microcosm: human being*
	Being seated, universal reality of Muhammad, sphere of Life[2]	spiritual reality (*laṭīfa*) and holy spirit
	the all-encompassing Throne	human body
	the Footstool, place of the Two Feet	human soul with all its faculties, place that receives command and prohibition, praise and blame
	the Visited House (*al-bayt al-maʿmūr*)	human heart
	the angels	spiritual faculties within the human
	Saturn (Zuḥal)[3]	faculty of knowledge, the breath
	Jupiter (Mushtarī)	power of memory, the back of the brain
	Mars (Mirrīkh/ Aḥmar)	power of intellect, the crown of the brain
	Sun	power of thinking, the centre of the brain
	Venus (Zuhara)	power of conjecture, the animal spirit
	Mercury (ʿUṭārid/Kātib)	power of imagination, the front of the brain
	Moon	power of sense-perception, the senses

[*Lower*] *world of change, annihilation* (*fanā'*)	Ether (hot and dry)	yellow bile, power of digestion
	Air (hot and wet)	blood, power of attraction
	Water (cold and wet)	phlegm, power of repulsion
	Ground[4] (cold and dry)	black bile, power of retention
	Earth: seven levels (black, dust-coloured, red, yellow, white, blue and green)	human body: seven levels (skin, fat, flesh, veins, nerves, muscles and bones)
the world of inhabitants, permanence and annihilation	spirit-beings	faculties within the human
	animals	the perceiving part of the human
	plants	the growing part of the human
	minerals	the non-perceiving part of the human

1. This table is drawn up on the basis of Ibn 'Arabī's description in chapter 6 of the *Futūḥāt* (I.120–1) and the treatise he wrote during his time in al-Andalus, *al-Tadbīrāt al-ilāhiyya*, chapter 17. This provides a complementary version of the conceptual framework employed in chapter 167. I have omitted a fourth category of world, that of relationships, which is found in the *Futūḥāt*, as well as his discussion of various precious stones in the *Tadbīrāt*.

2. Referring to Q.20.4–5: 'A revelation from Him who created the earth and the high heavens, the Compassionate (*al-Raḥmān*) who seated Himself upon the Throne.' In other words, the all-inclusive Compassion of God corresponds to the universal reality of Muhammad.

3. It is noteworthy that Ibn 'Arabī mostly uses a different vocabulary for the planets to that employed in chapter 167.

4. Ar: *turāb*, which means topsoil or dust, i.e. the potentially fertile layer of the Earth (*arḍ*).

BIBLIOGRAPHY

Ibn ʿArabī, Muḥyī al-Dīn, *Awrād al-usbūʿ/Wird* (London, 1979), trans. Stephen Hirtenstein and Pablo Beneito as *The Seven Days of the Heart* (Oxford, 2008)

—— *Dīwān al-maʿārif* (Paris BN MS 2348)

—— *Fuṣūṣ al-ḥikam*, ed. Mahmud Erol Kiliç and Abdurrahim Alkiş (Istanbul, 2016)

—— *al-Futūḥāt al-Makkiyya*, 4 vols. (Beirut, n.d.)

—— *al-Futūḥāt al-Makkiyya*, ed. ʿAbd al-Aziz Mansoub, 12 vols. (Sana'a, 1431/2010)

—— *The Meccan Illuminations*, ed. Michel Chodkiewicz (Paris, 1988)

—— *The Meccan Illuminations*, vol. 2, ed. Michel Chodkiewicz (New York, 2004)

—— *L'alchimie du bonheur parfait*, trans. of ch. 167 by Stéphane Ruspoli (Paris, 1981)

—— *K. al-Isfār ʿan natāʾij al-asfār*, ed. and trans. Angela Jaffray as *The Secrets of Voyaging* (Oxford, 2015)

—— *Mishkāt al-anwār*, ed. and trans. Stephen Hirtenstein and Martin Notcutt as *Divine Sayings* (Oxford, 2004)

—— *Rasāʾil* (Beirut, 1997)

—— *Rūḥ al-quds fī munāṣaḥat al-nafs*, ed. Abrar Ahmad Shahi (Rawalpindi, 2012)

—— *al-Tadbīrāt al-ilāhiyya fī iṣlāḥ al-mamlaka al-insāniyya*, ed. Abrar Ahmad Shahi (Rawalpindi, 2014)

Abū Dāwūd, *al-Sunan*, ed. A. S. ʿAli (Cairo, 1952)

Aladdin, Bakri, 'The Unity of Being', *JMIAS* 51 (2012), pp. 3–26

ʿAṭṭār, Farīd al-Dīn, *Ilāhī-nāma*, ed. Shafiʿi Kadkani (Tehran, 2014)

Austin, R. W. J., *Sufis of Andalusia*, partial trans. of Ibn ʿArabī's *Rūḥ al-quds* and *Durrat al-fākhira* (London, 1971)

Beneito, Pablo, and Stephen Hirtenstein, 'The Prayer of Blessing by ʿAbd al-ʿAzīz al-Mahdawī', *JMIAS* 34 (2003), pp. 1–57

van Bladel, Kevin, *The Arabic Hermes* (Oxford, 2009)
Bohm, David, *Wholeness and the Implicate Order* (London, 1983)
al-Bukhārī, *al-Ṣaḥīḥ* (n.p., 1378/1958–59)
Burckhardt, Titus, *Alchemy* (London, 1967, repub. Louisville, KY, 1997)
Chittick, William, *The Sufi Path of Knowledge* (Albany, NY, 1989)
—— *The Self-Disclosure of God* (Albany, NY, 1998)
—— 'Mysticism versus Philosophy in Earlier Islamic History: the al-Ṭūsī, al-Qūnawī Correspondence', *Religious Studies* 17/1 (1981), pp. 87–104
Chodkiewicz, Michel, *Seal of the Saints* (Cambridge, 1993)
Corbin, Henry, *Spiritual Body and Celestial Earth* (Princeton, 1977)
—— *Creative Imagination in the Sufism of Ibn 'Arabī* (Princeton, 1969)
The Dalai Lama and Howard Cutler, *The Art of Happiness* (London, 1998)
Ebstein, Michael, *Mysticism and Philosophy in al-Andalus* (Leiden, 2014)
Encyclopaedia of Islam, 2nd edition, P. Bearman et al. (Leiden, 1991–2004)
al-Ghazālī, *Iḥyā' 'ulūm al-dīn*, 5 vols. (Beirut, 1980)
—— *al-Munqidh min al-ḍalāl*, ed. F. Jabre (Beirut, 1959)
—— *Kīmiyā' al-sa'āda*, trans. Claud Field (London, 1980)
—— '*Adab* and Revelation', in *Muhyiddin Ibn 'Arabi*, ed. S. Hirtenstein and M. Tiernan (Shaftesbury, 1993)
al-Ḥabashī, Badr, *K. al-Inbāh 'alā ṭarīq Allāh*, trans. Denis Gril (*JMIAS* 15), 1994, pp. 1–36
Hafiz, *The Collected Lyrics of Háfiz of Shíráz*, trans. Peter Avery (Cambridge, 2007)
al-Ḥallāj, *Sharḥ Dīwān al-Ḥallāj*, ed. Kamil Mustafa Shaybi (Cairo, 2005)
Hirtenstein, Stephen, *The Unlimited Mercifier* (Oxford, 1999)
Hirtenstein, Stephen, and M. Tiernan (eds.), *Muhyiddin Ibn 'Arabi* (Shaftesbury, 1993)
Holmyard, Eric, and Desmond Mandeville, *Âvicennae de Congelatione et Conglutinatione Lapidum* (Paris, 1927)

Hopkins, Arthur, *Alchemy: Child of Greek Philosophy* (Morningside Heights, NY, 1934)
Ibn al-Nadīm, *The Fihrist*, ed. Ibrahim Ramadan (London, 1994)
Ibn Sawdakīn, *Lawāqiḥ al-asrār wa lawā'iḥ al-anwār min ma'ārif al-shaykh Muḥyī al-Dīn Ibn 'Arabī*, ed. Abdel Baqi Miftah (Damascus, 1436/2015)
Ikhwān al-Ṣafā', *Rasā'il*, 4 vols. (Beirut, 1957)
Jābir b. Ḥayyān, *K. Ikhrāj mā fī al-quwwa ilā al-fi'l* (*Essai sur l'histoire des idées scientifiques dans l'Islam*), vol. 1, ed. Paul Kraus (Paris, 1935)
Kazemi, Reza Shah, *The Spirit of Tolerance in Islam* (London, 2012)
Kazimirski, A. de B., *Dictionnaire Arabe Français*, 2 vols. (Paris, 1860)
Kingsley, Peter, *Ancient Philosophy, Mystery and Magic* (Oxford, 1995)
Kirk, G.S., J.E. Raven and M. Schofield, *The Presocratic Philosophers* (Cambridge, 1983)
Kirmānī, Awḥad al-Dīn, *Heart's Witness*, trans. Bernd Manuel Weischer and Peter Lamborn Wilson (Tehran, 1978)
Kraus, Paul (ed.), *Essai sur l'histoire des idées scientifiques dans l'Islam*, vol. 1 (Paris, 1935)
Lings, Martin, *Muhammad* (London, 1983)
Mason, Andrew, *Flow and Flux in Plato's Philosophy* (London, 2016)
McAuley, Denis, *Ibn 'Arabī's Mystical Poetics* (Oxford, 2012)
McGilchrist, Ian, *The Master and His Emissary* (New Haven, CN, 2009)
McGregor, Richard, 'Notes on the Transmission of Mystical Philosophy: Ibn 'Arabī according to 'Abd al-Wahhāb al-Sha'rānī', in *Reason and Inspiration in Islam*, ed. Hermann Landolt and Todd Lawson (London, 2005)
Mead, G.R.S., *Thrice-Greatest Hermes*, 3 vols. (London, 1906)
Morris, James W., 'Ibn 'Arabī's Spiritual Ascension', in *Les Illuminations de La Mecque*, ed. Michel Chodkiewicz (Paris, 1988)
Murata, Sachiko, *The Tao of Islam* (Albany, NY, 1992)
Muslim ibn Ḥajjāj, *al-Ṣaḥīḥ* (Cairo, 1334/1915–16)
Nasr, Seyyed Hossein, *Three Muslim Sages* (Cambridge, MA, 1964)
Nicholson, R. A., *Rūmī, Poet and Mystic* (London, 1964)

Patai, Raphael, *The Jewish Alchemists* (Princeton, 1994)
Pinés, Shlomo, *Studies in Arabic Versions of Greek Texts and in Medieval Science* (Leiden, 1986)
Plotinus, *The Enneads*, trans. A. H. Armstrong (Cambridge, MA, 2014)
al-Qūnawī, Ṣadr al-Dīn, *al-Nafaḥāt al-ilāhiyya* (Tehran, 1375/1996)
The Qur'ān, trans. Alan Jones (n.p., 2007)
al-Qushayrī, *Risāla fī al-taṣawwuf*, trans. Alexander Knysh as *Epistle on Sufism* (Reading, 2007)
Ritter, Hellmut, *The Ocean of the Soul*, trans. John O'Kane and Bernd Radtke (Leiden, 2003)
Rowson, Everett K., *A Muslim Philosopher on the Soul and its Fate* (New Haven, CN, 1988)
Schimmel, Annemarie, *Mystical Dimensions of Islam* (Chapel Hill, SC, 1975)
Sezgin, Fuat, *Geschichte des arabischen Schrifttums* (Leiden, 1967)
al-Sha'rānī, 'Abd al-Wahhāb, *K. al-Yawāqīt* (Cairo, 1277/1860)
Stieber, Mary, *The Poetics of Appearance in the Attic Korai* (Austin, 2004)
al-Suyūṭī, Jalāl al-Dīn, *Ḥusn al-muḥāḍara fī ta'rīkh Miṣr wa al-Qāhira*, ed. Abū al-Faḍl Ibrāhīm (Cairo, 1968)
al-Tirmidhī, *al-Jāmi' al-ṣaḥīḥ, wa huwa sunan al-Tirmidhī* (Cairo, 1938)
Wehr, Hans, *A Dictionary of Modern Written Arabic* (Wiesbaden, 1979)
Wensinck, A. J., *Concordance et indices de la Tradition musulmane*, 8 vols. (Leiden, 1992)
Wright, William, *A Grammar of the Arabic Language* (London, 1974)
Yahia, Osman, *Histoire et classification de l'oeuvre d'Ibn 'Arabī* (Damascus, 1964)
al-Zabīdī, Aḥmad, *al-Tajrīd al-ṣarīḥ li aḥādīth al-Jāmi' al-ṣaḥīḥ* (Beirut, 1386/1967)
Zargar, Cyrus, *Sufi Aesthetics* (Columbia, SC, 2013)

INDEX OF QURANIC REFERENCES

Bold indicates an entry in the translation text

INDEX OF *FUTŪḤĀT* EXTRACTS

Chapter numbers are in parentheses
Page numbers are from the 4-volume Beirut edition

GENERAL INDEX

People, places and key terms in English and Arabic

Bold indicates an entry in the translation text

في معرفة كيمياء السعادة
باب من الفتوحات المكّيّة

لمحيي الدين إبن عربي

تحقيق

إستيفن هيرتنستاين

المختصرات

اعتمدنا في التحقيق اصل المصنّف المدون بخط يده
(اوقاف 1859) و النسخ التالية

ص: طبعة الأستاذ عبد العزيز سلطان المنصوب (صنعاء، 1341ه).

ب: طبعة بيروت (4-أجزاء).

بسم الله الرحمن الرحيم

الباب السابع والستون ومائة

في معرفة كِيمِياءِ السعادة

إِنَّ الْأَكَاسِيرَ بُرْهَانٌ يَدُلُّ عَلَى ... مَا فِي الْوُجُودِ مِنَ التَّبْدِيلِ وَالْغِيَرِ
إِنَّ الْعَدُوَّ، بِإِكْسِيرِ الْعِنَايَةِ إِذْ ... يُلْقَى عَلَيْهِ بِمِيزَانٍ عَلَى قَدَرِ
فِي الْحِينِ يَخْرُجُ صِدْقًا مِنْ عَدَاوَتِهِ ... إِلَى وِلَايَتِهِ بِالْحُكْمِ وَالْقَدَرِ
فَصَحِّحِ الْوَزْنَ فَالْمِيزَانُ شِرْعَتُنَا ... وَقَدْ أَبَنْتُ فَكُنْ فِيهِ عَلَى حَذَرِ
الكِيمِيَاءُ مَقَادِيرٌ مُعَيَّنَةٌ ... لِأَنَّ كَمْ عَدَدٌ فِي عَالَمِ الصُّوَرِ
فَكُنْ بِهِ فَطِنًا إِنْ كُنْتَ ذَا نَظَرٍ ... وَلَا تَرُدَّنَّكَ الْأَهْوَا عَنِ النَّظَرِ
تَلْحَقْ بِرُتْبَةِ أَمْلَاكٍ مُطَهَّرَةٍ ... وَتَرْتَقِي رُتَباً عَنْ عَالَمِ الْبَشَرِ

الكيمياء عبارة عن العلم الذي يختصّ بالمقادير والأوزان في كلّ ما يدخله المقدار والوزن من الأجسام والمعاني محسوسا ومعقولا وسلطانها في الاستحالات، أعني تغيّر الأحوال على العين الواحدة. فهو علم طبيعيّ روحانيّ إلهيّ. وإنّما قلنا إلهيّ لورود الاستواء والنزول والمعيّة وتعدّد الأسماء الإلهيّة على المسمّى الواحد باختلاف معانيها.

فَالْأَمْرُ مَا بَيْنَ مَطْوِيٍّ وَمَنْشُورِ كَالْكَيْفِ وَالْكَمِّ أَحْوَالُ الْمَقَادِيرِ
تَاهَتْ مَرَاكِبُنَا عَلَى بَسَائِطِهَا تِيهَ امْتِيَازٍ بِسِرٍّ غَيْرِ مَقْهُورِ
وَالْوَحْيُ يُنْزِلُ أَحْكَامًا يُشَرِّعُهَا وَالْحُكْمُ مَا بَيْنَ مَنْهِيٍّ وَمَأْمُورِ

فعلم الكيمياء العلم بالإكسير، وهو على قسمين، أعني فِعله. إمّا إنشاءُ ذات ابتداء كالذهب المعدنيّ، وإمّا إزالة علّة ومرض كالذهب الصِناعيّ الملحق بالذهب المعدنيّ كنشأة الآخرة والدنيا في طلب الاعتدال.

فاعلم أن المعادن كلّها ترجع إلى أصل واحدٍ وذلك الأصل يطلب بذاته أن يلحق بدرجة الكمال وهي الذهبيّة. غير أنّه لمّا كان أمرا طبيعيّا عن أثر أسماء إلهيّة، متنوّعة الأحكام، طرأت عليه في طريقه علل وأمراض من اختلاف الأزمنة وطبائع الأمكنة، مثل حرارة الصيف وبرد الشتاء ويبوسة الخريف ورطوبة الربيع، ومن البقعة كحرارة المعدن وبرده. وبالجملة فالعلل كثيرة.

فإذا غلبتْ عليه علّة من هذه العلل في أزمان رحلته ونقْلته من طور إلى طور وخروجه من حكم دور إلى حكم دور، واستحكم فيه سلطان ذلك الموطن، ظهرت فيه صورة نقلت جوهرته إلى حقيقتها. فسمّي كبريتا أو زئبقا، وهما الأبوان لما يظهر من التحامهما وتناكحهما من المعادن لعلل طارئة على الولد. فهما إنّما يلتحمان ويتناكحان ليخرج بينهما جوهر شريف كامل النشأة يسمّى ذهبا فيشرف به الأبوان؛ إذ كانت تلك الدرجة مطلوبة لكلّ واحد من الأبوين من حيث

جوهريّتهما. إلّا أنّ ذلك الأصل في الإلهيّات نَفَس وفي الطبيعة بخار إلّا أنّ الأبوين أمر وطبيعة.

وإنّما قلنا إنّ ذلك الأمر كان مطلوبا للأبوين من حيث جوهرهما لا من حيث صورتهما، لأنّ الحكم في الجوهر الهيولائيّ إنّما هو للصور. فلمّا حالت العلّة التي طرأت عليه في معدنه؛ فصيّرته كبريتا وزئبقا. علمنا أيضا أنّ في قوّتهما إذا لم يطرأ عليهما علّة تخرجهما عن سلطان حكم اعتدال الطبائع وتعدل بهما عن طريقه أنّ الولد الخارج بينهما الذي يستحيل أعيانهما إليه، أنّهما يلحقان بدرجة الكمال وهو الذهب، الذي كان مطلوبا لهما ابتداء.

فإذا التحما وتناكحا في المعدن بحكم طبيعة ذلك المعدن الخاصّ وحكم قبوله لأثر طبيعة الزمان فيه، وهو على صراط مستقيم مثل الفطرة التي فطر الله الناس عليها، وأبواه هما اللذان يهوّدان الولد أو ينصّرانه أو يمجّسانه. كذلك إذا كثرت فيه كمّيّة الأب الواحد لعرض معدنيّ من عرض زمانيّ غَلَبَت بذلك إحدى الطبائع على أخواتها، فزاد وأربى، ونقص الباقي عن مقاومة الغالب، حكم على الجوهر، فردّه لما تعطيه حقيقة ذلك الطبع وعدل به عن طريق الاعتدال التي هي المحجّة، التي تخرج بك إلى المدينة الفاضلة الذهبيّة الكاملة، التي من حصل فيها لم يقبل الاستحالة إلى الأنقص عنها. فإذا غلب عليه ذلك الطبع، قلب عينه، فظهرت صورة الحديد أو النحاس أو القزدير أو الآنك أو الفضّة، بحسب ما يحكم عليه.

ومن هنا تعرف قوله تعالى في الاعتبار: ﴿مُخَلَّقَةٍ وَغَيْرِ مُخَلَّقَةٍ﴾ (الحجّ ٥) أي تامّة الخلقة وليس إلّا الذهب، وغير تامّة الخلقة وهي بقيّة المعادن.

فتتولّاه في ذلك الوقت روحانيّة كوكب من الكواكب السيّارة السبعة وهو ملك من ملائكة تِلك السماء يجري مع ذلِك الكوكب المسخّر في سباحته لأنّ الله هو الذي وجّهه إلى غاية يقصدها عن أمر خالقه إبقاء لعين ذلك الجوهر. فيتولّى صورة الحديد، ذلك المَلَك، الذي جواده هذا الكوكب السابح من السماء السابعة من هنا. وصورة القزدير وغيره، وكذلك كلّ صورة معدنيّة، يتولّاها ملك يكون جواده هذا الكوكب السابح في سمائه وفلكه الخاصّ به الذي وجّهه فيه ربّه تعالى.

فإذا جاء العارف بالتدبير نظر في الأمر الأهون عليه، فإن كان الأهون عليه إزالة العلّة من الجسد حتّى يردّه إلى المجرى الطبيعيّ المعتدل الذي انحرف عنه، فهو أَوْلى. فإنّ الكوكب السابح يراه صاحب الرصد وقتا في المنزلة عينها ووقتا عادلا عنها، منحرفا فوقها أو تحتها، فيعمد العارف بالتدبير إلى السبب الذي ردّه حديدا أو ما كان. ويعلَم أنّه ما غلب الجماعة إلّا بما فيه من الكمّيّة. فنقص من الزائد وزاد في الناقص. وهذا هو الطبّ والعامل به العالم هو الطبيب.

فيزيل عنه بهذا الفعل صورة الحديد مثلا أو ما كان عليه من الصور. فإذا ردّه إلى الطريق أخذ يحفظ عليه تقويم الصحّة وإقامته فيها. فإنّه قد يعافى من مرضه وهو ناقه، فيخاف عليه،

فهـو يعاملـه بتلطيـف الأغذيـة، ويحفظـه مـن الأهويـة. ويسـلك بـه علـى الصـراط القويـم؛ إلـى أن يكسـو ذلـك الجوهـر صـورة الذهـب. فـإذا حصلـت لـه خـرج عـن حكـم الطبيـب وعـن علّتـه. فإنّـه بعـد ذلـك الكمـال لا ينـزل إلـى درجـة النقصـان، ولا يقبلـه. ولـو رامهـا الطبيـب لـم يتمكّـن لـه ذلـك.

فإنّ القاضي ما عنده نصّ في هذه المسألة، حتّى يحكم فيها بما يراه. وسبب ذلك على الحقيقة أنّ القاضي عادل ولا يحكم إلّا على من خرج عن طريق الحقّ، وهذا الذهب عليه فلا يقضي عليه بشيء، لأنّه لم يتوجّه للخصم عليه حقٌّ فهذا سببه. فمن لزم طريق الحقّ ارتفع عن درجة الحكم عليه وصار حاكما على الأشياء. فهذه طريقة إزالة العلل. وما رأيت عليها أحدا يعرف ذلك، ولا نبّه عليه ولا أشار ولا تجده إلّا في هذا الباب أو في كلامنا.

وأمّا إذا أراد صاحب هذه الصنعة إنشاء العين المسمّى إكسيرا، ليحمله على ما يشاء من الأجساد المعدنيّة، فيقلّبها لما تحكم به طبيعة ذلك الجسَد القابل. والدواء واحد الذي هو الإكسير. فمن الأجساد مَن يردّه الإكسير إلى حكمه، فيكون إكسيرا يعمل عمله وهو المسمّى بالنائب. فيقوم في باقي الأجساد المعدنيّة ويحكم بحكمه. مثل أن يأخذ وزن درهم أو أيّ وزن شاء من عين الإكسير، فيلقيه على ألف وزن من أيّ جَسَد شئت من الأجساد. فإن كان قزديرا أو حديدا أعطاه صورة الفِضّة، وإن كان نحاسا أو رصاصا أسود أو فضّة أعطاه صورة الذهب. وإن كان الجسدُ زئبِقا أعطاه قوّته وتركه

نائبا عنه، يحكم في الأجساد حُكمه ولكن بوزن يخالف وزن باقي الأجساد وذلك وزن درهم من الإكسير. فيلقيه على رطل الحكمة خاصّة من الزئبق، فيردّه إكسيرا كلّه. فيلقي من ذلك النائب وزنا على ألف وزن من بقيّة الأجساد مثل الإكسير، فيجري في الحكم مجراه. فهذه صورة الإنشاء والأولى صنعة إزالة المرض.

وإنّما جئنا بهذا لِنُعلمك بارتباط الحكمة في مسمّى الكيمياء بين الطريقين. ولماذا سمّيت كيمياء السعادة لأنّ فيها سعادة الأبد، وزيادة ما عند الناس من أهل الله خير منها وهو أنّه يعطيك درجة الكمال الذي للرجال. فإنّه ما كلّ صاحب سعادة يُعطَى الكمال. فكلّ صاحب كمال سعيد وما كلّ سعيد كامل. والكمال عبارة عن اللحوق بالدرجة العليا وهو التشبّه بالأصل. ولا يتخيّل أنّ قول النبيّ 'صلّى الله عليه وسلّم': {كُمّلٌ من الرجال كثيرون} أنّه أراد الكمال الذي ذكره الناس، وإنّما هو ما ذكرناه وذلك بحسب ما يعطي الاستعداد العلميّ في الدنيا. فلنتكلّم إن شاء الله على كيمياء السعادة بعد هذا التمهيد. والله الموفّق لا ربّ غيره.

وَصْل في فَصْل

اعلم أنّ الكمال المطلوب الذي خُلِق له الإنسان إنّما هو الخِلافة. فأخذها آدم، عليه السلام، بحكم العناية الإلهيّة. وهو مقام أخصّ من الرسالة في الرسل لأنّه ما كلّ رسول

خليفة. فإنّ درجة الرسالة إنّما هي التبليغ خاصّة. قال تعالى: ﴿مَا عَلَى الرَّسُولِ إِلَّا الْبَلَاغُ﴾ (المائدة ٩٩). وليس له التحكّم في المخالف، إنّما له تشريع الحكم عن الله أو بما أراه الله خاصّة. فإذا أعطاه الله التحكّم فيمن أُرسل إليهم، فذلك هو الاستخلاف والخلافة، والرسول الخليفة. فما كلّ من أُرْسِل حُكِّمَ. فإذا أعطي السيف وأمضى الفعل، حينئذ يكون له الكمال، فيظهر بسلطان الأسماء الإلهيّة: فيعطي ويمنع ويعزّ ويذلّ ويحيي ويميت ويضرّ وينفع. ويظهر بأسماء التقابل مع النبوّة، لا بدّ من ذلك. فإن ظهر بالتحكّم من غير نبوّة فهو مَلِك وليس بخليفة.

فلا يكون خليفة إلّا من استخلفه الحقّ على عباده، لا مَن أقامه الناس وبايعوه، وقدَّموه لأنفسهم وعلى أنفسهم. فهذه هي درجة الكمال.

وللنفوس تعمّل مشروع في تحصيل مقام الكمال وليس لهم تعمّل في تحصيل النبوّة. فالخلافة قد تكون مكتسبة، والنبوّة غير مكتسبة. لكن لَمّا رأى بعض الناس الطريقَ الموصل إليها ظاهر الحكم ومن شاء الله يَسلك فيه، تخيّل أن النبوّة مكتسبة، وغلط.

فلا شكّ أن الطريق يُكتسب، فإذا وصل إلى الباب يكون بحسب ما يخرج له في توقيعه، وهنالك هو الاختصاص الإلهيّ. فمن الناس من يخرج له توقيع بالولاية، ومنهم من يخرج له توقيع بالنبوّة وبالرسالة، وبالرسالة والخلافة، ومنهم من يخرج له توقيع بالخلافة وحدها. فلمّا رأى من رأى أنّ

هؤلاء ما خرج لهم هذا التوقيع إلّا بعد سلوكهم بالأفعال والأقوال والأحوال إلى هذا الباب، تخيّل أن ذلك مكتسب للعبد، فأخطأ.

واعلم أنّ النفس من حيث ذاتها مهيّأة لقبول استعداد ما تخرج به التوقيعات الإلهيّة. فمنهم من حصل له استعداد توقيع الولاية خاصّة فلم يزد عليها. ومنهم من رُزق استعداد ما ذكرناه من المقامات كلّها أو بعضها. وسبب ذلك أنّ النفوس خلقت من معدن واحد كما قال تعالى: ﴿خَلَقَكُم مِّن نَّفْسٍ وَاحِدَةٍ﴾ (النساء ١) وقال بعد استعداد خلْق الجسد: ﴿وَنَفَخْتُ فِيهِ مِنْ رُوحِي﴾ (الحجر ٢٩). فمِن روح واحد صحّ السرّ المنفوخ في المنفوخ فيه، وهو النفس. وقوله: ﴿فِي أَيِّ صُورَةٍ مَّا شَاءَ رَكَّبَكَ﴾ (الانفطار ٨) يريد الاستعدادات، فيكون بحكم الاستعداد في قبول الأمر الإلهيّ.

فلمّا كان أصل هذه النفوس الجزئيّة الطهارة من حيث أبيها ولم يظهر لها عين إلّا بوجود هذا الجسد الطبيعيّ، فكانت الطبيعة الأب الثاني خرجت ممتزجة فلم يظهر فيها إشراق النور الخالص المجرّد عن الموادّ، ولا تلك الظلمة الغائيّة التي هي حكم الطبيعة.

فالطبيعة شبيهةٌ بالمعدن والنفس الكلّيّة شبيهة بالأفلاك التي لها الفعل وعن حركاتها يكون الانفعال في العناصر. والجسد المكوّن في المعدن بمنزلة الجسم الإنسانيّ. والخاصّيّة التي هي روح ذلك الجسد المعدنيّ بمنزلة النفْس الجزئيّة التي للجسم الإنسانيّ وهو الروح المنفوخ.

وكما أن الأجساد المعدنيّة على مراتب لعلل طرأت عليهم في حال التكوين مع كونهم يطلبون درجة الكمال التي لها ظهرت أعيانهم، كذلك الإنسان خُلِق للكمال. فما صرفه عن ذلك الكمال إلّا علل وأمراض طرأت عليهم، إمّا في أصل ذواتهم وإمّا بأمور عرَضيّة. فاعلم ذلك.

فلنبتدئ بما ينبغي أن يليق بهذا الباب وهو أن نقول: إنّ النفوس الجزئيّة لما ملّكها الله تدبير هذا البدن واستخلفها عليه وبيّن لها أنّها خليفة فيه، لتتنبّه على أنّ لها موجِدا استخلفها، فيتعيّن عليها طلب العلم بذلك الذي استخلفها: هل هو من جنسها؟ أو شبيه بها بضربٍ مّا من ضروب المشابهة؟ أو لا يشبهها؟. فتوفّرت دواعيها لمعرفة ذلك من نفسها. فبينما هي كذلك على هذه الحالة في طلب الطريق الموصلة إلى ذلك وإذا بشخص قد تقدّمها في الوجود من النفوس الجزئيّة، فأنِسوا به للشّبه. فقالوا له: أنت تقدّمتنا في هذه الدار فهل خطر لك ما خطر لنا؟ قال: وما خطر لكم؟ قالوا: طلب العلم بمن استخلفنا في تدبير هذا الهيكل. فقال: عندي بذلك علم صحيح جئت به ممن استخلفكم. وجعلني رسولًا إلى جنسي لأبيّن لهم طريق العلم الموصل إليه الذي فيه سعادتهم. فقال الواحد: إيّاه أطلب فعرّفني بذلك الطريق حتّى أسلك فيه. وقال الآخر: لا فرْق بيني وبينك فأريد أن أستنبط الطريق إلى معرفته من ذاتي ولا أقلّدك في ذلك. فإن كنتَ أنت حصل لك ما أنت عليه وما جئت به بالنظر الذي خطر لي، فلماذا أكون ناقص الهمّة وأقلّدك؟ وإن كان حصل لك باختصاص منه

كما خصّنا بالوجود بعد أن لم نكن، فدعوى بلا برهان. فلم يلتفت إلى قوله وأخذ يفكّر وينظر بعقله في ذلك.

فهذا بمنزلة من أخذ العِلم بالأدلّة العقليّة من النظر الفكريّ، ومثال الثاني مثال أتْبَاع الرسول ومقلّديه فيما أخبر به من العلم بصانعهم. ومثال ذلك الشخص الذي اختلَفَ في اتّباعه هذان الشخصان مثال الرسول المعلِّم. فشرع هذا المعلِّم يبيّن الطريق الموصل إلى درجة الكمال والسعادة على ما اقتضاه نظر الشخص الواحد من الشخصين اللذين نظرا في شأن هذا المعلِّم وهو الذي لم يتّبعه. ولكن ما وقعت الموافقة معه إلّا في بعض ما يقتضيه الأمر الطبيعيّ من مخالفة الطبع. ولا كلّ مخالفة الطبع إلّا بوزن خاصٍّ ومقدار معيّن. وبهذا سمّي كيمياء لدخول التقدير والوزن.

فلمّا رأى ذلك هذا الشخص فرح بذلك حيث استقلّ به دون تقليده. ورأى أنّ له شفوفا على صاحبه الذي قلّده، فاغترّ به. وأمّا المقلِّد فبقي على ما كان عليه من تقليد المعلِّم. وزاد غير المقلِّد وهو ذلك الشخص بما رأى من الموافقة زهدًا في تقليد هذا الشخص وانفرادا بنظره من أجل هذه الموافقة.

فسلك الرجلان أو الشخصان إن كانا امرأتين أو أحدهما امرأة في الطريق، الواحد بحكم النظر والآخر بحكم التقليد. وأخذا في الرياضة وهو تهذيب الأخلاق، والمجاهدة وهي المشاقّ البدنيّة من الجوع، والعبادات العمليّة البدنيّة كالقيام الطويل في الصلاة والدؤوب عليها والصيام والحجّ والجهاد والسياحة. هذا بنظره وهذا بما شرع له أستاذه ومعلّمه،

المسمّى شارعا. فلمّا فرغا من حكم أسْر الطبيعة العنصريّة وما بقي واحد منهما يأخذ من حكم الطبيعة العنصريّة إلّا الضروريّ الذي يحفظ به وجود هذا الجسم، الذي بوجوده واعتداله وبقائه يحصل لهذه النفس الجزئيّة مطلوبُها من العلم بالله الذي استخلفها خاصّة.

فإذا خرجا عن حكم الشهوات الطبيعيّة العنصريّة وفتح لهما باب السماء الدنيا، تلقّى المقلّدَ آدمُ، عليه السلام، ففرح به وأنزله إلى جانبه. وتلقّى صاحب النظر المستقلِّ روحانيّة القمر، فأنزله عنده.

ثمّ إنّ صاحب النظر الذي هو نزيل القمر في خدمة آدم، عليه السلام، وهو كالوزير له مأمورا من الحقّ بالتسخير له، ورأى جميع ما عنده من العلوم لا يتعدّى ما تحته من الأكر ولا علم له بما فوقه وأنّه مقصور الأثر على ما دونه. ورأى آدمَ أنّ عنده علْم ما دونه وعلم ما فوقه من الأمكنة وأنّه يُلقي إلى نزيله ممّا عنده ممّا ليس في وسع القمر أن يعرفه، وعلم أنّه ما أنزله عليه إلّا عناية ذلك المعلِّم الذي هو الرسول. فاغتمّ صاحب النظر وندم حيث لم يسلك على مدرجة ذلك الرسول، واعتقد الايمان به وأنّه إذا رجع من سفرته تلك أن يتّبع ذلك الرسول ويستأنف من أجله سفرا آخر.

ثمّ إنّ هذا التابع نزيل آدم علّمه أبوه من الأسماء الإلهيّة على قدر ما رأى أنّه يحمله مزاجه. فإنّ للنشأة الجسميّة العنصريّة أثرا في النفوس الجزئيّة، فما كلّها على مرتبة واحدة في القبول: فتقبل هذه ما لا تقبل غيرها. وفي أوّل سماء يقف

من علم آدم على الوجه الإلهيّ الخاصّ الذي لكلّ موجود سِوَى الله الذي يحجبه عن الوقوف مع سببه وعلّته. وصاحب النظر لا علم له بذلك الوجْه أصلاً. والعلم بذلك الوجْه هو العلم بالإكسير في الكيمياء الطبيعيّة فهذا هو إكسير العارفين. وما رأيت أحدا نبّه عليه غيْرة. ولولا أنّي مأمور بالنصيحة لهذه الأمّة، بل لعباد الله، ما ذكرته.

فعَلِم كلّ واحد منهما ما لهذا الفلك من الحكم الذي ولّاه الله به في هذه الأركان الأربعة والمولّدات وما أوحى الله في هذه السماء من الأمر المختصّ بها، في قوله: ﴿وَأَوْحَى فِي كُلِّ سَمَاءٍ أَمْرَهَا﴾ (فصّلت ١٢). وما علم صاحب النظر نزيل القمر من ذلك إلّا ما يختصّ بالتأثيرات البدنيّة والاستحالات في أعيان الأجسام المركّبة من الطبيعة العنصريّة. وحصّل التابع ما فيها من العلم الإلهيّ الحاصل للنفوس الجزئيّة ممّا هو لهذا الفلك خاصّة وما نسبة وجود الحقّ من ذلك وما له فيهم من الصور ومن أين صحّت الخلافة لهذه النشأة الإنسانيّة، ولا سيّما وآدم المنصوص عليه صاحب هذه السماء. فعَلم التابع صورة الاستخلاف في العلم الإلهيّ، وعلم صاحب النظر الاستخلاف العنصريّ في تدبير الأبدان وعلل الزيادة والربوّ والنموّ في الأجسام القابلة لذلك والنقص.

فكلّ ما حصل لصاحب النظر حصل للتابع، وما كلّ ما حصل للتابع حصل لصاحب النظر. فما يزداد صاحب النظر إلّا غمًّا على غمّ وما يصدِّق متى ينقضي سفره ويرجع إلى بدنه. فإنّهم في هذا السفر مثل النائم فيما يرى في نومه

وهو يعرف أنّه في النوم. فلا يصدّق متى يستيقظ ليستأنف العمل ويستريح من غمّه. وإنّما يتقلّق خوفا ممّا حصل له في سفره أن يقبض فيه فلا يصحُّ له تَرَقٍّ بعد ذلك فهذا هو الذي يزعجه. والتابع ليس كذلك فإنّه يرى الترقّي يَصْحَبُه حيث كان من ذلك الوجْهِ الخاصّ الذي لا يعرفه إلّا صاحب هذا الوجه.

فإذا أقاما في هذه السماء ما شاء الله وأخذا في الرحلة وودع كلّ واحد منهما نزيله وارتقيا في معراج الأرواح إلى السماء الثانية. وفي هذه السماء الأولى هو النائب السابع الإلهيّ الموكّل بالنطفة الكائنة في الأرحام التي تظهر فيها هذه النشأة الإنسانيّة؛ وهو يتوكّل بها في الشهر السابع من سقوط النطفة، والطفل في هذا الشهر الجنين يزيد وينمو في بطن أُمّه بزيادة القمر ويذبل وتقلّ حركته في بطن أُمّه في نقص القمر وذلك هو العلامة. فإن وُلد في هذا الشهر لم يكن في القوّة مثلَ الذي يولد في الشهر السادس.

فإذا قرعا السماء الثانية وفُتحت لهما صعدا. فنزل التابع عند عيسى، عليه السلام، وعنده يحيى ابن خالته ونزل صاحب النظر عند الكاتب. فلمّا أنزله الكاتب عنده وأكرم مثواه اعتذر إليه وقال له: لا تستبطئني فإنّي في خدمة عيسى ويحيى عليهما السلام. وقد نزل بهما صاحبك فلا بدّ لي من الوقوف عندهما حتّى أرى ما يأمراني به في حقّ نزيلهما. فإذا فرغتُ من شأنه رجعت إليك. فيزيد صاحب النظر غمّا إلى غمّه وندامة حيث لم يسلك مسلك صاحبه ولا ذهب في مذهبه.

فأقام التابع عند ابني الخالة ما شاء الله. فأوقفاه على صحّة رسالة المعلِّم رسول الله، صلّى الله عليه وسلّم، بدلالة إعجاز القرآن، فإنّها حضرة الخطابة والأوزان وحسن مواقع الكلام وامتزاج الأمور وظهور المعنى الواحد في الصور الكثيرة. ويحصل له الفرقان في مرتبة خرق العوائد. ومِن هذه الحضرة يعلم علم السيمياء الموقوفة على العمل بالحروف والأسماء لا على البخورات والدماء وغيرها. ويعرف شرف الكلمات وجوامع الكلم وحقيقة 'كن' واختصاصها بكلمة الأمر لا بكلمة الماضي ولا المستقبل ولا الحال وظهور الحرفين من هذه الكلمة مع كونها مركّبة من ثلاثة، ولماذا حُذِفت الكلمة الثالثة المتوسّطة البرزخيّة التي بين حرف الكاف وحرف النون، وهي حرف الواو الروحانيّة التي تعطي ما للملَكِ في نشأة المُكوّن من الأثر مع ذهاب عيْنِها.

ويعلَمَ سرّ التكوين من هذه السماء وكون عيسى يحيي الموتَى وإنشاءِ صورة الطير ونفخه في صورته وتكوين الطائر طائرا. هل هو بإذن الله؟ أو تصوير عيسى خلق الطير ونفخَه فيه هو بإذن الله؟ وبأيّ فعل من الأفعال اللفظيّة يتعلّق قوله: ﴿بِإِذْنِي﴾ (المائدة ١١٠) و﴿بِإِذْنِ اللهِ﴾ (آل عمران ٤٩)؟ هل العامل فيه: ﴿يَكُونُ﴾ (آل عمران ٤٩) أو ﴿تَنْفُخُ﴾ (المائدة ١١٠)؟. فعند أهل الله العامل فيه: ﴿يَكُونُ﴾ وعند مثبتي الأسباب وأصحاب الأحوال العامل فيه: ﴿تَنْفُخُ﴾. فيحصل لمن دخل هذه السماء واجتمع بعيسى ويحيى، عِلْمُ ذلك ولا بدّ. ولا يحصل ذلك لصاحب النظر وأعني حصول ذوق.

وعيسى روح الله ويحيى له الحياة. فكما أنّ الروح والحياة لا يفترقان، كذلك هذان النبيّان عيسى ويحيى لا يفترقان لما يحملانه من هذا السرّ. فإنّ لعيسى من علم الكيمياء الطريقين: الإنشاء وهو خلقه الطائر من الطين والنفخ، فظهر عنه الصورة باليدين والطيران بالنفخ الذي هو النفَس. فهذه طريقة الإنشاء في علم الكيمياء الذي قدّمناه في أوّل الباب.

والطريق الثانية إزالة العلل الطارئة وهو في عيسى إبراء الأكمه والأبرص وهي العلل التي طرأت عليهما في الرحم الذي هو بوطيقى التكوين.

فمن هنا يحصل لهذا التابع علم المقدار والميزان الطبيعيّ والروحانيّ لجمع عيسى بين الأمرين. ومن هذه السماء يحصل لنفس هذا التابع الحياة العلميّة التي تحيا بها القلوب كقوله ﴿أَوَ مَنْ كَانَ مَيْتًا فَأَحْيَيْنَاهُ﴾ (الأنعام ١٢٢) وهي حضرة جامعة فيها من كلّ شيء وفيها الملك الموكّل بالنطفة في الشهر السادس. ومن هذه الحضرة يكون الإمداد للخطباء والكتّاب لا للشعراء. ولمّا كان لمحمّد، صلّى الله عليه وسلّم، جوامع الكلم خوطب من هذه الحضرة. وقيل: ﴿مَا عَلَّمْنَاهُ الشِّعْرَ﴾ (يس ٦٩) لأنّه أرسِل مبيّنا مفصّلا. والشعر من الشعور فمحلّه الإجمال لا التفصيل وهو خلاف البيان.

ومن هنا تُعلم تقليبات الأمور ومن هنا توهب الأحوال لأصحابها. وكلّ ما ظهر في العالم العنصريّ من النيرنجيّات الأسمائيّة فمن هذه السماء. وأمّا الفلقطيرات فمن غير هذه الحضرة ولكن إذا وُجدت فأرواحها من هذه السماء لا أعيان

صورها الحاملة لأرواحها. فإذا حصل علم هذه الكائنات وسرعة الإحياء فيها من شأنه أن لا يقبل ذلك إلّا في الزمان الطويل، فإنّ ذلك من علم عيسى لا من الأمر الموحَى به في ذلك الفَلَك ولا في سباحة كوكبه. وهو من الوجه الخاصّ الإلهيّ الخارج عن الطريق المعتادة في العلم الطبيعيّ الذي يقتضي الترتيب النسبيّ الموضوع بالترتيب الخاصّ.

وهذه مسألة يغمض دركها. فإنّ العالم المحقّق يقول بالسبب فإنّه لا بدّ مِنه ولكن لا يقول بهذا الترتيب الخاصّ في الأسباب. فعامّة هذا العلم إمّا ينفون الكلّ وإمّا يثبتون الكلّ، ولم أر منهم من يقول ببقاء السبب مع نفي ترتيبه الزمانيّ. فإنّه علم عزيز يُعلم من هذه السماء. فما يكون عن سبب في مدّة طويلة يكون عن ذلك السبب في لمح البصر أو هو أقرب. وقد ظهر ذلك فيما نقل في تكوين عيسى، عليه السلام، وفي تكوين خلْق عيسى الطائر وفي إحياء الميّت من قبره قبل أن يأتي المخاض الأرضَ في إبراز هذه المولّدات ليوم القيامة، وهو يوم ولادتها. فألْق بالَك وأشحذ فؤادك عسى أن يهديك ربّك سواء السبيل. ومن هذه السماء قوله في ناشئة الليل: إنّها ﴿أَقْوَمُ قِيلًا﴾ (المزمّل ٦).

فإذا حصّل التَابع هذه العلوم وانصرف الكاتب إلى نزيله وردّ النظر إليه، أعطاه من العلم المودع في مجراه ما يعطيه استِعداده ممّا له من الحكم في الأجسام التي تحته في العالم العنصريّ لا من أرواحه. فإذا كمل فذلك قِرَاهُ يطلب الرحيل عنه فجاء إلى صاحبه التابع.

وخرجا يطلبان السماء الثالثة وصاحبُ النظر بين يدي التابع مثل الخادم بين يدي مخدومه، وقد عرف قدره ورتبة معلِّمه وما أعطاه من العناية اتّباعُه لذلك المعلِّم.

فلمّا قرعا السماء الثالثة فتحت فصعدا فيها. فتلقّى التابعَ يوسفُ، عليه السلام، وتلقّى صاحب النظر كوكب الزهرة فأنزلتْه وذكرتْ له ما ذكره من تقدّم من كواكب التسخير فزاده ذلك غمّا إلى غمّه.

فجاء كوكب الزهرة إلى يوسف، عليه السلام، وعنده نزيله وهو التابع، وهو يلقي إليه بما خصّه الله به من العلوم المتعلّقة بصور التمثّل والخيال، فإنّه كان من الأئمّة في علم التعبير. فأحضر الله بين يديه الأرض التي خلقها الله من بقيّة طينة آدم، عليه السلام، وأحضر له سوق الجنّة، وأحضر له أجساد الأرواح النوريّة والناريّة والمعاني العلويّة. وعرّفه بموازينها ومقاديرها ونِسَبها ونَسَبها. فأراه السنين في صور البقر وأراه خصبَها في سِمانها، وأراه جدبها في عجافها. وأراه العلم في صورة اللبن وأراه الثبات في الدين في صورة القيد. وما زال يعلّمه تجسّد المعاني والنِّسب في صورة الحسّ والمحسوس. وعرّفه معنى التأويل في ذلك كلّه فإنّها سماء التصوير التامّ والنظام.

ومن هذه السماء يكون الإمداد للشعراء والنظْم والإتقان والصور الهندسيّة في الأجسام وتصويرها في النفس من السماء التي ارتقى عنها. ومن هذه السماء يعلم معنى الإتقان والإحكام والحسن الذي يتضمّن بوجوده الحكمة والحسن الغرضيّ الملائم لمزاج خاصّ.

وفي هذه السماء هو النائب الخامس الذي يتلقّى تدبير النطفة في الرحم في الشهر الخامس. ومن الأمر الموحي من الله في هذه السماء حصل ترتيب الأركان التي تحت مقعّر فَلَك القمر، فجعل ركن الهواء بين النار والماء وجعل ركن الماء بين الهواء والتراب. ولولا هذا الترتيب ما صحّ وجود الاستحالة فيهنّ ولا كان منهنّ ما كان من المولّدات ولا ظهر في المولّدات ما ظهر من الاستحالات. فأين النطفة من كونها استحالت لحما ودما وعظامًا وعروقا وأعصابا؟

ومن هذه السماء رتّب الله في هذه النشأة الجسميّة الأخلاط الأربعة على النظم الأحسن والإتقان الأبدع. فجعل ممّا يلي نظر النفس المدبّرة المرّة الصفراء ثمّ يليها الدم ثمّ يلي الدم البلغم ثمّ يلي البلغم المرّة السوداء وهو طبع الموت. ولولا هذا الترتيب العجيب في هذه الأخلاط (لما حصلت) المساعدة للطبيب فيما يرومه من إزالة ما يطرأ على هذا الجسد من العِلل أو فيما يرومه من حفظ الصحّة عليه.

ومن هذه السماء ظهرت الأربعة الأصول التي يقوم عليها بيت الشعر كما قام الجسد على الأربعة الأخلاط. وهم السببان والوتدان: السبب الخفيف والسبب الثقيل، والوتد المفروق والوتد المجموع. فالوتد المفروق يعطي التحليل والوتد المجموع يعطي التركيب، والسبب الخفيف يعطي الروح والسبب الثقيل يعطي الجسم. وبالمجموع يكون الإنسان فانظر ما أتقن وجود هذا العالم كبيره وصغيره.

فإذا حصّلا هذه العلوم هذان الشخصان وزاد التابع على الناظر بما أعطاه الوجه الخاصّ من العلم الإلهيّ، كما اتّفق في كلّ سماء لهما، انتقلا يطلبان السماء الوسطى التي هي قلب السماوات كلّها.

فلمّا دخلاها تلّقى التابعَ إدريسُ، عليه السلام، وتلقّى صاحبَ النظر كوكبُ الشمس. فجرى لصاحب النظر معه مثل ما تقدّم فزاد غمّا إلى غمّه. فلمّا نزل التابع بحضرة إدريس، عليه السلام، علم تقليب الأمور الإلهيّة ووقف على معنى قوله، عليه السلام: {القلب بين إصبعين من أصابع الرحمن}، وبماذا يقلّباه. ورأى في هذه السماء غشيان الليل النهار والنهار الليل، وكيف يكون كلّ واحد منهما لصاحبه ذَكَرا وقتا وأنثى وقتا، وسرّ النكاح والالتحام بينهما، وما يتولّد فيهما من المولّدات بالليل والنهار، والفرق بين أولاد الليل وأولاد النهار. فكلّ واحد منهما أبٌ لما يولد في نقيضه وأمّ لما يولد فيه.

ويعلم من هذه السماء علم الغيب والشهادة وعلم الستر والتجلّي وعلم الحياة والموت واللباس والسكن والمودّة والرحمة، وما يظهر من الوجه الخاصّ من الاسم الظاهر في المظاهر الباطنة، ومن الاسم الباطن في الظاهر من حكم استعداد المظاهر. فتختلف على الظاهر الأسماء لاختلاف الأعيان.

ثمّ رحلا يطلبان السماء الخامسة. فنزَل التابع بهرون، عليه السلام، ونزل صاحبُ النظر بالأحمر. فاعتذر الأحمر

لصاحبه ونزيله في تخلّفه عنه مدّة اشتغاله بخدمة هرون، عليه السلام، من أجل نزيله. فَلمّا دخل الأحمر على هرون وجد عنده نزيلَه وهو يباسطه. فتعجّب الأحمر من مباسطته فسأل عن ذلك. فقال: إنّها سماء الهيبة والخوف والشدّة والبأس وهي نعوت توجب القبض. وهذا ضيفٌ ورد من أتباع الرسول تجب كرامته. وقد ورَد يبتغي عِلْمًا ويلتمس حكما إلهِيّا يستعين به على أعداء خواطره خوفًا من تعدّي حدود سيّده فيما رسم له. فأكْشِفُ له عن محيّاها وأباسِطه حتّى يكون قبوله لما التمسه على بَسْط نفْسٍ بروح قُدسٍ.

ثمّ ردّ وجهه إليه وقال له: هذه سماء خلافة البشر فضعف حكم إمامها وقد كان أصلها قويّ المباني، فأُمر باللين بالجبابرة الطغاة. فقيل لنا: ﴿قُولَا لَهُ قَوْلًا لَيِّنًا﴾ (طه ٤٤) وما يؤمَر بلين المقال إلّا مَن قوّته أعظم من قوّة من أرْسِل إليه وبطشه أشدّ.

لكنّه لمّا علّم الحقّ أنّه قد طبع على كلّ قلب مُظْهِر للجبروت والكبرياء، وأنّه في نفسه أذلّ الأذلّاءِ، أُمِرَا أن يعاملاه بالرحمة واللين لمناسبة باطنِه واستنزال ظاهره من جبروته وكبريائه ﴿لَعَلَّهُ يَتَذَكَّرُ أَوْ يَخْشَى﴾ (طه ٤٤). و'لعلّ' و'عسى' من الله واجبتان. فيتذكّر بما نقابله به من اللين والمسكنة ما هو عليه في باطنه، ليكون الظاهر والباطن على السواء.

فما زالت تلك الخميرة معه تعمل في باطنه مع الترجّي الإلهيّ الواجب وقوع المترجَّى. ويتقوّى حكمُها إلى حين

انقطاع يأسه من أتباعِه وحال الغرق بينه وبين أطماعِه، لجأ إلى ما كان مستترًا في باطنه من الذلّة والافتقار، ليتحقّق عند المؤمنين وقوع الرجاءِ الإلهيّ. فقال: ﴿آمَنْتُ أَنَّهُ لَا إِلَهَ إِلَّا الَّذِي آمَنَتْ بِهِ بَنُو إِسْرَائِيلَ وَأَنَا مِنَ الْمُسْلِمِينَ﴾ (يونس ٩٠). فأظهر حالة باطنه وما كان في قلبه من العلم الصحيح بالله. وجاء بقوله: ﴿الَّذِي آمَنَتْ بِهِ بَنُو إِسْرَائِيلَ﴾ لرفع الإشكال عند الأشكال كما قالت السحرة لمّا آمنت: ﴿آمَنَّا بِرَبِّ الْعَالَمِينَ. رَبِّ مُوسَى وَهَارُونَ﴾ (الأعراف ١٢١، ١٢٢) أي الذي يدعوان إليه. فجاءت بذلك لرفع الارتياب. وقوله: ﴿وَأَنَا مِنَ الْمُسْلِمِينَ﴾ خطاب منه للحقّ لعلمه أنّه تعالى يسمعه ويراه. فخاطبه الحقّ بلسان العتب وأسمعه: ﴿آلْآنَ﴾ أظهرتَ ما قد كنتَ تعلمه ﴿وَقَدْ عَصَيْتَ قَبْلُ وَكُنْتَ مِنَ الْمُفْسِدِينَ﴾ (يونس ٩١) في أتباعك. وما قال له: "وأنت من المفسدين". فهي كلمة بشرى له عرّفنا بها لنرجو رحمته مع إسرافنا وإجْرامنا.

ثمّ قال: ﴿فَالْيَوْمَ نُنَجِّيكَ﴾ فبشّره قبل قبض روحه ﴿ بِبَدَنِكَ لِتَكُونَ لِمَنْ خَلْفَكَ آيَةً﴾ (يونس ٩٢) يعني لتكون النجاة لمن يأتي بعدك ﴿آيَةً﴾ علامة، إذا قال ما قلتَه تكون له النجاة مثل ما كانت لك. وما في الآية أنّ بأس الآخرة لا يرتفع ولا أنّ إيمانه لم يُقبل. وإنّما في الآية أن بأس الدنيا لا يرتفع عمّن نزل به إذا آمن في حال رؤيته إلّا قوم يونس. فقوله: ﴿فَالْيَوْمَ نُنَجِّيكَ بِبَدَنِكَ﴾ إذ العذاب لا يتعلّق إلّا بظاهرك وقد أرَيْتُ الخلق نجاته من العذاب. فكان ابتداء الغرق عذابا فصار الموت فيه شَهادة خالصة بريئة لم تتخلّلها معصيةٌ،

فقبضت على أفضل عمل وهو التلفّظ بالإيمان. كلّ ذلك حتّى لا يقنط أحد من رحمة الله. والأعمال بالخواتم. فلم يزل الإيمان بالله يجول في باطنه وقد حال الطابع الإلهيّ الذاتيّ في الخلق بين الكبرياء واللطائف الإنسانيّة، فلم يدخلها قطّ كبرياء.

وأمّا قوله: ﴿فَلَمْ يَكُ يَنْفَعُهُمْ إِيمَانُهُمْ لَمَّا رَأَوْا بَأْسَنَا﴾ (غافر ٨٥) فكلام محقّق في غاية الوضوح، فإنّ النافع هو الله فما نفعهم إلّا الله. وقوله: ﴿سُنَّتَ اللَّهِ الَّتِي قَدْ خَلَتْ فِي عِبَادِهِ﴾ يعني الإيمان عند رؤية البأس الغير المعتاد.

وقد قال: ﴿وَلِلَّهِ يَسْجُدُ مَنْ فِي السَّمَاوَاتِ وَالْأَرْضِ طَوْعًا وَكَرْهًا﴾ (الرعد ١٥) فغاية هذا الإيمان أن يكون كرها وقد أضافه الحقّ إليه سبحانه. والكراهة محلّها القلب والإيمان محلّه القلب. والله لا يأخذ العبد بالأعمال الشاقّة عليه من حيث ما يجده من المشقّة فيها، بل يضاعف له فيها الأجر.

وأمّا في هذا الموطن فالمشقّة منه بعيدة، بل جاء طوعًا في إيمانه وما عاش بعد ذلك. كما قال في راكب البحر عند ارتجاجه: ﴿ضَلَّ مَنْ تَدْعُونَ إِلَّا إِيَّاهُ﴾ (الإسراء ٦٧) فنجّاهم.

فلو قبضهم عند نجاتهم لماتوا موحّدين وقد حصلت لهم النجاة. فقبض فرعون ولم يؤخّر في أجله في حال إيمانه لئلّا يرجع إلى ما كان عليه من الدعوى.

ثمّ قوله تعالى في تتميم قصّته هذه: ﴿وَإِنَّ كَثِيرًا مِنَ النَّاسِ عَنْ آيَاتِنَا لَغَافِلُونَ﴾ (يونس ٩٢). وقد أظهرت نجاتك آية

أي علامة على حصول النجاة، فغفل أكثر الناس عن هذه الآية وقضوا على المؤمن بالشقاء. وأمّا قوله: ﴿فَأَوْرَدَهُمُ النَّارَ﴾ (هود ٩٨) فما فيه نَصٌّ أنّه يدخلها معهم. بل قال الله: ﴿أَدْخِلُوا آلَ فِرْعَوْنَ﴾ (غافر ٤٦) ولم يقل: "أدخلوا فرعون وآله".

ورحمة الله أوسع من حيث أن لا يقبل إيمان المضطرّ. وأيّ اضطرار أعظم من اضطرار فرعون في حال الغرق؟ والله يقول: ﴿أَمَّنْ يُجِيبُ الْمُضْطَرَّ إِذَا دَعَاهُ وَيَكْشِفُ السُّوءَ﴾ (النمل ٦٢) فقرن للمضطرّ إذا دعاه الإجابة وكشف السوء عنْه. وهذا آمَنَ لله خالصا وما دعاه في البقاء في الحياة الدنيا خوفا من العوارض أو يحال بينه وبين هذا الإخلاص الذي جاءه في هذه الحال. فرجّح جانب لقاء الله على البقاء بالتلفّظ بالإيمان، وجعل ذلك الغرق ﴿نَكَالَ الْآخِرَةَ وَالْأُولَى﴾ (النازعات ٢٥). فلم يكن عذابه أكثر من غمّ الماء الأجاج وقبضه على أحسن صفة. هذا يعطي ظاهر اللفظ، وهذا معنى قوله: ﴿إِنَّ فِي ذَلِكَ لَعِبْرَةً لِمَنْ يَخْشَى﴾ (النازعات ٢٦) يعني في أخذه ﴿نَكَالَ الْآخِرَةَ وَالْأُولَى﴾ وقدّم ذِكْر الآخرة وأخّر الأُولَى ليعلم أن ذلك العذاب، أعني عذاب الغرق، هو نكال الآخرة فلذلك قدّمها في الذِّكْر على الأولى. وهذا هو الفضل العظيم.

فانظر يا وليّ ما أثّرت مخاطبة اللين وكيف أثمرت هذه الثمرة. فعليك أيّها التابع باللين في الأمور، فإنّ النفوس الأبيّة تنقاد بالاستمالة.

ثمّ أمره بالرفق بصاحبه، صاحب النظر. وكان سبب هذا الأمر من هرون لأنّه حصل له هذا ذوقا من نفسه حين أخذ

موسى برأسه يجرّه إليه. فأذاقه الذلّ بأخذ اللحية والناصية. فناداه بأشفق الأبوين فقال: ﴿يَبْنَؤُمَّ لَا تَأْخُذْ بِلِحْيَتِي وَلَا بِرَأْسِي﴾ (طه ٩٤) و﴿لَا تُشْمِتْ بِيَ الْأَعْدَاءَ﴾ (الأعراف ١٥٠) لمّا ظهر عليه أخوه موسَى بصفة القهر. فلمّا كان لهرون ذلّة الخلق ذوقا مع براءته مِمّا أذِلّ فيه، تضاعفت المذلّة عنده، فناداه بالرحم. فهذا سبب وصيّته لهذا التابع.

ولو لم يُلق موسى الألواح ما أخذ برأس أخيه، فإنّ في نسختها الهدى والرحمة تذكرة لموسى. فكان يرحم أخاه بالرحمة، وتتبيّن مسألته مع قومِهِ بالهدى. فلمّا سكت عنه الغضب أخذ الألواح، فما وقعت عينه ممّا كتب فيها إلّا على الهدى والرحمة. فقال: ﴿رَبِّ اغْفِرْ لِي وَلِأَخِي وَأَدْخِلْنَا فِي رَحْمَتِكَ وَأَنْتَ أَرْحَمُ الرَّاحِمِينَ﴾ (الأعراف ١٥١).

ثمّ أمره أن يجعل ما تقتضيه سماؤه من سَفْكِ الدماء في القرابين والأضاحي ليلحق الحيوان بدرجة الأناسي، إذ كان لها الكمال في الأمانة. ثمّ خرج من عنده بخلعة نزيله وأخذ بيد صاحبه، وقد أفاده ما كان في قوّته من المعارف بما يقتضيه حكمه في الدور لا غير.

وانصرفا يطلبان السماء السادسة فتلقّاه موسى، عليه السلام، ومعه وزيره البرجيس. فلم يعرف صاحب النظر موسى، عليه السلام، فأخذه البرجيس فأنزله. ونزل التابع عند موسى، فأفاده اثني عشر ألف علمٍ من العِلم الإلهيّ سِوَى ما أفاده من علوم الدور والكور. وأعلمه أنّ التجلّي الإلهيّ إنّما يقع في صور الاعتقادات وفي الحاجات فتحفّظ. ثمّ ذكر له طلبه النار

لأهله فما تجلّى له إلّا فيها إذ كانت عين حاجته، فلا يُرى إلّا في الافتقار. وكلّ طالب فهو فقير إلى مطلوبه ضرورة.

وأعلمَه في هذه السماء خلع الصور من الجوهر وإلباسه صورا غيرها، ليعلمه أن الأعيان أعيان الصور لا تنقلب. فإنّه يؤدّي إلى انقلاب الحقائق. وإنّما الإدراكات تتعلّق بالمدركات تلك المدركات لها صحيحة، لا شكّ فيها. فيتخيّل من لا علم له بالحقائق أن الأعيان انقلبت وما انقلبت. ومن هنا يعلم تجلّي الحقّ في القيامة في صورة يتعوّذ أهل الموقف منها وينزّهوا الحقّ عنها ويستعيذون بالله منها. وهو الحقّ ما هو غيره. وذلك في أبصارهم فإنّ الحقّ منزّه عن قيام التغيير به والتبديل.

قال عُلَيْم الأسود لرجل: وقف. فضرب بيده عليم إلى أسطوانة في الحرم فرآها الرجل ذهبا. ثمّ قال له: يا هذا إنّ الأعيان لا تنقلب ولكن هكذا تراه لحقيقتك بربّك، يشير إلى تجلّي الحقّ يوم القيامة وتحوّله في عين الرائي.

ومن هذه السماء يعلم العلم الغريب الذي لا يعلمه قليل من الناس، فأحْرَى أن لا يعلمه الكثير. وهو معنى قوله تعالى لموسى، عليه السلام، وما علِم أحد ما أراد الله إلّا موسى ومن اختصّه الله: ﴿وَمَا تِلْكَ بِيَمِينِكَ يَا مُوسَى. قَالَ هِيَ عَصَايَ﴾ (طه ١٧، ١٨). والسؤال عن الضروريّات ما يكون من العالِم بذلك إلّا لمعنى غامض. ثمّ قال في تحقيق كونها عصا: ﴿أَتَوَكَّأُ عَلَيْهَا وَأَهُشُّ بِهَا عَلَى غَنَمِي وَلِيَ فِيهَا مَآرِبُ أُخْرَى﴾ (طه ١٨) كلّ ذلك من كونها عصا. أرأيتم أنّه أعلم الحقّ

تعالى بما ليس معلوما عند الحقّ؟ وهذا جواب علم ضروريّ عن سؤال عن معلوم مدرَك بالضرورة. فقال له: ﴿أَلْقِهَا﴾ (طه ١٩) يعني عن يدك مع تحقّقك أنّها عصا. ﴿فَأَلْقَاهَا﴾ موسى ﴿فَإِذَا هِيَ﴾ يعني تلك العصا ﴿حَيَّةٌ تَسْعَى﴾ (طه ٢٠). فلمّا خلع الله على العصا أعني جوهرها صورة الحيّة، استلزمها حكم الحيّة وهو السعي، حتّى يتبيّن لموسى، عليه السلام، بسعيها أنّها حيّة. ولولا خوفه منها خوف الإنسان من الحيّات لقلنا إنّ الله أوجد في العصا الحياة، فصارت حيّة من الحياة فسعت لحياتها على بطنها إذ لم يكن لها رجل تسعى به. فصورتها لشكلها عصا صورة الحيّات.

فلمّا خاف منها للصورة قال له الحقّ: ﴿خُذْهَا وَلَا تَخَفْ﴾، وهذا هو خوف الفُجْأة إذ كان. ثمّ قال له: ﴿سَنُعِيدُهَا﴾ الضمير يعود على العصا ﴿سِيرَتَهَا الْأُولَى﴾ (طه ٢١).

فجواهِرُ الأشياء متَماثلة وتختلف بالصوَر والأعراض، والجوهر واحدٌ. أي ترجع عصا مثل ما كانت في ذاتها وفي رأي عينك، كما كانت حيّة في ذاتها وفي رأي عيْنِك، ليعلم موسى من يرى وما يرى وبمن يَرى. وهذا تنبيه إلهيّ له ولنا. وهو الذي قاله علَيم سواء، من أنّ الأعيان لا تنقلب. فالعصا لا تكون حيّة ولا الحيّة عصا، ولكن الجوهر القابل صورة العصا قَبل صورة الحيّة. فهي صور يخلعها الحقّ القادر الخالق عن الجوهر إذا شاء ويخلع عليه صورة أخرى.

فإن كنت فطِنا فقد نبّهتُك على علم ما تراه من صور الموجودات. وتقول: هو ضروريّ، من كونك لا تقدر على

إنكاره، وقد بان لك أن الاستِحالات محال. ولله أعين في بعض عباده يدركون بها العصا حيّة في حال كونها عصا، وهو إدراك إلهيّ وفينا خياليٌّ. وهكذا في جميع الموجودات سواء.

انظر لولا قوّة الحسّ ما قلتَ هذا جماد لا يحسّ ولا ينطق وما به من حياة، وهذا نبات، وهذا حيوان يحسّ ويدرِك، وهذا إنسان يعقل. هذا كلّه أعطاه نظرك. ويأتي شخص آخر يقف معك فيرى ويسمع تسليم الجمادات والنبات والحيوان عليْه. وكلّا الأمرين صحيح. وبالقوّة التي تستدلّ بها على إنكار ما قاله هذا بها بعينها يستدلّ هذا الآخر. فكلّ واحد من الشخصين دليله عين دليل الآخر، والحكم مختلف. فوالله ما زالت حيّة عَصا موسَى وما زالت عصا! كلّ ذلك في نفس الأمر، لم تُخْطِ رؤية كلّ واحد ما هو الأمر عليه في نفسه.

وقد رأينا ذلك وتحقّقناه رؤية عيْن، فهو الأوّل والآخر من عين واحدة. وهو في التجلّي الأوّل لا غيره، وهو في التجلّي الآخر لا غيره. فقل 'إله' وقل 'عالَم'، وقل 'أنا' وقل 'أنت' وقل 'هو'، والكلّ في حضرة الضمائر ما برح وما زال. فزيد يقول في حقّك 'هو'، وعمرو يقول عنك 'أنت'، وأنت تقول عنك 'أنا'. فـ 'أنا' عينُ 'أنت' وعينُ 'هو'. وما هو 'أنا' عين 'أنت' ولا عين 'هو'! فاختلفت النِّسب. وهنا بحور طامية لا قعر لها ولا ساحل. وعزّةِ ربّي، لو عرفتم ما فُهْتُ به في هذه الشذور لطربتم طربَ الأبد ولخفتم الخوف الذي لا يكون معه أمْنٌ لأحد. تدكْدك الجبل عينُ ثباته، وإفاقة موسى عينُ صعْقته.

انْظُرْ إِلَى وَجْهِهِ فِي كُلِّ حَادِثَةٍ مِنَ الْكِيَانِ وَلَا تُعْلِمْ بِهِ أَحَدَا

أيّها التابع المحمّديّ، لا تغفل عمّا نبّهتك عليه ولا تبرح في كلّ صورة ناظرا إليه. فإنّ المجلى أجلى. ثمّ أخذ بيده البرجيس وجاء به إلى صاحب النظر، فعرّفه ببعض ما يليق به ممّا علمه التابع من علم موسى بما يختصّ من تأثيرات الحركات الفلكيّة في النشآت العنصريّة. لا غير. فارتحلا من عنده، المحمّديّ على رفرف العناية وصاحب النظر على براق الفكر.

ففتح لهما السماء السابعة وهي الأولى من هناك على الحقيقة. فتلقّاه إبراهيم الخليل، عليه السلام، وتلقّى صاحب النظر كوكب كيوان. فأنزله في بيتٍ مظلم قَفْر موحشٍ وقال له: هذا بيت أخيك، يعني نفسه، فكن به حتّى آتِيَك فإنّي في خدمة هذا التابع المحمّديّ من أجل مَن نزل عليه، وهو خليل الله.

فجاء إليه، فوجده مسندا ظهره إلى البيت المعمور والتابع جالس بين يديه جلوس الابن بين يدي أبيه، وهو يقول له: نِعم الولد البارّ. فسأله التابع عن الثلاثة الأنوار فقال: هي حجّتي على قومي آتانيها الله عناية منه بي، لم أقُلْها أشراكا، لكن جعلتُها حبالةَ صائد أصيد بها ما شرد من عقول قومي. ثمّ قال له: أيّها التابع ميّز المراتب واعرِف المذاهب. وكن على بيّنة من ربّك في أمرك، ولا تهمل حديثك فإنّك غير مهمَل ولا متروك سُدى. اجعل قلبك مثل هذا البيت المعمور بحضورك مع الحقّ في كلّ حال. واعلم أنّه ما وسع الحقّ شيء ممّا رأيت سِوى قلب المؤمن وهو أنت.

فعندما سمع صاحب النظر هذا الخطاب، قال: ﴿يَا حَسْرَتَا عَلَى مَا فَرَّطْتُ فِي جَنْبِ اللهِ وَإِنْ كُنْتُ لَمِنَ السَّاخِرِينَ﴾ (الزمر ٥٦). وعلم ما فاته من الإيمان بذلك الرسول واتّباع سنَنِه ويقول: يا ليتني لم أتّخذ عقلي دليلا ولا سلكت معه إلى الفكر سبيلا.

وكلّ واحد من هذين الشخصين يدرك ما تعطيه الروحانيّات العلى وما يسبّح به الملأ الأعلى، بما عندهما من الطهارة وتخليص النفس من أسْر الطبيعة. وارتقم في ذات نفس كلّ واحد منهما كلّ ما في العالَم، فليس يخبر إلّا بما شاهده من نفسه في مرآة ذاته.

فحكاية الحكيم الذي أراد أن يُرِي هذا المقام للملِك، فاشتغل صاحب التصوير الحسن بنقش الصور على أبدع نظام وأحسن إتقان، واشتغل الحكيم بجلاء الحائط الذي يقابِل موضع الصُّوَر، وبينهما ستر معَلّقٌ مسدَل. فلمّا فرغ كلّ واحد من شغله وأحكم صنعته فيما ذهب إليه جاء الملك. فوقف على ما صوّره صاحب الصور، فرأى صورا بديعةً يبهر العقول حسن نظمها وبديع نقشها. ونظر إلى تلك الأصبغة في حسن تلك الصنعة، فرأى أمرًا هاله منظره.

ونظر إلى ما صنع الآخر من صقالة ذلك الوجه، فلم ير شيئا. فقال له: أيّها الملك صنعتي ألطف من صنعته وحكمتي أغمض من حكمته. ارفع الستر بيني وبينه حتّى ترى في الحالة الواحدة صِنعتي وصنعته. فرفع الستر. فانتقش في ذلك الجسم الصقيل جميع ما صوّره هذا الآخر بألطف صورة

ممّا هو ذلِك في نفسِه، فتعجّب الملِك. ثمّ إنّ الملك رأى صورة نفسه وصورة الصاقِل في ذلك الجسم فحار وتعجّب. وقال: كيف يكون هكذا؟ فقال: أيّها الملك ضربته لك مثلا لنفسك مع صور العالم. إذا أنت صقلتَ مرآة نفسك بالرياضات والمجاهدات حتّى تزكو وأزلتَ عنها صدأ الطبيعة وقابلتَ بمرآة ذاتك صور العالم انتقش فيها جميع ما في العالم كلّه.

وإلى هذا الحدّ ينتهي صاحب النظر وأتباع الرسل، وهذه الحضرة الجامعة لهما. ويزيد التابع على صاحب النظر بأمور لم تنتقش في العالَم جملة واحدة من حيث ذلك الوجه الخاصّ الذي لله في كلّ ممكن محدث ممّا لا ينحصر ولا ينضبط ولا يتصوّر، يمتاز به هذا التابع عن صاحب النظر.

ومن هذه السماء يكون الاستدراج الذي لا يُعلم والمكر الخفيّ الذي لا يُشْعَر به والكيد المتين والحجاب والثبات في الأمور والتأنّي فيها.

ومن هنا يعرف معنى قوله: ﴿لَخَلْقُ السَّمَاوَاتِ وَالْأَرْضِ أَكْبَرُ مِنْ خَلْقِ النَّاسِ﴾ (غافر ٥٧) لأنّ لهما في الناس درجة الأبوّة فلا يلحقهما أبدا. قال تعالى: ﴿أَنِ اشْكُرْ لِي وَلِوَالِدَيْكَ﴾ (لقمان ١٤).

ومن هذه السماء يعلم أن كلّ ما سوى الإنس والجانّ سعيد لا دخول له في الشقاء الأخرويّ، وأنّ الإنس والجانّ منهم شقيّ وسعيد. فالشقيّ يجري إلى أجلٍ في الأشقياء، لأنّ الرحمة سبقت الغضب، والسعيد إلى غير أجل.

ومن هنا يعرف تفضيل خلق الإنسان وتوجُّه اليدين على خلق آدم دون غيره من المخلوقات. ويعلم أنّه ما ثَمّ جنس من المخلوقات إلّا وله طريقة واحدة في الخلق، لم تتنوّع عليه صنوف الخلق تنوّعَها على الإنسان. فإنّه تَنَوَّع عليه الخَلق: فخلْق آدم يخالف خلق حوّاء، وخلق حوّاء يخالف خلق عيسى، وخلق عيسى يخالف خلق سائر بني آدم، وكلّهم إنسان.

ومن هنا زيّن للإنسان سوء عمله فرآه حسنا. وعند تجلّي هذا التزيين يشكر الله تعالى التابع على تخلّصه من مثل هذا. وأمّا صاحب النظر فلا يجد فرجًا إلّا في هذا التجلّي يعطيه الحسن في السوء وهو من المكر الإلهيّ. ومن هنا تثبت أعيان الصور في الجوهر التي تحت هذا الفلك إلى الأرض خاصّة.

ومن هنا تعرف ملّة إبراهيم أنّها ملّة سمحاء ما فيها من حرج. فإذا عِلم هذه المعاني ووقف على أبوّة الإسلام أراد صاحب النظر القربَ منه. فقال إبراهيم للتابع: من هذا الأجنبيّ معك؟ فقال: هو أخي. قال: أخوك من الرضاعة أو أخوك من النَّسب؟ قال: أخي من الماء. قال: صدقتَ، لهذا لا أعرفه. لا تصاحب إلّا من هو أخوك من الرضاعة، كما أنّي أبوك من الرضاعة. فإنّ الحضرة السعاديّة لا تقبل إلّا إخوان الرضاعة وآباءها وأمّهاتها، فإنّها النّافعة عند الله. ألا ترى العلم يظهر في صورة اللبن في حضرة الخيال؟ هذا لأجل الرضاع.

وانقطع ظهر صاحب النظر لما انقطع عنه نسب أبوّة إبراهيم، عليه السلام. ثمّ أمره أن يدخل البيت المعمور، فدخله

دون صاحبه. وصاحبه منكوس الرأس، ثمّ خرج من الباب الذي دخل ولم يخرج من باب الملائكة، وهو الباب الثاني، لخاصّيّة فيه، وهو أنّه من خرجَ منه لا يرجع إليه.

ثمّ ارتحل من عنده يطلب العروج. ومسك صاحبَه صاحب النظر هناك. وقيل له: قف حتّى يرجع صاحبُك، فإنّه لا قَدم لك هنا، هذا آخر الدخان. فقال: أسْلِم وأدخل تحت حكم ما دخل فيه صاحبي. قيل له: ليس هذا موضع قبول الإسلام. إذا رجعت إلى موطنك الذي منه جئت أنت وصاحِبَك، فهناك. إذا أسلمت وآمنت واتّبعت سبيل من أناب إلى الله إنابة الرسل المبلّغين عن الله، قُبلْتَ كما قُبل صاحبك.

فبقي هنالك، ومشى التابع فبلغ به سدرة المنتهى. فرأى صور أعمال السعداء من النبيّين وأتباع الرسل، ورأى عمله في جملة أعمالهم. فشكر الله على ما وفّقه إليه من اتّباع الرسول المعلِّم.

وعاين هنالك أربعة أنهار: منها نهر كبير عظيم وجداول صغار تنبعث من ذلك النهر الكبير، وذلك النَهر الكَبير تتفجّر منه الأنهار الكبار الثلاثة. فسأل التابعُ عن تلك الأنهار والجداول فقيل له: هذا مَثَل مضروبٌ أقيم لك. هذا النهر الأعظم هو القرآن، وهذه الثلاثة الأنهار الكتب الثلاثة التوراة والزبور والإنجيل. وهذه الجداول الصحف، المنزلة على الأنبياء. فمن شرب من أيّ نهر كان أو أيّ جدول، فهو لمن شرب منه وارث. وكلّ حقّ فإنّه كلام الله. و{العلماء ورثة الأنبياء} بما

شربوا من هذه الأنهار والجداول. فاشرع في نهر القرآن تَفُزْ بكلّ سبيل للسعادة، فإنّه نهر محمّد، صلّى الله عليه وسلّم، الذي صحّت له النبوّة وآدم بين الماء والطين، وأوتي جوامع الكلم، وبُعِث عامّة، ونُسخت به فروع الأحكام، ولم يُنسخ له حكمٌ بغيره.

ونظر إلى حسن النور الذي غشّى تلك السدرة فرأى قد غشّاها منه ذاك الذي غشّى. فلا يستطيع أحد أن ينعتها للغشاء النوريّ الذي لا تنفذُه الأبصار، بل لا تدركه الأبصار. ثمّ قيل له: هذه شجرة الطُّهُور فيها مرضاة الحقّ. ومن هنا شرع السدْر في غسل الميّت للقاء الله، الماء والسدر ليناله طهور هذه السدرة. وإليها تنتهي أعمال بني آدم السعادِيّة وفيها مخازنها إلى يوم الدين. وهنا أوّل أقدام السعداء. والسماء السابعة التي وقف عندها صاحبك منتهى الدخان، ولا بدّ لها ولمن هو تحتها من الاستحالة إلى صور، كانت عليها أو على أمثالها قبل أن تكون سماء.

ثمّ قيل لهذا التابع: اِرْقَ. فَرَقِي في فلك المنازل. فتلقّاه من هنالك من الملائكة والأرواح الكوكبيّة ما يزيد على ألف، وعشرات من الحضرات تسكنها هذه الأرواح. فعاين منازل السائرين إلى الله تعالى بالأعمال المشروعة. وقد ذكر من ذلك الهرويّ في جزء له سمّاه منازل السائرين، يحوي على مائة، كلّ مقام يحوي على عشرة مقامات وهي المنازل. وأمّا نحن فذكرنا من هذه المنازل في كتاب لنا سمّيناه مناهج الارتقاء، يحوي على ثلاث مائة مقام، كلّ مقام يحوي على عشرة

منازل، ففيه ثلاثة آلاف منزل. فلم يزل يقطعها منزلة منزلة بسبع حقائق هو عليها، كما يقطع فيها السبع الدراريّ ولكن في زمان أقرب، حتّى وقف على حقائقها بأجمعها، وقد كان أوصاه إدريس بذلك.

فلمّا عاين كلّ منزل منها رآها وجميع ما فيها من الكواكب تقطع في فلك آخر فوقها. فطلب الارتقاء فيه ليرى ما أودع الله في هذه الأمور من الآيات والعجائب الدالّة على قدرته وعلمه. فعندما حصل على سطحه، حصل في الجنّة الدهماء فرأى ما فيها ممّا وصف الله في كتابه من صفة الجنّات. وعاين درجاتها وغرفها وما أعدّ الله لأهلها فيها. ورأى جنّته المخصوصة به، واطّلع على جنّات الميراث وجنّات الاختصاص وجنّات الأعمال. وذاق من كلّ نعيم منها بحسب ما يعطيه ذوق موطن القوّة الجنانيّة.

فلمّا بلغ من ذلك أمنيته، رُقِيَ به إلى المستوى الأزهى والستر الأبْهَى. فرأى صور آدم وبنيه السعداء من خلف تلك الستور فعلِم معناها وما أودع الله من الحكمة فيها وما عليها من الخلع التي كساهنّ بني آدم. فسلّمت عليه تلك الصور فرأى صورته فيهنّ. فعانقها وعانقتْه، واندفعت معه إلى المكانة الزلفى.

فدخل فلك البروج الذي قال الله فيه فأقسم به: ﴿وَالسَّمَاءِ ذَاتِ الْبُرُوجِ﴾ (البروج ١). فعلم أنّ التكوينات التي تكون في الجنان من حركة هذا الفلك. وله الحركة اليوميّة في العالَم الزمانيّ كما أنّ حركة الليل والنهار في الفلك الذي

فيه جرْم الشمس. والتكوينات التي تكون في جهنّم من حركة فلك الكواكب وهو سقف جهنّم، أعني مقعّره وسطحه أرض الجنّة. والذي يسقط من الكواكب وينتثر ضوءُها فتبقى مظلمة وفعلها المودع فيها باقٍ. وهذا كلّه سبب التبديل الذي يقع في جهنّم: ﴿كُلَّمَا نَضِجَتْ جُلُودُهُمْ بَدَّلْنَاهُمْ جُلُودًا غَيْرَهَا﴾ (النساء ٥٦) كلّ ذلك بإذن الله مرتّب الأشياء مراتِبَها.

كما أنّ الشمس إذا حلّتْ بالحمل جاء زمن الربيع. فظهرت زينَة الأرض، وأورقت الأشجار، وازّينت ﴿وَأَنْبَتَتْ مِنْ كُلِّ زَوْجٍ بَهِيجٍ﴾ (الحجّ ٥). وإذا حلّتْ بالجدي أظهرت النقيض. والقوابلُ تقبل بحسب ما هي عليه من المزاج: فمهما اختلف مزاجها، كان قبولها لما يحدث الله عند هذه الحركات الفلكيّة بحسب ما هي عليه.

وكذلك في الجنان في كلّ حين من خلق جديد ونعيم جديد حتّى لا يقع مَلل. فإنّ كلّ شيء طبيعي إذا توالى عليه أمر ما من غير تبدّل، لا بدّ أن يصحب الإنسان فيه ملل. فإنّ الملل نعت ذاتي له. فإن لم يغذّه الله بالتجديد في كلّ وقت ليدوم له النعيم بذلك. وإلّا كان يدركهم الملل. فأهل الجنان يدركون في كلّ نظرة ينظرونها إلى ملكهم أمرا وصورة لم يكونوا رأوها قبل ذلك، فينعمون بحدوثها. وكذلك في كلّ أَكلة وشَرْبَةٍ يجدون طعما جديدا لذيذا لم يكونوا يجدونه في الأكلة الأولى، فينعمون بذلك وتعظم شهوتهم.

والسبب في سرعة هذا التبدّل وبقائه أنّ الأصل على ذلك. فيعطي في الكون بحسب ما تعطيه حقيقة مرتبته،

ليكون خلّاقا على الدوام ويكون الكون فقيرا على الدوام. فالوجود كلّه متحرّك على الدوام دنيا وآخرة، لأنّ التكوين لا يكون عن سكون. فمن الله توجّهات دائمة وكلِمات لا تنفد، وهو قوله: ﴿وَمَا عِنْدَ اللَّهِ بَاقٍ﴾ (النحل ٩٦). فعند الله التوجّه وهو قوله تعالى: ﴿إِذَا أَرَدْنَاهُ﴾ (النحل ٤٠)، وكلمة الحضرة وهي قوله لكلّ شيء يريده: ﴿كُنْ﴾ بالمعنى الذي يليق بجلاله. و'كن' حرف وجوديّ، فلا يكون عنه إلّا الوجود. ما يكون عنه عدم لأنّ العدم لا يكون، لأنّ الكون وجود.

وهذه التوجّهات والكلمات في خزائن الجود لكلّ شيء يقبل الوجود. قال تعالى: ﴿وَإِنْ مِنْ شَيْءٍ إِلَّا عِنْدَنَا خَزَائِنُهُ﴾ وهو ما ذكرناه. وقوله: ﴿وَمَا نُنَزِّلُهُ إِلَّا بِقَدَرٍ مَعْلُومٍ﴾ (الحجر ٢١) من اسمه الحكيم فالحكمة سلطانة هذا الإنزال الإلهيّ. وهو إخراج هذه الأشياء من هذه الخزائن إلى وجود أعيانها.

وهو قولنا في أوّل خطبة هذا الكتاب: "الحمد لله الذي أوجد الأشياء عن عدم وعدمه". وعدم العدم وجود. فهو نسبة كون الأشياء في هذه الخزائن محفوظة، مَوجُودةً لله، ثابتة لأعيانها غير موجودة لأنفسها. فبالنظر إلى أعيانها هي موجودة عن عدم؛ وبالنظر إلى كونها عند الله في هذه الخزائن هي موجودة عن عدم العدم، وهو وجود. فإن شئت رجّحت جانب كونها في الخزائن، فتقول: أوجد الأشياء من وجودها في الخزائن إلى وجودها في أعيانها للنعيم بها أو غير ذلك. وإن شئت قلت: أوجد الأشياء عن عدم، بعد أن تقف

على معنى ما ذكرتُ لك. فقل ما شِئت، فهو المُوجِد لها على كلّ حال في الموطن الذي ظهرت فيه لأعيانها.

وأمّا قوله: ﴿مَا عِنْدَكُمْ يَنْفَدُ﴾ (النحل ٩٦) فهو صحيح في العلم، لأنّ الخطاب هنا لعين الجوهر والذي عنده، أعني عند الجوهر من كلّ موجود. إنّما هو ما يوجده الله في محلّه من الصفات والأعراض والأكوان، وهي في الزمان الثاني أو في الحال الثاني، كيف شئت. قل: من زمان وجودها أو حال وجودها، تنعدم من عندنا وهو قوله: ﴿مَا عِنْدَكُمْ يَنْفَدُ﴾. وهو يجدّد للجوهر الأمثال أو الأضداد دائما من هذه الخزائن. وهذا معنى قول المتكلّمين: إنّ العرض لا يبقى زمانين، وهو قول صحيح، خبرٌ لا شبهة فيه، لأنّه الأمر المحقّق الذي عليه نعت الممكنات. وبتجدّد ذلك على الجوهر يبقى عينه دائما ما شاء الله، وقد شاء أنّه لا يفنى، فلا بدّ من بقائه.

فيعلم التابع من هذه الحضرة التكوينات الجنانيّة وجميع ما ذكرناه. وأمّا صاحب النظر رفيق التابع، فما عنده خبر بشيء من هذا كلّه، لأنّه تنبيه نبويٌّ لا نظر فكري. وصاحب النظر مقيّد تحت سلطان فكره، وليس للفكر مجال إلّا في ميدانه الخاصّ به، وهو معلومٌ بين الميادين. فإنّه لكلّ قوّة في الإنسان مَيدان يجول فيه لا يتعدّاه. ومهما تعدّت ميدانها وقعتْ في الغلط والخطأ، ووُصفت بالتحريف عن طريقها المستقيم. وقد يشهد الكشف البصريّ بما تعثر فيه الحجج العقليّة، وسبب ذلك خروجها عن طورها. فالعقول الموصوفة بالضلال إنّما أضلّتها أفكارها، وإنّما ضلّت

أفكارها لتصرّفها في غير موطنها. وإنّما تصرّف ما تصرّف منها في غير موطنه وجال في غير ميدانه ليظهر فضل بعض الناس على بعضهم. وإنّما ظهر الفضل في العالَم ليُعلم أنّ الحقّ له عناية ببعض عباده، وله خذلان في بعض عباده، وليُعلم أنّ الممكن لم يخرج عن إمكانه. وأنّ المرجّح له نظر خصوصيّ لمن شاء من هذه القوى بما شاء ﴿وَهُوَ الْعَلِيمُ الْقَدِيرُ﴾ (الروم ٥٤).

ثمّ يخرج بالتابع مع حامله إلى الكرسيّ. فيرى فيه انقسام الكلمة التي وُصفتْ قبل وصولها إلى هذا المقام بالوحدة. ويرى القدمين اللتين تدلّتا إليه فينكبّ من ساعته إلى تقبيلهما: القدم الواحدة تعطي ثبوت أهل الجنّات في جنّاتهم وهي قدم الصدق، والقدم الأخرى تعطي ثبوت أهل جهنّم في جهنّم على أيّ حالة أراد وهي قدم الجبروت. ولهذا قال في أهل الجنان: ﴿عَطَاءً غَيْرَ مَجْذُوذٍ﴾ (هود ١٠٨) فما وصفه بالانقطاع. وقال في أهل جهنّم الذين شقوا لحكم هذا القدم الجبروتيّ: ﴿إِنَّ رَبَّكَ فَعَّالٌ لِمَا يُرِيدُ﴾ (هود ١٠٧). وما قال إنّ الحال التي هم فيها لا تنقطع كما قال في السعداء. والذي منع من ذلك قوله: ﴿وَرَحْمَتِي وَسِعَتْ كُلَّ شَيْءٍ﴾ (الأعراف ١٥٦) وقوله: {إنّ رحمتي سبقت غضبي} في هذه النشأة. فإنّ الوجود رحمة في حقّ كلّ موجود، وإن تعذّب بعضهم ببعض. فتخليدهم في حال النعيم غير منقطع وتخليدهم في حال الانتقام موقوف على إرادة. فقد يعود الانتقام منهم عذابا عليهم لا غير، ويزول الانتقام.

ولهذا فسّره في مواضع بالألم المؤلم وقال: ﴿عَذَابٌ أَلِيمٌ﴾ (البقرة ١٠) و: ﴿الْعَذَابَ الْأَلِيمَ﴾ (يونس ٨٨) وفي مواضع لم يقيّد العذاب بالأليم وأطلقه. فقال: ﴿لَا يُخَفَّفُ عَنْهُمُ الْعَذَابُ﴾ (البقرة ١٦٢) يعني وإن زال الألم. وقال: ﴿فِي عَذَابِ جَهَنَّمَ﴾ (الزخرف ٧٥) ولم ينعته بأنّه أليم وقال: ﴿لَا يُفَتَّرُ عَنْهُمْ﴾ (الزخرف ٧٥) من كونه عذابا ﴿وَهُمْ فِيهِ﴾ أي في العذاب ﴿مُبْلِسُونَ﴾ أي مبعَدون من السعادة العرَضيّة في هذا الموطن. لأنّ الإبلاس لفظة مختصّة بأهل جهنّم في بُعْدهم. فلهذا جاء بذكْر الإبلاس ليوقع هذا الاصطلاح اللغويّ في موضعه عند أهله ليعلموه. فإنّه لموطن جهنّم لغة ليست لأهل الجنان، والإبلاس منها. فيعرف التابع من هذا المقام ما لكلّ دار.

ثمّ إنّه يفارق هذا الموضع ويزجّ به في النور الأعظم فيغلبه الوجد. وهذا النور هو حضرة الأحوال الظاهر حكمها في الأشخاص الإنسانيّة. وأكثر ما يظهر عليهم في سماع الألحان. فإنّها إذا نزلت عليهم تمرّ على الأفلاك. ولحركات الأفلاك نغمات طيّبة مستلذّة تستلذّ بها الأسماع، كنغمات الدولاب. فتكسو الأحوال وتنزل بها على النفوس الحيوانيّة في مجالس السماع. فإن كانت النفس في أيّ شيء كانت من تعلّق بجارية أو غلام أو يكون من أهل الله، فيكون تعلّقه حبّ جمال إلهيّ متخيّل. اكتسبوه من ألفاظ نبويّة مثل قوله في الصحيح: {إنّ الله جميل يحبّ الجمال}، وقوله في التجريد: ﴿اعبد الله كأنك تراه﴾. فيأخذه الوجد على ما تخيّله.

ومنهم من يغمره الحال لا من حضرة التخيّل، بل يجد أمرا لا يكيّف ولا يدخل تحت الحصر والمقدار. ومنهم من تَهبّ عليه من هذه الأحوال التي تعطي الوجد روائح على نفوس غير عاشقة إلّا بنسبة جزئيّة لا كلّيّة. فتعطيه من الحكم لذلك معنى يسمّى التواجد.

ثمّ يخرج من ذلك النور إلى موضع الرحمة العامّة التي وسِعت كلّ شيء وهو المعبّر عنه بالعرش. فيَجد هنالك من الحقائق الملكيّة: إسرافيل وجبريل وميكائيل ورضوان ومالك. ومن الحقائق الملكيّة البشريّة: آدم وإبراهيم ومحمد سلام الله عليهم. فيجد عند آدم وإسرافيل علم الصور الظاهرة في العالم المسمّاة أجساما وأجسادا وهياكل، سواء كانت نوريّة أو غير نوريّة. ويجد عند جبريل ومحمد، عليهما السلام، علم الأرواح المنفوخة في هذه الصور التي عند آدم وإسرافيل. فيقف على معاني ذلك كلّه ويرى نسبة هذه الأرواح إلى هذه الصور وتدبيرها إيّاها، ومن أين وقع فيها التفاضل مع انبعاثها من أصل واحد، وكذلك الصور، يعلم من هذه الحضرة ذلك كلّه.

ويعلم من هذه الحضرة علم الأكاسير التي تقلّب صور الأجساد بما فيه من الروح. وينظر إلى ميكائيل وإبراهيم، عليهما السلام، فيجد عندهما علم الأرزاق وما يكون به التغذّي للصور والأرواح وبماذا يكون بقاؤها. ويقف على كون الإكسير غذاء مخصوصا لذلك الجسد الذي يردّه ذهبا أو فضّة بعد ما كان حديدا أو نحاسا: وهو صحّة ذلك الجسم وإزالة

مرضه الذي كان قد دخل عليه في معدنه فصيّره حديدا أو غير ذلك. وكلّ هذا من هذه الحضرة يعلمه.

ثمّ ينظر إلى رضوان ومالك. فيجد عندهما عِلْمَ السعادة والشقاء، والجنّة ودرجاتها وجهنّم ودركاتها. وهو علم المراتب في الوعد والوعيد، ويعلم حقيقة ما تعطي كلّ واحدة منهما. وإذا علم هذا كلّه عَلِمَ العرش وحملَتَه وما تحت إحاطته. وهو منتهى الأجسام وليس وراءه جسم مركّبٌ ذو شكل ومقدار.

فإذا علم هذا كلّه، عرج به معراجا آخر معنويا في غير صورة متخيّلة إلى مرتبة المقادير. فيعلم منها كمّيّات الأشياء الجسميّة وأوزانها في الأجسام المقدّرة من المحيط إلى التراب، وما فيهنّ وما بينهنّ من أصناف العالم الذين هم عمّار هذه الأمكنة.

ثمّ ينتقل إلى علم الجوهر المظلم الكلّ الذي لا جزء له ولا صورة فيه. وهو غيب كلّ ما وراءه من العالم، ومنه ظهرت هذه الأنوار والضياءات في عالم الأجسام. وهي الأنوار المركّبة سُلخت من هذا الجوهر فبقي مظلما، كما سُلخ النهار من الليل فبانت الظلمة. وهذا هو أصل الظلمة في العالم وأصل العالم في الأحكام الناموسيّة.

ثمّ ينتقل من هذا المقام إلى حضرة الطبيعة البسيطة. فيعلم حكمها في الأجسام مطلقا من اختلاف تركيباتها وأحوالها، ومن أين وقع الغلط لبعض الطبيعيّين فيما غلطوا فيه من العلم بأحكامها، وذلك لجهلهم بالعلم بذاتها، فصاحب هذا الكشف يعلم ذلك كلّه.

ثمّ ينتقل من النظر في ذلك إلى شهود اللوح المحفوظ وهو الموجود الانبعاثيّ عن القلم. وقد رقم الله فيه ما شاءه من الكوائن في العالَم. فيعلم هذا التالي لما في هذا اللوح علم القوّتين، وهما علم العلم وعلم العمل، ويعلم الانفعالات الانبعاثيّة. ومن كون هذا الروح لوحا يعلم ما سطّره فيه من سمّاه لوحا بالقلم الإلهيّ ممّا أملاه الحقّ عليه. وكتابته فيه نقش صور المعلومات التي يجريها[1] الله في العالَم في الدنيا إلى يوم القيامة خاصّة. وهي علوم محصورة مسطّرة صورا كصور الحروف المرقومة في الألواح والكتب المسمّاة كلمات. وعدد أمّهاتها ما يكون من ضرب درجات الفلَك في مثلها سواء، من غير زيادة ولا نقصان.

ومن هنا جعل الله في الفلك الذي تقطع فيه الكواكب بسباحتها ثلاث مائة درجة وستّين درجة، وفيها انحصرت السنة في الدار الدنيا بسباحة الشمس والقمر. قال تعالى ﴿الشَّمْسُ وَالْقَمَرُ بِحُسْبَانٍ﴾ (الرحمن ٥). وتتكرّر بالسنين من أوّل وجودها، وما هو تكرار على الحقيقة، إلى أن ينتهي إلى قدر ما خرج من ضرب الثلاث مائة والستين في مثلها من السنين يكون عمر عالم الدنيا.

ثمّ يُمْلِي أمرا آخر وعلوما تختصّ بالقيامة وبالموازين أيضا إلى أجل مسمّى بتميّز في الدارين، وهو انتهاء مدّة الانتقام على أهل دار الشقاء خاصّة. ثمّ يستأنف فيه كتابة

١ يحدثه (م) يجربها (ب).

العذاب في هذه الدار مع الخلود الدائم في الدارين لأهلها، غير أنّه لا بُدّ مهما كانت الكتابة أن تجري إلى أجل مسمّى، لاستحالة دخول ما لا يتناهى في الوجود.

ثمّ ينتقل هذا التابع من هذا المقام إلى مشاهدة القلم الأعْلى. فيحصل له من هذا المشهد علم الولاية. ومن هنالك هو ابتداء مرتبة الخلافة والنيابة. ومن هناك دُوّنت الدواوين وظهر سلطان الاسم المدبِّر والمفصِّل. وهو قوله: ﴿يُدَبِّرُ الْأَمْرَ يُفَصِّلُ الْآيَاتِ﴾ (الرعد ٢)، وهذا هو علم القلم. ويشاهد تحريك اليمنى إيّاه التحريك المعنويّ اللطيف، ومن أين يستمدّ، وأنّه من ذاته له علم الإجمال والتفصيل. والتفصيل يظهر بالتسطير وهو عين ذواته. فلا افتقار له إلى معلّم يستمدّ منه سوى خالقه، عزّ وجلّ. وكتابته نقش ولهذا تثبت فلا تقبل المحوَ. وبهذا سمّي اللوح بالمحفوظ، يعني عن المحو. فلو كانت كتابته مثل الكتابة بالمداد قبلت المحو، كما يقبله لوح المحو في عالم الكون بالقلم المختَصّ به، الذي هو بين إصبعي الرحمن.

فيفرّق من هذا المشهد بين الأقلام والألواح وأنواع الكتبة. ويعلم علم الأحكام والإحكام. ومن هنا يعلم أنّه لم يبق في الإمكان ما ينبغي أن يكون دليلا على الله إلّا وقد ظهر من كونه دليلا، وإن كثرت الأدلّة فيجمعها كماليّة الدلالة خاصّة.

ثمّ ينظُر عن يمين هذا المشهد فينظر إلى عالم الهيمان، وهو العالم المخلوق من العماء.

ثمّ ينتقل إلى العماء وهو مستوى الاسم الربّ، كما كان العرش مستوى الرحمن. والعماء هو أوّل الأينيّات، ومنه ظهرت الظروف المكانيّات والمراتب فيمن لم يقبل المكان وقَبِل المكانة. ومنه ظهرت المَحالّ القابلة للمعاني الجسمانيّة حسًّا وخيالا. وهو موجود شريف الحقُّ معناه، وهو الحقّ المخلوق به كلّ موجود سوى الله. وهو المعنى الذي ثبتت فيه واستقرّت أعيان الممكنات. ويقبل حقيقة الأين وظرفة المكان ورتبة المكانة واسم المحلّ.

ومن عالم الأرض إلى هذا العماء ليس فيها من أسماء الله تعالى سوى أسماء الأفعال خاصّة، ليس لغيرها أثر في كون ممّا بينهما من العالم المعقول والمحسوس.

غير أنّ صاحب التابع الذي هو صاحب النظر لمّا تركه صاحبه بالسماء السابعة ورحل عنه، امتدّتْ منه رقيقة على غير معراج التابع: ظهرت للتابع في الفلك المكوكب، وفَقَدها في الجنّة، ثمّ ظهرت له في فلك البروج، ثمّ فقدها أيضا في الكرسيّ وفي العرش، ثمّ ظهر له في مرتبة المقادير وفي الجوهر المظلم، ثمّ فقده في الطبيعة، ثمّ ظهر له في النفس من جهة كونها نفسا لا من جهة كونها لوحا، ثمّ ظهر له في العقل الإبداعيّ من كونه عقلا لا من كونه قلما، ثمّ فارقه بعد ذلك فلم ير له عينا.

ومن هذا العماء يبتدئ بالترقّي والمعراج في أسماء التنزيه إلى أن يَصِل إلى الحضرة التي يشهد فيها أن التنزيه يحدّه ويشير إليه ويقيّده. ويستشرف على العالَم بأسره المعنويّ

والروحانيّ، والجسميّ والجسمانيّ، فلا يجد في مشهده ذلك ما ينبغي أن ينزّه عنه من ظهر فيه، ويرى ارتباطه به ارتباط المرتبة بصاحبها. فلا يتمكّن له التنزيه الذي كان يتخيّله ولا يتمكّن له التشبيه، فإنّه ليس ثَمَّ بِمَنْ:

فَمَا ثَمَّ إِلَّا اللهُ لَا شَيْءَ غَيْرُهُ وَمَا ثَمَّ إِلَّا وَحْدَةُ الْوَحَدَاتِ

ثمّ فارق أسماء الأفعال وتسلّمته أسماء التنزيه. فرأى صاحبَه صاحب النظر يرافقه إلى أن وصل إلى الحضرة التي لا تقبل التنزيه ولا التشبيه. فيتنزّه عن الحدّ بنفي التنزيه وعن المقدار بنفي التشبيه، فيفقد رفيقَه صاحب النظر هنالك.

ثمّ ينقلب يطلب ما منه خرج. فسلك به الحقُّ تعالى طريقا غير طريقه الأوّل وهو طريق لا يتمكّن أن ينقال. ولا يعرفه إلّا مَن شاهده ذوقا.

ورجع صاحبه على معراجه ذلك، إذ لم يكن تابعا إلى أن وصل إلى جسده. فاجتمع مع رفيقه. فبادر من حينه صاحبُ النظر إلى الرسول إن كان حاضرا أو لوارثه، فيُبَايِعُه بيعة الإيمان والرضوان على بيّنة من ربّه وآية من نفسه. وتلاه شاهد منه وهو التابع. فآمن بالله من حيث ما شرع له الإيمان به، لا من حيث دليله. فوجد عنده وفي قلبه نورا لم يكن يجده قبل ذلك. فرأى في اللمحة الواحدة وهو في مكانه بذلك النور جميع ما رآه مع التابع، في معراجه الأوّل، ولم يقف. بل ترقّى مرقى التابع حتّى بلغ العماءَ والغاية القصوى. ورأى الشيء في

الأشياء، ورأى وجوب وجود مَا أحال وجوده فكرةً وعقلًا، وهو في مكانه ذلك لم يبرح.

وأُعطى إكسير التكوين، ورأى حشر الأجساد من طور إلى طَور باختلاف حكم لاختلاف دَور، فتغيّرت الأشكال وتقلّبت الأحوال. ورأى ما قلناه في مثل ذلك:

إِذَا السَّمَاءُ انْفَطَرَتْ حَقِيقَةُ تَصَوَّرَتْ
فَمَنْ لَهَا بِهَا لَهَا إِذَا النُّجُومُ انْكَدَرَتْ
تَطْلُبُ بِانْكِدَارِهَا جِبَالَ صَخْرٍ سُيِّرَتْ
تَنْظُرُ فِي تَسْيِيرِهَا جَحِيمَ نَارٍ سُعِّرَتْ
سَعَّرَهَا مُوقِدُهَا لِجَنَّةٍ قَدْ أُزْلِفَتْ
تَدْخُلُهَا طَائِفَةٌ مِنْ قَبْرِهَا قَدْ بُعْثِرَتْ
قُلْتُ لَهَا مَا تَبْتَغِي قَالَتْ وُحُوشٌ حُشِرَتْ
وَأَنْ تَرَى نَفْسِي مَا قَدْ قَدَّمَتْ وَأَخَّرَتْ

ولمّا أسلم صاحب النظر وآمن ورأى من مقامه جميع ما رآه التابع في معراجه مشاهدة عين، سأل أن يرى مقام المجرمين. وهم المستحقّون تلك الدار التي دخلوها بحكم الاستحقاق، وعلموا أن العلم أشرف حُلّة وأن الجهل أقبح حليةَ، وأن جهنّم ليست بدار لشيء من الخير كما أنّ الجنّة ليست بدار لشيء من الشرّ. ورأى الإيمان قد قام بقلب من لا علم له بما ينبغي لجلال الله، ورأى العلم بجلال الله وما ينبغي له قد قام بمن ليس عنده شيء من الإيمان. وهذا العالِم بعَدم الإيمان قد

استحقّ دار الشقاء، وأنّ الجاهل المؤمن قد استحقّ بالإيمان دار السعادة والدرجات في مقابلة الدركات. فسُلِب هذا العالِم المستحقّ دار الشقاء عِلْمُه، حتّى كأنّه ما عَلِمه أو لم يعلم شيئا. فيتعذّب بجهله أشدّ منه من عذابه بحسِّه، وهو أشدّه عليه. فخُلِع عِلمُه على هذا الجاهل المؤمن الذي دخل الجنّة بإيمانه. فنال المؤمن بذلك العلم الذي خلع عن هذا الذي استحقّ الإقامة بدار الشقاء، درجةَ ما يطلبه ذلك العلم، فيتنعّم به نفسا وحسّا وفي الكثيب عند الرؤية.

ويعطى ذلك الكافرُ جهل هذا المؤمن الجاهل، فينال بذلك الجهل دَرَكَ ذلك من النار. وتلك أشدّ حسرة تمرّ عليه، فإنّه يتذكّر ما كان عليْه من العلم ولا يعلم ذلك الآن، ويعلم أنّه سُلِبه. ويكشف الله عن بصره حتّى يرى مرتبة العلم الذي كان عليه في الجنان، ويرى حلّة عِلمه على غيره ممّن لم يتعب في تحصيله، ويطلب شيئا منه في نفسه فلا يقدر عليه. وينظر هذا المؤمن ويطّلع على سواء الجحيم. فيرى شرّ جهله على ذلك العالِم الذي ليس بمؤمن، فيزيد نعيما وفرحا. فما أعظمها من حسرة!

واتّفق لي في هذه المسألة عجبا، وذلك أنّ بعض علماء الفلاسفة سمع منّي هذه المقالة. فربّما أحالها في نفسه أو استخفّ عقلي في ذلك. فأطلعه الله بكشف لم يشكّ فيه في نفسه، بحيث أن تحقّق الأمر على ما قلناه. فدخل عليّ باكيا على نفسه وتفريطه. وكانت لي معه صحبة، فذكر لي الأمر وأناب واستدرك الفائتَ وآمنَ. وقال لي: ما رأيت أشدّ

منها حسرة، وتحقّق قوله تعالى: ﴿إِنِّي أَعِظُكَ أَنْ تَكُونَ مِنَ الْجَاهِلِينَ﴾ (هود ٤٦)، وقوله: ﴿فَلَا تَكُونَنَّ مِنَ الْجَاهِلِينَ﴾ (الأنعام ٣٥). فهذا قد جمع بين خطاب لطفٍ ولين وعنفٍ وشدّة، لأنّ الواحد شيخ فخاطبه باللطف، والآخر شابّ فخاطبه بالشدّة.

نفعنا الله بالعلم وجعلنا من أهله، ولا يجعلنا ممّن يسعى بخيره في حقّ غيره ويشقى. آمين بعزّته.

انتهى الجزء الثامن ومائة.